TIM O'BRIEN

Courtesy of Texas State University.

TIM O'BRIEN

A Critical Companion

Patrick A. Smith

CRITICAL COMPANIONS TO POPULAR CONTEMPORARY WRITERS
Kathleen Gregory Klein, Series Editor

Greenwood Press
Westport, Connecticut • London

Library of Congress Cataloging-in-Publication Data

Smith, Patrick A., 1967–
    Tim O'Brien : a critical companion / Patrick A. Smith.
        p.   cm. — (Critical companions to popular contemporary writers,
    ISSN: 1082–4979)
    Includes bibliographical references and index.
    ISBN 0–313–33055–7 (alk. paper)
        1. O'Brien, Tim, 1946—Criticism and interpretation. 2. Vietnamese Conflict,
    1961–1975—Literature and the conflict. 3. War stories, American—History and
    criticism. I. Title. II. Series.
    PS3565.B75Z86   2005
    813'.54—dc22   2005007695

British Library Cataloguing in Publication Data is available.

Library of Congress Catalog Card Number: 2005007695
ISBN: 0–313–33055–7
ISSN: 1082–4979

First published in 2005

Greenwood Press, 88 Post Road West, Westport, CT 06881
An imprint of Greenwood Publishing Group, Inc.
www.greenwood.com

Printed in the United States of America

The paper used in this book complies with the
Permanent Paper Standard issued by the National
Information Standards Organization (Z39.48–1984).

10   9   8   7   6   5   4   3   2   1

For Matthew Guiler Smith
True hope is swift, and flies with swallow's wings

Contents

Contents

Series Foreword

The authors who appear in the series Critical Companions to Popular Contemporary Writers are all best-selling writers. They do not simply have one successful novel, but a string of them. Fans, critics, and specialist readers eagerly anticipate their next book. For some, high cash advances and breakthrough sales figures are automatic; movie deals often follow. Some writers become household names, recognized by almost everyone.

But their novels are read one by one. Each reader chooses to start and, more importantly, to finish a book because of what she or he finds there. The real test of a novel is in the satisfaction its readers experience. This series acknowledges the extraordinary involvement of readers and writers in creating a best-seller.

The authors included in this series were chosen by an advisory board composed of high school English teachers and high school and public librarians. They ranked a list of best-selling writers according to their popularity among different groups of readers. For the first series, writers in the top-ranked group who had received no book-length, academic, literary analysis (or none in at least the past 10 years) were chosen. Because of this selection method, Critical Companions to Popular Contemporary Writers meets a need that is being addressed nowhere else. The success of these volumes as reported by reviewers, librarians, and teachers led to an expansion of the series mandate to include some writers with wide critical attention—Toni Morrison, John Irving, and Maya Angelou, for example—to extend the usefulness of the series.

The volumes in the series are written by scholars with particular expertise in analyzing popular fiction. These specialists add an academic focus to the popular success that these writers already enjoy.

The series is designed to appeal to a wide range of readers. The general reading public will find explanations for the appeal of these well-known writers. Fans will find biographical and fictional questions answered. Students will find literary analysis, discussions of fictional genres, carefully organized introductions to new ways of reading the novels, and bibliographies for additional research. Whether browsing through the book for pleasure or using it for an assignment, readers will find that the most recent novels of the authors are included.

Each volume begins with a biographical chapter drawing on published information, autobiographies or memoirs, prior interviews, and, in some cases, interviews given especially for this series. A chapter on literary history and genres describes how the author's work fits into a larger literary context. The following chapters analyze the writer's most important, most popular, and most recent novels in detail. Each chapter focuses on one or more novels. This approach, suggested by the advisory board as the most useful to student research, allows for an in-depth analysis of the writer's fiction. Close and careful readings with numerous examples show readers exactly how the novels work. These chapters are organized around three central elements: plot development (how the story line moves forward), character development (what the reader knows of the important figures), and theme (the significant ideas of the novel). Chapters may also include sections on generic conventions (how the novel is similar to or different from others in its same category of science fiction, fantasy, thriller, etc.), narrative point of view (who tells the story and how), symbols and literary language, and historical or social context. Each chapter ends with an "alternative reading" of the novel. The volume concludes with a primary and secondary bibliography, including reviews.

The alternative readings are a unique feature of this series. By demonstrating a particular way of reading each novel, they provide a clear example of how a specific perspective can reveal important aspects of the book. In the alternative reading sections, one contemporary literary theory—way of reading, such as feminist criticism, Marxism, new historicism, deconstruction, or Jungian psychological critique—is defined in brief, easily comprehensible language. That definition is then applied to the novel to highlight specific features that might go unnoticed or be understood differently in a more general reading. Each volume defines two or three specific theories, making them part of the reader's understanding of how diverse meanings may be constructed from a single novel.

Taken collectively, the volumes in the Critical Companions to Popular Contemporary Writers series provide a wide-ranging investigation of the complexities of current best-selling fiction. By treating these novels seriously as both literary works and publishing successes, the series demonstrates the potential of popular literature in contemporary culture.

Kathleen Gregory Klein
Southern Connecticut State University

Acknowledgments

The following people and organizations were instrumental in bringing this book to life: Wynton C. Hall, Rob Gingras, Bainbridge College Library, Florida State University Libraries, and, for giving me much-needed energy and focus, my creative writing class at Bainbridge College, fall semester 2004, including Jacqui Fisher, Drew Hall, Basil Lucas, Trilla Pando, Chris Timmons, and Jamie Williams. Thanks also to Don Anders and Media Relations at Texas State University–San Marcos; Debby Adams and Kathy Klein, for their encouragement and forbearance; my mother, Martha Smith, a lifelong English teacher, for her keen editing eye and Grammy skills; and, of course, Lori, for her love and support—and extraordinary patience.

List of Editions

The most readily available editions of O'Brien's novels and memoir are quoted in the text that follows. Pagination in other editions may vary slightly.

If I Die in a Combat Zone, Box Me Up and Ship Me Home	New York: Delacorte, 1989
Northern Lights	New York: Broadway, 1999
Going after Cacciato	New York: Broadway, 1999
The Nuclear Age	New York: Knopf, 1985
The Things They Carried	New York: Broadway, 1998
In the Lake of the Woods	Boston: Houghton Mifflin, 1994
Tomcat in Love	New York: Broadway Books, 1998
July, July	Boston: Houghton Mifflin, 2002

1

The Words Are All: A Brief Biography of Tim O'Brien

Vietnam is what we had instead of happy childhoods.
—Michael Herr, *Dispatches*

William Timothy—or, as the literary world knows him, simply "Tim"—
O'Brien may not embrace his narrow reputation as one of a small handful
of his generation's greatest chroniclers of the Vietnam experience. Still, he
comes by the moniker honestly. O'Brien, the author of eight books to date,
all of which deal with issues related to Vietnam, is the son of William T.
and Ava E. (Schultz) O'Brien, both of whom were involved in World War
II—his father in the Pacific theater and his mother as a WAVE (Women
Accepted for Voluntary Emergency Service, a division of the navy).
O'Brien writes in his memoir, *If I Die in a Combat Zone, Box Me Up and Ship
Me Home*—his first published book and, according to O'Brien, a mostly
true account of his tour of duty—"I was bred with the haste and dispatch
and careless muscle-flexing of a nation giving bridle to its own good for-
tune and success. I was fed by the spoils of 1945 victory" (11).

Having come of age as the war in Vietnam became more an obligation
than an option, particularly for a young midwestern man from a solid
family, regardless of education, O'Brien recalls doubting his initial vehe-
ment opposition to the war and giving in to the persistent pressures of
life in small-town America. In addition to his own indecision, he writes,

there was the influence of "the town, my family, my teachers, a whole history of the prairie. Like magnets, these things pulled in one direction or the other, almost physical forces weighting the problem so that, in the end, it was less reason and more gravity that was the final influence" (*If I Die* 18). That sentiment appears repeatedly in O'Brien's work.

But before Vietnam, there was Minnesota. After World War II, O'Brien's parents settled back into daily life, his father as an insurance salesman and his mother as an elementary-school teacher. O'Brien was born October 1, 1946, in Austin, Minnesota, the first of three children. After 10 years in Austin, he was raised in nearby Worthington, which touts itself, the author relates with no small irony, as "The Turkey Capital of the World" for its large number of poultry farms and a penchant for spectacle. Of the town, a community of fewer than 10,000 inhabitants on the country's middle plains, near the Iowa and North Dakota state lines and 170 miles north of Omaha, Nebraska, O'Brien says,

> If you look in a dictionary under the word "boring," you will find a little pen-and-ink illustration of Worthington. . . . Every September in my home town, on September fifteenth, there is an event called "Turkey Day." And what Turkey Day consists of is the farmers will put their turkeys in their trucks, drive them into town, dump them in front of the Esso gas station on one end of Main Street, and then they'll herd the turkeys up Main Street, and we, the citizens of Worthington, will all sit on the curbs and watch the turkeys go by. And then we'd go home. That's our big day! Well, you can imagine what the rest of the days are like. ("Tim O'Brien, President's Lecture")

O'Brien concedes that many towns across the United States are similar, with their share of stereotypical housewives, ministers, and Kiwanis and country-club members. Perhaps one of his most caustic and telling remarks on the reasons for going to war—or what he saw as the ultimate lack of purpose in the war—however, is that Worthington's town fathers, "the people in that town [who] sent me to war . . . couldn't spell the word 'Hanoi' if you spotted them three vowels" ("Tim O'Brien, President's Lecture"). More than half the town's residents are of German and Scandinavian descent, committed to a work ethic that has fallen out of favor in much of the country; many families whose ancestors settled the area in the last century have remained, fighting rugged winters and an unpredictable job market. Those geographic and economic facts are the source for much of O'Brien's philosophical and social commentary in his first novel, *Northern Lights.*

In fact, many of O'Brien's ideas concerning the effects of place on his characters were formed as he memorized the hard, inscrutable, yet subtle landscapes of his youth. The contradictions that arise in a consideration of O'Brien the author and O'Brien the soldier, who releases his soul into words by way of organizing the horror of war, are apparent from the outset of what would come to be, above all and often to the exclusion of all else, a literary life. Don Lee writes, "For a brief time, he contemplated being a writer, inspired by some old clippings he'd found of his father's— personal accounts about fighting in Iwo Jima and Okinawa that had been published in the *New York Times* during World War II" (196). The early promise of a life in books would come true, in a way, when O'Brien, like his father, published personal accounts of his own war—Vietnam—in various Minnesota newspapers.

To be sure, O'Brien was more cut out for the literary life than for the games that his peers played. In explaining the difficulties of being a distinctly unathletic child and a failed shortstop on his Little League team in Minnesota in the 1950s, O'Brien writes with typical matter-of-factness, "I couldn't hit a baseball. Too small for football, but I stuck it out through junior high, hoping something would change. When nothing happened, I began to read. I read Plato and Erich Fromm, the Hardy boys and enough Aristotle to make me prefer Plato" (*If I Die* 14). To satisfy his passion for books, especially stories of any kind, O'Brien recalls spending his days in the Noble County Library, one of the places where he felt most comfortable, immersing himself in literature. One favorite of the young Tim, *Larry of the Little League,* tells a great deal about O'Brien's preference for the intellectual life over sports; O'Brien claims that he wrote his first novel, *Timmy of the Little League,* as a 10-year-old immediately after first reading *Larry.* Decades later, the intertwining of memory and imagination, as well as the author's obsessive attention to language and meaning-making, would inform much of O'Brien's fiction. O'Brien says of *Cacciato* that "the premise ... was essentially *Timmy of the Little League*—a book about a soldier walking away from Vietnam, heading for Paris" ("Tim O'Brien, President's Lecture").

To dull the edge of his boredom, O'Brien practiced magic tricks. The image of the magician and the machinations of a performer seemingly able to subvert reality influenced O'Brien and would become an important metaphor in the novel *In the Lake of the Woods,* which dissects the tour of duty of John Wade, "the Sorcerer." Many other characters would experience events based on various aspects of O'Brien's childhood, particularly the historical lens through which O'Brien viewed his own early life, which was relatively unscathed by tragedy. Still, the observant O'Brien felt many of the same fears of returning to war that most children felt. With World War II barely a memory, the Korean War captured the headlines; with Korea out of the way, the country was gearing up to send its sons to Vietnam. Always in the background was the cold war.

Although he does not speak often of the details of his childhood, preferring instead to remain on the topic of writing, one may assume, given his interest in using autobiographical details as the basis for many of his characters' fears and ambitions, that he thought much about the cold war. The proximity of nuclear warheads to their homes affected many children during this time. His character Cowling (both Cowling and O'Brien share a given name: William) faces those fears in *The Nuclear Age* as he imagines compulsively that a group of ICBMs situated near his boyhood home in Montana becomes the catalyst for Armageddon. O'Brien's concern over the response of his neighbors, friends, and family to his duty in Vietnam is also a major issue for his characters, not the least in *If I Die* (1973), *Northern Lights* (1975), and *The Things They Carried* (1990).

O'Brien's experiences in Vietnam are well documented, either in his memoir, which critics take more or less at face value, or nested in novels and short stories that combine experiential and fictional components. O'Brien had been out of college for barely a month—he was class president and graduated summa cum laude and Phi Beta Kappa from Macalester College with a degree in political science—when he received his draft notice one mid-June day upon returning to his parents' home from the golf course. "I took it into the kitchen where my mother and father were having lunch, and I dropped it on the table," he says. "My father looked at it, and my mom looked at it, and I looked at it, and there was absolute silence in that kitchen. They knew about my feeling toward the war, how much I despised it, but they also knew I was a child of Worthington" ("Tim O'Brien, President's Lecture"). Already an outspoken supporter for diplomacy, he marched in protest of the war and had designs on joining the State Department after college. He tells Lee, "I thought we needed people who were progressive and had the patience to try diplomacy instead of dropping bombs on people" (196). He also mentions to Steven Kaplan that "from 1964 to 1968, while I attended Macalester College, there were no real demonstrations against the war. Four or five local activists might wave signs saying 'End the War.' I wasn't among those four or five people. I was, however, a big supporter of Gene McCarthy. . . . I knocked on doors for him, took trips up to Wisconsin to help out during the primaries" (*Understanding Tim O'Brien* 2–3).

One of the defining moments of O'Brien's young adulthood was the soul-searching he underwent while considering whether to accept his conscription. A story that O'Brien often relates in his readings and lectures, most notably in "On the Rainy River" from *The Things They Carried*, takes him to International Falls, Minnesota, on the Canadian border, to a lake where he considers heading across the border to avoid serving in Vietnam. Although the old man accompanying him knows why O'Brien is there (the younger man, not wanting to give himself away, makes a poor show of fishing and enjoying himself; not a good actor, he cannot hide the truth), he talks around the issue, letting O'Brien make his own decision. When O'Brien finishes his story, his audience is held in rapt attention by the man who admits his weakness. Only then does he astonish his audience by explaining that the story he has just presented as fact is instead fabricated, a tale created and told to define the experience of wanting to run but being unable to gather the courage to do so. A former student of O'Brien's describes the experience of hearing the story live: "He leans in over the microphone, like he's confessing, though the look on his face made it seem more like he was the priest and we were the sinners, and he tells us everything he just said was fiction—all true, he says, but fiction nonetheless. Most people familiar at all with O'Brien's works have heard this from him before" (Dayley 317). Regardless of its genesis, the story is indicative of O'Brien's state of mind at the time and explains, at least in part, his later reputation as a stylist who, perhaps more than any other writer focusing on Vietnam, combines reality and fiction with little regard for the story's surface relation to the "truth."

When he finally accepted his fate in the military, O'Brien, with the optimism of naïveté, assumed that he would be assigned a position as a cook or clerk. Instead, he was made an infantryman in the U.S. Army's Fifth Battalion, 46th Infantry, better known as the Americal Division. Once engaged in battle, the troops would fight an enemy that had become difficult to define. O'Brien's Vietnam experience is marked by his assignment on the ground in the My Lai area, a series of hamlets in the Vietnamese countryside that would become infamous when it was revealed that Lieutenant William Calley had led a massacre on one of the villages in March 1968, leaving an estimated 500 Vietnamese dead, many of them women and children (see chapter 2 for an in-depth discussion of the historical importance of that event). O'Brien tells Bruckner, "When the unit I went with got [to Vietnam] in February 1969, we all wondered why the place was so hostile. We did not know there had been a massacre there a year earlier" (C15).

O'Brien earned a Purple Heart for a shrapnel wound sustained from an exploding grenade. He returned from Vietnam as a sergeant in 1970 and considered giving up writing altogether—he had yet to publish any significant writing at this point—instead enrolling in Harvard's Kennedy School for graduate work in political science with a focus on American military intervention. He stopped short of finishing his dissertation, deciding instead to work as a national-affairs reporter for the *Washington Post* (he had interned there during his time at Harvard) for a short time before becoming a full-time writer. *If I Die* was published in 1973, the same year O'Brien married a magazine production manager. The memoir introduces readers to O'Brien's trademark style and draws on a long tradition of American war writers with journalistic backgrounds, including Stephen Crane, Ernest Hemingway, Norman Mailer, and Philip Caputo. Importantly, *If I Die* provides a context within which to read O'Brien's subsequent novels and short stories, as he comments on issues relating to the war, literature, philosophy, and an American sensibility that would be reexamined and reassessed in both O'Brien's work and by society at large. The memoir is a synthesis of imagination and experience and a means of sense-making for O'Brien, who explains the simple and brutal truth behind what he witnessed and what he will spend most of his adult life writing about: "Now, war ended, all I am left with are simple, unprofound scraps of truth. Men die. Fear hurts and humiliates. It is hard to be brave. It is hard to know what bravery is. Dead human beings are heavy and awkward to carry, things smell different in Vietnam . . . " (*If I Die* 23).

Northern Lights, an essentially realist book that takes the landscape of O'Brien's youth for its setting and the return of a Vietnam veteran for its backdrop, was published two years later. Although O'Brien openly regrets some of the stylistic decisions he made in the novel, *Going after Cacciato,* which followed in 1978 and had little in common with the straightforward plot and characterization of the earlier novel, owes much to the failed experiment (to paraphrase O'Brien) that was *Northern Lights. Cacciato,* which came during a time rich in explorations of Vietnam's effect on the American psyche, won the National Book Award and earned O'Brien a reputation alongside Philip Caputo, Michael Herr, and David Halberstam, among others, as the writers who most powerfully evoked the Vietnam experience. The late 1970s was the pinnacle period of art focused on the study of Vietnam, Samuel G. Freedman points out, only two or three years removed from the fall of Saigon. Herr and Caputo published their seminal works in 1977. *Cacciato* followed a year later.

After publishing his sixth book and fifth novel, *In the Lake of the Woods*, in 1994, O'Brien maintained in several published interviews and profiles that he was seriously considering giving up writing. Before the year's end, however, he had published the most poignant exploration of his time in Vietnam, an essay titled "The Vietnam in Me." The lengthy *New York Times Magazine* piece describes O'Brien's return to Vietnam earlier in the year with Kate, a Harvard graduate student. Their lengthy romance, begun after O'Brien's earlier divorce, is winding down to an inevitably painful end. Still, he attempts to explain to Kate the significance of the war in his life and the connection of that experience, finally, with his current state of mind: "Later in the night, as on many other nights, we talk about the war. I try to explain—ineptly, no doubt—that Vietnam was more than terror. For me, at least, Vietnam was partly love. With each step, each light-year of a second, a foot soldier is always almost dead, or so it feels, and in such circumstance you can't *help* but love" (51).

The tone of the passage is not unusual in O'Brien's work—the numbing shock of war mingled with the heartbreaking loss and intense love that define human experience. Returning to his apartment in Cambridge, Massachusetts, O'Brien draws the inevitable connection between his present reality and recollection by implying that, regardless of how intricately we plan our own disappearances, memories find us. Ruminating on his relationships and his war experiences, O'Brien admits, "Last night suicide was on my mind. Not whether, but how. Tonight it will be on my mind again. Now it's 4 a.m., June the 5th. The sleeping pills have not worked. I sit in my underwear at this unblinking fool of a computer and try to wrap words around a few horrid truths" (50). That statement is a rare glimpse into the mind of the writer, stripped of everything save the essential humanity of his work and the importance of words in his life. Perhaps not coincidentally, the novels published after O'Brien's 1994 return to Vietnam—*Tomcat in Love* (1998) and *July, July* (2002)—are decidedly less obsessed with the direct influence of Vietnam on the characters' lives three decades after the fact (although, to be sure, the protagonists of both novels are keenly aware of the sacrifices they made all those years before), focusing instead on the characters' lives in the interim.

As of late 2004, O'Brien, active on the workshop and reading circuits, is Mitte Chair in Creative Writing at Texas State University–San Marcos (ironically, the alma mater of President Lyndon B. Johnson, who was instrumental in escalating American involvement in Vietnam after the death of John F. Kennedy). O'Brien accepted the position in 1999. Dayley, a former student, recalling his time with O'Brien in the program, writes,

> When it was your turn to have a conference with him, you didn't meet him in his office—there wasn't much in there, blank walls, a chair, a desk, and a computer which I don't think he ever used. In fact, I don't think he ever even went in his office. . . . He chain smoked all during the conference, holding the cigarette in one hand and a marked-up copy of your story in the other. And it was marked-up. O'Brien takes words seriously, and he did his best to pull us up to his high standards. On one of my stories, frustrated with my apathy or laziness regarding grammar, he wrote, "PROOFREAD! The words are all we have." (316)

O'Brien's attitude toward workshop teaching is only an extension of his own work ethic, envied in writing circles and described by O'Brien himself as the antithesis of the romantic-writer approach. His writing sessions are endless cycles of hard, continuous work that one day, with luck, will appear between covers. After having thrown away thousands of pages of prose that most writers would gladly have taken as their own — *The Nuclear Age,* published in 1985, was apparently the worst instance of this—O'Brien still adheres to a regimen that he likens to that of one of his great influences, Joseph Conrad, who claimed that the "sitting-down" is the most important aspect of the act of writing. O'Brien demystifies the process when he says, "Beyond anything, it seems to me, a writer performs this sitting-down act primarily in search of those rare, very intense moments of artistic pleasure that are as real in their way as the pleasures that can come from any other source" ("Tim O'Brien, President's Lecture"). For O'Brien, the act of writing itself, taken apart from the results, is hardly the Byronic endeavor one might imagine. Commenting on his critical reception and his status as a cult figure in the closed world of fiction workshops and M.F.A. programs, O'Brien reminds Robert Birnbaum, "I'm the guy who sits in his underwear in front of the computer all day. People forget that. That's how I spend my days for four years in a row."

O'Brien's career has been ascendant since *Cacciato* won the National Book Award in 1979, besting the favorites that year, John Irving's *The World According to Garp* and John Cheever's *Stories. The Things They Carried,* whether considered a collection of short stories or a novel, is one of the most celebrated works to come out of Vietnam. His short work, much of which has found its way in one form or another into subsequent books, has been published in the *New Yorker, Ploughshares, Harper's,* the *Atlantic, Esquire, Best American Short Stories,* and the *O. Henry Prize Stories,* among other national venues. Despite having given numerous interviews over the years, O'Brien's personal life has managed—except in his own writing, on his own terms, in prose that often blurs the boundary between fact and fiction—to remain well hidden. In late 2004 O'Brien, recently married and a first-time father (despite having included a 9-year-old daughter in *The Things They Carried,* she never existed), published a poignant, bittersweet letter to his 16-month-old son. Discussing the advantages and disadvantages of late fatherhood and the importance of work in his life until his son was born, he writes, "I had defined myself, for better and for worse, by the novels and stories I had written. I had sought myself in sentences. I had loved myself only insofar as I loved a chapter or a scene or a scrap of dialogue. . . . I doubt that at 28 or even 38 I would have been so willing—so eager—to walk away from my work to warm your bottle" (15).

The events of O'Brien's life, combined with his intense passion for great literature, inform his style. In explaining the inevitable connection between Vietnam and the characters that inhabit his texts, O'Brien says, "All writers revisit terrain. Shakespeare did it with kings, and Conrad did with the ocean, and Faulkner did with the South. It's an emotional and geographical terrain that's given to us by life. Vietnam is there the way childhood is for me" (Lee 201).

2

Creating Art from the Ashes of War: Context and Style in O'Brien's Fiction

"War is the best subject of all," Ernest Hemingway once wrote. "It groups the maximum of material and speeds up the action and brings out all sorts of stuff that normally you would have to wait a lifetime to get."
——Samuel G. Freedman, "The War and the Arts"

The literature of war is as old as war itself—Homer's epic *The Iliad*, for instance, dates back 3,000 years or more—though descriptions of war in America up to World War I are confined primarily to generals' accounts of battles and military strategies, leaving much of war's confusion and chaos to the imagination. In 1895, Stephen Crane published *The Red Badge of Courage*, a journal of a young soldier's introduction to battle in the Civil War, illustrating how battlefield exploits (despite the fact that Crane had never been on the battlefield) might make viable literature in a society more inclined to write and read forward-looking tomes of hope, expansion, and country building. But it was not until the horror of World War I—in which new ways of fighting war meant new ways of dying for hundreds of thousands of young men on the cusp of advances in science and technology that would bring the world into the modern era—that writers began to take wholesale a revised, more cynical attitude toward war. That notion is corroborated by the journalistic style of Ernest Hemingway who, despite his participation in World War I, would become better known for his writing on the Spanish Civil War and social commentary in general; John Dos Passos's stinging indictment of the war specifically and society in general in *Three Soldiers* (1921); and the poetics of Robert Graves and his British counterparts Wilfred Owen and Siegfried Sassoon, men disillusioned by the war and frightened by its possibilities.

World War II, a conflict much more popular with the American people than any other of the century's wars, produced a number of powerful works of literature ranging from correspondent Ernie Pyle's war dispatches, James Jones's *The Thin Red Line* (1962), and John Hersey's *Hiroshima* (1946) to Kurt Vonnegut's *Slaughterhouse-Five* (1972). Richard Hooker's *MASH* (1968) came out of the brief Korean conflict and became a popular television show for more than a decade in the 1970s and 1980s. With the advent of new ways of expression in writing—particularly the modernism that had been translated to an American idiom after World War I and allowed American writers to describe war in all its sublime violence—the literature of war began to express meanings outside the traditional sphere of "war stories." Joseph Heller's *Catch-22* (1961) insinuated itself into mainstream literature not as a war book, but as a novel that explored American optimism and the apprehension of our post–World War II society. "The most obvious generic label for *Catch-22* is that of war novel. The book is often characterized as such and is treated as a major text in several recent critical studies of American war fiction," Robert Merrill writes. "Yet Heller has done everything possible to dissuade us from reading his book as a war novel 'about World War II'" (16). Instead, explains Heller, *Catch-22* deals with "the contemporary regimented business society" (30). In the same way, O'Brien's work, which has become the Vietnam literature of record for many students introduced to contemporary war fiction, challenges the boundaries of genre writing.

O'Brien and his contemporaries were influenced by the introduction in the 1960s of the New Journalism, a style popularized by journalist Tom Wolfe, who used a stream-of-consciousness narrative, creative details, and a conversational style to transform what had to that point been a traditional, objective news story into something that reflected the chaotic, surreal qualities of the subject—in this case, the Vietnam experience. The literature that resulted, Stewart O'Nan observes, expressed a "pronounced split in methods or modes of portraying the war. While some authors choose a documentary realism, others, hoping to come closer to the emotional and intellectual effect of the experience, shoot for a more poetic or metaphorical truth. . . . When an author purposefully mixes real and metaphorical forms, the result can leave the reader with more questions than answers" (6). Such is the nature of O'Brien's work. The chaos in the words themselves is a linguistic metaphor for war, and Herr, Caputo, and others take full advantage of the quasi-fictional aspects of the memoir to further explore their Vietnam experiences.

In assessing the art and literature that came out of the Vietnam War, whether created by those who had experienced the war firsthand—O'Brien; memoirists Philip Caputo, Michael Herr, and Ron Kovic; poet Bruce Weigl; dramatist David Rabe; and novelists Stephen Wright and John Del Vecchio, for instance—or by those who had stayed behind for various reasons, Freedman writes,

> To the usual chemistry of combat, the Vietnam War added even more volatile elements. Vietnam was America's ideological civil war, pitting hawk against dove, hard hat against peacenik. Patriotism gave way to revulsion, to a questioning of the national character. And most important for the men who fought the war—as it seemed to be for the country—Vietnam had no clear ending, neither victory nor surrender. Their art is a search for that final, missing piece. ("War and the Arts" 51)

The push and pull of competing ideologies and attitudes is strong in O'Brien's work. The ambiguity of outcome and the uncertainty of purpose in the war combine with tales of genuine courage and humanity to create viable art. O'Brien's novels are just as important for the themes of everyday life that they develop in the context of the war as they are for their vivid, claustrophobic descriptions of the war itself.

It is a milieu, Don Ringnalda writes, that threatened to erase the possibility of retelling: "what they knew of reality before war was nothing more than a publicly-agreed-upon fiction—a communally embraced shadow. That communal shadow was quickly blasted by war. Language itself seemed to stop casting shadows. There seemed to be an entropic void between word and object" ("Tim O'Brien's Understood Confusion" 95). Much of the literature that O'Brien read as a young man influenced his later decision to write fiction, even if the author's first effort was a memoir, *If I Die in a Combat Zone*. (Critics fail to mention that O'Brien's poignant memoir was begun by a man in his early 20s.) Early in the memoir, a young soldier, the narrator Tim O'Brien (for the sake of argument, most critics emphasize the memoir's fictional elements by viewing the character as an entity separate from the author Tim O'Brien), refers to reading Plato, Aristotle, and the philosopher Erich Fromm. That he read widely is hardly a surprise: his novels are filled with readers, lovers of literature who happen also, incongruously, to be involved in life-and-death struggles on the Vietnam killing grounds. In fact, the well-being of those characters often depends upon their ability to organize their thoughts into a usable reality. They learn those skills not through brute-force training, but through literature.

O'Brien's later style, beginning with *Going after Cacciato*, is a powerful synthesis of descriptive prose and dreamlike, surreal flights of fancy. Those images arise from O'Brien's fragmented experiences in Vietnam—the schizophrenic chaos of the battlefield, simultaneously raucous and desolate—rendered in terms that engage both the layperson and the veteran. The difficulty of capturing in its totality any notion of war is explained in *Cacciato* by Captain Rhallon, an Iranian soldier the men run into in their search for the eponymous soldier of the title. Rhallon observes, "The soldier is not a photographic machine. He is not a camera. He registers, so to speak, only those few items that he is predisposed to register and not a single thing more. Do you understand this? So I am saying to you that after a battle each soldier will have different stories to tell, vastly different stories, and that when a war is ended it is as if there have been a million wars, or as many wars as there were soldiers" (196). Similar observations would be made in various stories in *The Things They Carried* and in the novel *The Nuclear Age,* and, importantly, although more than two decades removed from its Vietnam context, through Wade's tormented conscience in *In the Lake of the Woods.*

Eric James Schroeder compares O'Brien's work to that of the New Journalists Hunter S. Thompson and Tom Wolfe, asserting that "while O'Brien's authorial stance is not as megalomanic as Thompson's, the narrative nonetheless depends on the author's first person viewpoint for its formal cohesion; furthermore, his content, his participation in the Vietnam War . . . is presented as a shared experience and, more importantly, as a *believable* one" ("The Past and the Possible" 117). To be sure, as Freedman concludes, "From the veterans has come a view of the war dramatically different from the one propounded by the antiwar artists of the 1960's and early 70's" ("War and the Arts" 51). Although Caputo's *A Rumor of War* had won a Pulitzer for the author's depiction of his tours of duty in Indochina—a book that, like O'Brien's own *If I Die,* describes the transforming power of war in a decidedly literary way—it is O'Brien's work that continues to enthrall readers of the Vietnam generation, as well as subsequent generations who may not fully grasp the historical importance of the novels' events. Writing in 1994, in his now-famous *New York Times* essay "The Vietnam in Me," O'Brien implies his unease at the notion that little time passes before events that once held an audience rapt in righteous indignation—in this case, the My Lai massacre—have been forgotten: "More than 25 years later, the villainy of that Sunday morning in 1968 has been pushed off to the margins of memory. In the colleges and high schools I sometimes visit, the mention of My Lai brings on null stares, a sort of puzzlement, disbelief mixed with utter ignorance" (52). It is from the ashes of his experiences and through the pain of memory that O'Brien creates his most powerful literature.

HISTORICAL CONTEXTS

> Men who do not expect to receive mercy eventually lose their inclination to grant it.
> —Philip Caputo, *A Rumor of War*

In the Lake of the Woods details one of the most misunderstood events of the Vietnam War, the My Lai massacre. The massacre is the basis for John Wade's humiliation and the catalyst for his wife's disappearance and Wade's own suicidal plunge into the Minnesota wilderness. Lieutenant William Calley, an unassuming draftee from Columbus, Georgia, perpetrated the worst documented war crime in U.S. history during a four-hour attack that claimed the lives of some 500 or more Vietnamese, many of them women and children. Calley, whose justification for his actions was published as a memoir, *Lieutenant Calley: His Own Story* (1971), details his naive and rather nonchalant response to having killed, by his own admission, at least 22 unarmed Vietnamese (the number of deaths for which he was held culpable at trial; most estimates go much higher). Calley recalls that his goal in Vietnam was to become, above all, a good soldier: "We thought, *We will go to Vietnam and be Audie Murphys. Kick in the door, run in the hooch, give it a good burst*—kill. And get a big kill ratio in Vietnam. Get a big kill count" (28). After the trial, Calley was the only one of the 30 indicted participants to receive prison time. He was pardoned by President Nixon after spending less than six months in the stockade. His actions would further divide a country unsure, exactly, of what it expected from its decades-long participation in a war that would eventually cost nearly 60,000 American lives.

In O'Brien's work, the influence of My Lai is felt most strongly in *If I Die* and *In the Lake of the Woods*, particularly in the sections of the later work that include transcribed passages from court-martial proceedings. Despite his obvious disgust with what transpired, O'Brien offers commentary from both sides of the issue. He has spoken openly about the difficulty of being on the ground in the My Lai area in 1969, a year after the event, when anti-American sentiment in Vietnam had reached a crescendo, and he discusses the war's profound impact on the American myth on which he and his generation were raised:

> So along comes Vietnam, which disrupted all of these myths and stereotypes—"disrupted" is the wrong word, but erased all these myths—and substituted a kind of hard, tough reality: America is not always good. It's hard to distinguish the white hats and the black hats. You can't always tell them apart. Sometimes they commingle. Sometimes a man can do something beautiful and sublime one moment and something horrendous the next. Witness My Lai. So, in a sense, all of my writing about Vietnam has been a kind of delayed response to the simplistic images and icons that were presented to me as a young man through pop art. (Marquiss 11)

In *If I Die,* O'Brien describes the reaction of Major Callicles, his commanding officer, to news of the massacre: "You ever been to My Lai? Well, I'll tell you, those civilians—you call them civilians—they kill American GI's. They plant mines and spy and snipe and kill us. Sure, you all print color pictures of dead little boys, but the live ones—take pictures of the live ones digging holes for mines" (188).

The attitude of distrust toward the Vietnamese that engendered such a crime is a matter of a great deal of scrutiny in histories of the war. James R. Ebert contends that, although the Viet Cong—the identified true enemy of the Americans and the South Vietnamese—used civilians to undermine American efforts, "civilian duplicity was undoubtedly exaggerated, but the tales were taken to heart by American soldiers, and often provided the basis for soldiers' attitudes and, more tragically, their actions" (296). In addition, "as soldiers progressed in their tours of duty and became more and more desensitized by the war, their attitude and self-control often eroded. The change was often evident in the men's writing" (301). In a letter home, Ebert reports, soldier Ed Austin wrote, "We make more VC than we kill by the way these people are treated. I won't go into detail but some of the things that take place would make you ashamed of good old America" (315). The sentiment echoes words reported by Ebert and others, social historians who, like O'Brien in *If I Die,* focus on the reasons for the war and the extravagant cost in lives, money, and reputation that the United States paid for its participation. "Even in the abstract, I get angry at the stunning, almost cartoonish narcissism of American policy on this issue," O'Brien writes. "I get angrier at the narcissism of an American public that embraces and breathes life into the policy—so arrogant, so ignorant, so self-righteous, so wanting in the most fundamental qualities of sympathy and fairness and mutuality" ("The Vietnam in Me" 55). A great number of historical accounts and social histories describe experiences similar to O'Brien's and are useful as background, among them Ebert's *A Life in a Year* (1993), Wilbur H. Morrison's *The Elephant and the Tiger* (1990), James S. Olson and Randy Roberts's *Where the Domino Fell* (1991), and Stanley Karnow's comprehensive *Vietnam: A History* (1983).

Of course, the Vietnam War is only one in a litany of transformative historical events to be cataloged by O'Brien's characters over the span of the memoir and the body of fiction. *The Nuclear Age* focuses on the rise and escalation of the cold war between the United States and the Soviet Union, a result of animosity spawned by losses incurred in World War II and the possibilities—for both advancement and destruction—inherent in the advent of the atomic age. The dispute, heightened by Soviet leader Joseph Stalin's rabid hatred of the West, arose originally from a clash of ideologies. The Americans, according to the Soviets, were the imperialist state, and the Soviets the "progressive" Communist state (or, as the Americans would have it, the conflict was one of democracy versus oppression, myopic economic policies, and bureaucracy). The confrontation arose as a postwar land grab that prompted the Soviets, through its East German puppet government, to raise an Iron Curtain that would stand until the late 1980s.

A metaphor for the decades-long dispute is Sputnik, which in October 1957 became the first satellite to orbit Earth and was a wake-up call for Americans, who had become comfortable with their position as world leaders. The *New York Times*, first describing the event and its impact on October 6, reports,

> The Soviet announcement inevitably was a sobering one for the West, particularly the United States. It tended to confirm the claim by Moscow six weeks ago of the first successful test of an intercontinental ballistic missile, and indicated that the U.S.S.R. was—for the moment, at least—ahead of the U.S. in the crucial rocket race. The Russians sought to make political capital of their satellite—*Sputnik*, in Russian—by calling the achievement that of "the new socialist society." ("Round the World in 96 Minutes" 193)

Four days later, the *Times* further developed the story's implications for Soviet/American relationships, contending, "It is becoming increasingly evident that the main purpose of the sputnik, the man-made moon launched by the Soviets, is political rather than scientific" ("Politics of the Sputnik" 32). A later generation would remember the cold war in terms of its epicenter at Checkpoint Charley, the dividing line between East and West Berlin; the Cuban Missile Crisis, an October 1962 standoff between President John F. Kennedy and Soviet leader Nikita Khrushchev that nearly resulted in the use of nuclear weapons; and the Olympics struggles that resulted in boycotts, allegations of drug use by Eastern Bloc athletes, and memorable confrontations between American and Soviet teams—particularly in the 1972 basketball final, which the United States lost in a controversial late-game referee's decision, and the 1980 hockey tournament, which the United States won by defeating a juggernaut Soviet team.

The cold war figures prominently in *The Nuclear Age* and less directly impacts the characters in *Tomcat in Love* and *July, July*, acting as historical shorthand, similar to the role of Vietnam in those same novels. Although O'Brien insists that *The Nuclear Age* contains dark comic qualities, the overarching emotion of protagonist William Cowling's quest is fear, and his only goal the elimination of that fear. O'Brien mingles images of the young William cowering beneath a Ping-Pong table in his family's basement with later images of the adult Cowling protesting a war he refuses to fight. By combining the two images—one a scene recognizable by many who lived through the early days of the cold war and one defining the thin edge of the wedge that had become the Vietnam War—the author suggests the continued and pervasive influence of violence or, at the very least, the anticipation of imminent violence. The cold war represents clearcut notions of good versus evil, a democratic way of life versus the oppression of the Soviet socialist system, a good-natured détente set against the perceived unbending iron will of the Soviets. Vietnam was a relatively small war fought for parcels of land that were, in retrospect, laughably small; the cold war, ostensibly fought for the same reason—the protection of America from the threat of communism—engendered paralyzing fear but cost relatively few lives.

The upshot of Vietnam and the emergence of the cold war was a counterculture that has become a cliché only two generations later. In *July, July*, many of the old friends who meet for their 30th class reunion in 2001 to trade stories and listen to ersatz Rolling Stones music arranged for clarinet are profoundly aware of the earnest absurdity of their actions as young adults in college all those years before. Even the men who fought valiantly in the war and the women who married well have their regrets. None of the returnees are as happy as they should be, O'Brien implies, and the unanswerable question asked in various forms throughout the novel is, if we are not proud of what we did in response to the war, then what have we to show for our lives?

O'Brien's continued increasing disillusionment with the war in his later novels signals his disdain for Americans who accept the ubiquity of war and believe in the infallibility of American ideology, the very attitudes that allow us to fight in a war such as Vietnam in the first place. In "The Vietnam in Me," O'Brien writes, "Evil has no place, it seems, in our national mythology. We erase it. We use ellipses. We salute ourselves and take pride in America the White Knight, America the Lone Ranger, America's sleek laser-guided weaponry beating up on Saddam and his legion of devils" (52). He posits in his later fiction that the horror of Vietnam and the nagging fear and frustrating inactivity of the cold war are not entirely separable. Still, Vietnam is the starting point for any reading of O'Brien's fiction, a defining point in the lives of a generation, so that "when Saigon fell in 1975, it was as if those last helicopters left behind not only Vietnam but memory itself. A collective amnesia set in" (Freedman 54). Perhaps that amnesia is the necessary result of a war that engaged its soldiers on every level, the psychological torment coupled with a loathing of the place itself that approached the pathological: "Alpha Company began to regard Quang Ngai itself as the true enemy—the physical place, the soil and the paddies. What had started for us as a weird, vicious little war soon evolved into something far beyond vicious, a hopped-up killer strain of nihilism, waste without want, aimlessness of deed mixed with aimlessness of spirit" (*If I Die* 54). That sentiment forms the basis for the confusion and alienation of O'Brien's characters, the ones living "out on the peripheries of human experience" (Rosica), who equate a land and its history with physical and spiritual death. It is the process of reconciliation for those characters, perceptions filtered through the smudged lens of history, that O'Brien describes so well.

O'BRIEN'S FICTION

Although O'Brien, not unlike Caputo, first expressed his Vietnam experience through the memoir form as a way of lessening the psychological impact of the war, the writers who influence O'Brien's work—he cites Jorge Luis Borges, Joseph Conrad, Ernest Hemingway, William Faulkner, and others—represent an eclectic mix of styles, genres, and backgrounds.

Undoubtedly those writers helped to mold O'Brien's style, which ranges from memoir (*If I Die*) to realist fiction (*Northern Lights, The Nuclear Age*) to magical realism (*Going after Cacciato*), comedy (*Tomcat in Love*), and experimental short fiction (*The Things They Carried*). Still, O'Brien contends, "the huge 'influence,' finally, is the life that surrounds me—people, places, events" (Rosica).

Despite the range of styles that he employs, O'Brien uses Vietnam as a common contextual grounding. Surviving the war and transcending the historical limitations of the fiction are the characters themselves, each protagonist as different as the style with which O'Brien approaches a particular story. Within the subject of war, the author explores the world from the perspective of both the dispassionate observer—particularly when the emotion evoked by an action exceeds a character's ability to articulate it, as in the serio-ironic death of Ted Lavender in *The Things They Carried*— and the first-person protagonist tuned to life's intricate harmonies. Points of view shift as well, from the introspection of the first-person narrator that employs a modified stream-of-consciousness style (*If I Die, Tomcat in Love*) to the more objective third-person narrator, both limited and omniscient, that records events in graphic, though necessarily distanced (and distancing), detail. O'Brien's approach to fiction, discovering and exploring the truth and recording his perceptions, wherever they take him, owes much to the writing that came out of World War I. The modernists, appalled by man's ability to wreak unprecedented havoc on man, began to question the future. There is a direct link—a human link—between the experiences of World War I soldiers exposed to mustard gas, months-long sieges, and high casualty rates and their Vietnam counterparts half a century later, similarly subjected to napalm, guerilla attacks, and body bags. The literature that comes out of both wars reflects the fragmented self, and, as Freedman points out, "Vietnam literature makes a conscious connection to the disillusioned writing that emerged after World War I from the British and from American expatriate Ernest Hemingway" (56).

O'Brien takes *Cacciato*'s epigraph from Siegfried Sassoon, a talented young British poet and a dedicated soldier who became disgusted by what he witnessed. Caputo took a similar interest in Sassoon, and the memoirs of both writers seem to have followed related tracks. Caputo, whose own Pulitzer Prize–winning work is often seen as a parallel text to *If I Die* and was published just a year before *Going after Cacciato* changed the landscape of Vietnam fiction, expresses a similar sentiment to that of O'Brien when he tells Robert Dahlin, "I'd put my own [book] aside for months because I didn't know what I wanted it to be. Besides, the war kept going on. There was no closure, so it was hard to write about. . . . I found that fiction wasn't supple enough. . . . I was too much a who-what-where kind of guy" (81).

The depth with which O'Brien views his subject results, in part, from the thematic similarity of his work to that of his modernist predecessors. The modernists—among them James Joyce, T. S. Eliot, Thomas Mann, and Joseph Conrad—gained strength for their convictions in the wake of World War I and reveled in new ways of articulating perception and experience. As Vicki Mahaffey points out, the advent of modern literature marked either a new height of literary prowess or the end of the novel, depending upon the perceiver: "In its positive sense, 'modernism' signals a revolutionary break from established orthodoxies, a celebration of the present, and an experimental investigation into the future. As a negative value, 'modernism' has connoted an incoherent, even opportunistic heterodoxy, an avoidance of the discipline of tradition" (*Guide to Literary Theory and Criticism* 512). It is important to note that the modern does not imply that art has changed the world, but rather that art has responded to a world in flux.

A scene from *If I Die* illustrates that principle: Tim O'Brien's friend Erik acts as the narrator's muse, leading O'Brien, through discussions on the works of the modernists Robert Frost, Marianne Moore, and Ezra Pound, to a better understanding of his role as soldier. Erik, after reciting stanzas from Pound's poem "Hugh Selwyn Mauberly," which details the different reasons that men go to war, explains to O'Brien, "Pound is right. . . . Look into your own history. Here we are. Mama has been kissed goodbye, we've grabbed our rifles, we're ready for war. All this not because of conviction, not for ideology; rather it's from fear of society's censure, just as Pound claims" (37). That sentiment colors O'Brien's response to his own participation in the war and makes its way, in various forms, into many retellings of his own history. Critic Stephen Spender sees that continuous re-visioning of one's past as natural in the modern, when "artists have to learn the idiom of changed speech, vision and hearing, and mould the modern experience into forms either revolutionized or modified" (50).

The character Tim O'Brien undergoes a similar transformation, awakened from his torpor after being bludgeoned by the banality of Middle America in the late 1960s. He is thrown into the horror of war, compelled by his sense of duty to fulfill his obligation to the townsfolk steeped in the history of small-town Minnesota. He remarks on the first pages of *If I Die*, "Piled on top of this was the town, my family, my teachers, a whole history of the prairie. Like magnets, these things pulled in one direction

or the other, almost physical forces weighting the problem, so that, in the
end, it was less reason and more gravity that was the final influence" (18).
O'Brien's contradictory impulses—one to run, the other to fight for his
country when "certain blood was being shed for uncertain reasons" (*The
Things They Carried* 40)—are a result of his having had the ambition and
the heart, despite deep ambivalence toward his role in the war, to pen the
memoir. Most of his characters feel the burden of contradiction, an illus-
tration of the Romantic poet John Keats's articulation of a "Negative Ca-
pability," the ability of a writer to work within contradictions in order to
discover truth. It is a notion with which O'Brien is keenly familiar. He
tells Karen Rosica, "There's a frustration that comes from uncertainty and
ambiguity, but there's also a beguiling fascination that comes with it. It's
maybe why I'm captivated by gambling—the uncertainty of it. . . . I, as a
writer and as a human being, make do with what I can [in terms of]
ambiguity and uncertainty and try to plod onward writing these novels."
That ambiguity and uncertainty found voice in his first two published
books in a realism deeply rooted in his Minnesota childhood. Both books
are the observations of a young man writing his thoughts for the first
time; the later style, beginning with *Cacciato,* is certainly the more intricate,
more mature style. Although O'Brien does not deny that *If I Die* contains
certain fictional elements—the recording of conversations, for instance,
and various shifting of events to give the "plot" a continuity it might
otherwise lack—the style is journalistic. The characters' emotions, despite
being predicated upon such volatile situations as battle and the return of
a wounded brother (as in *Northern Lights,* for instance), are controlled.
Similar emotions, seen through the eyes of an older, wiser writer, find
voice in new, less constrained, ways.

   Although magical realism often connotes a prose style practiced primarily by Latin American writers—particularly Gabriel García Márquez,
most notably in *One Hundred Years of Solitude,* and Borges in his intricately
organized short fictions—O'Brien grounds his style in the reportage of
Vietnam. The term *magical realism,* Karen Castellucci Cox points out, was
"coined by German art critic Franz Roh in the 1920s to describe painters
experimenting with reality on their canvases, [and] the term came to represent a particular literary mode that proliferated in the works of Latin
American novelists who . . . adapted conventional realism to make it distinctly their own" (15–16). Magical realism implies flights of fancy in fiction, though it applies equally to fiction whose tragedy is mitigated by
the protagonist's escapism (aside from O'Brien's own *Cacciato* and *The
Things They Carried,* Toni Morrison's *Beloved* is a good example). Ringnalda

defines magical realism in O'Brien's fiction when he writes, "The task O'Brien seems to have assigned himself in *Cacciato,* and even more so in *Carried,* is to see himself metafictionally seeing himself as a writer, like Berlin seeing himself outside a labyrinthine tunnel while looking at himself—future to the past—through a periscope inside the tunnel" ("Tim O'Brien's Understood Confusion" 100). That O'Brien should attempt such a style in *Cacciato* is natural, it seems, as he had written the memoir and his first novel, *Northern Lights,* before writing the more complicated—and in many ways, since it is not bound by the rules of realist prose, more expressive—style that drives *Cacciato.*

The protagonist Paul Berlin's fascination with the story of Cacciato, a characterless soldier who deserts and improbably heads on foot for Paris, some 8,000 miles distant, is born of his own desire to be out of Vietnam (the Quang Ngai landscape that figures so prominently in *If I Die* appears again in *Cacciato*) and, on a more immediate level, to complete his night guard duty in the observation post during the several hours of narrative time that comprise the novel's action. A third narrative thread has Berlin recalling his experiences through the first six months of his tour in Vietnam. O'Brien's strength in the novel is his ability to intertwine all three storylines into a sensible whole. For much of the novel, the truth or fiction of Cacciato's situation is not known absolutely (an echo of Captain Rhallon's speech to the Americans), but only through the observations of the other soldiers who, like Berlin, would rather not be in country.

Although the novel's title suggests a chase and perhaps capture, if it offers closure at all—Cacciato is the ostensible target of their search, but is conspicuous only by his absence throughout much of the novel—the story focuses on Paul Berlin more than any other figure. In that sense, the novel is a bildungsroman, the transition of a young man from aimless college student to hard-bitten Vietnam soldier. In chapter 28, one of 10 "Observation Post" chapters, the limited-omniscient narrator (the reader may logically conflate the narrator and Berlin in these chapters) insists that "he did have a history" (180).

Notwithstanding the many quick deaths that O'Brien describes in the course of his memoir and novels, the slower spiritual death and historical erasure of the infantryman is nearly as insidious, the crushing sameness of everyday life grinding away at the soldiers' resolve until nothing remains as incentive and no events—including death—strike the men as being particularly remarkable. As O'Brien the soldier points out after an attack on a Vietnamese village, "things happened, things came to an end. There was no sense of developing drama. All that remained was debris, four smoldering holes in the dirt, a few fires that would burn themselves out" (*If I Die* 7). The scene is played out with heavy irony in the later *July, July,* in which Amy Robinson, one of the story's many protagonists, reminisces, "Used to be, we'd talk about the Geneva Accords, the Tonkin Gulf Resolution. Now it's down to liposuction and ex-husbands. Can't trust anybody over sixty" (18). The remark is an ironic adjunct to the counterculture mantra "Don't trust anyone over thirty." O'Brien's characters have become the people they once despised.

Still, those characters are important to O'Brien, whose writing has joined the canon of American literature not for its examination of Vietnam per se, but for its ability to seamlessly combine a keen historical sense with a humanity absent from much literature that details the war and its consequences. Near the conclusion of "The Vietnam in Me," O'Brien, holding the hand of the woman who was bound to break his heart when they returned to Boston, recalls in a rush of words the experiences that occurred a quarter-century ago on the very spot where he now stood: "I hear myself talking about what happened here so long ago, motioning out at the rice, describing chaos and horror beyond anything I would experience until a few months later. I tell her how Paige lost his lower leg, how we had to probe for McElhaney in the flooded paddy, how the gunfire went on and on, how in the course of two hell-on-earth hours we took 13 casualties" (56). Of the impression that the stories may have had on his companion, O'Brien muses, "I doubt Kate remembers a word. Maybe she shouldn't" (56). It is for the ones who don't remember—or never knew—that O'Brien writes.

3

If I Die in a Combat Zone, Box Me Up and Ship Me Home (1973)

> I couldn't relate that I had changed. But everybody I knew couldn't figure me out. "Hey, what is this? Patriotic Jim all of a sudden, going to this great war—doesn't know what for."
>
> —Mark Baker, *Nam*

"It wasn't the material that Vietnam presented me with so much as it was a revolution of personality," O'Brien says of his decision to pen a memoir. "I'd been an academic and intellectual sort of person, and Vietnam changed all that" (Shostak and Bourne 75). That understated response to the war is an ideal starting point for an analysis of O'Brien's fiction as seen through the lens of his single full-length work of nonfiction. The result is what Philip Beidler compares, on the one hand, to the "central tradition of spiritual biography" of Jonathan Edwards, John Woolman, Benjamin Franklin, and Henry David Thoreau; on the other hand, the book reveals "in its own profound humanity and its distinctly literary quality of aspiration toward some large and perhaps enduring significance, the depictions of men at war by Whitman, Melville, Crane, and Hemingway" (*American Literature* 99).

The book's title comes from a marching song that young soldiers on their way to Vietnam learn while in basic training, the violent and vulgar words ringing in their ears as their instructors turn raw recruits into more efficient soldiers—and killers. The nonchalance with which the words are chanted masks the soldiers' fears of going to war and marks their indoctrination into a system that exists only to perpetuate itself. Explaining his initial response to basic training, O'Brien recalls doggedly maintaining his individuality for as long as possible: "Without sympathy or compassion, I instructed my intellect and eyes: ignore the horde" (33). O'Brien would soon realize, as so many of his comrades before him had discovered, the futility of fighting the system.

The memoir, told in 23 chapters more thematically linked than connected by plot, contains the elements that would make O'Brien's fiction so recognizable: alternating scenes of intense description and introspection, the ironic juxtaposition of images, observations that blend fact and fiction. In fact, much of the criticism commenting on the memoir explores O'Brien's blurring of the boundaries between truth and fiction, an issue that comes to the fore in similar discussions of *Going after Cacciato, The Things They Carried*, and *In the Lake of the Woods*. Many of the memoir's images prefigure the events and plotlines that appear in the fiction, not the least by creating "a complex dialectic between what [O'Brien] calls 'story-truth' and 'happening-truth,'" a perspective that "many critics have interpreted . . . as validating their own view of the Vietnam War as unknowable or crazy or 'unreal'" (Franklin 34–35).

That view of the war as somehow unknowable and therefore unavailable for analysis is, O'Brien says, an attempt on the part of the people who took part in the war to expiate their own guilt and rationalize their unthinking involvement. O'Brien does not shun his responsibility for having been in the war; still, more than 30 years later, he harbors a sense of cowardice and anger at having taken part. The "happening-truth" that he articulates in *If I Die* is the most direct statement of his disdain for war, though the fiction would transform that raw material into stories whose arc at times allows for the possibility that the characters may transcend their situations. And although O'Brien professes great admiration for the war stories of Hemingway (he quotes a conversation on bravery between Frederic Henry and Catherine Barkely from the author's *A Farewell to Arms*), he wonders how such stories can be written without fully exploring the thoughts of the men who fight. The author's answer to that question would become important to the work that followed.

Not until he returned from Vietnam did O'Brien decide to take on the memoir form. While in Vietnam, he had written articles for the *Washington*

Post and newspapers in Minnesota, though only a small portion of *If I Die*, notably the pages that became the chapter "Step Lively," was written in-country over a period of months during which O'Brien felt compelled to record his experiences. During his tour of duty, O'Brien recalls briefly having tried his hand at poetry and short fiction. Upon his return to the United States, he considered a career as a journalist, reporting for the *Washington Post* during and after his graduate studies at Harvard.

PLOT DEVELOPMENT

The plot, based as it is on the life of young Tim O'Brien the soldier, is constrained by the text's function as memoir, an ostensible record of the author's activities in and around his time in Vietnam. In the book, O'Brien combines intimate descriptions of war with thoughts on a young man's history, offering the reader one version—of many, he makes clear—of the Vietnam experience. O'Brien manipulates the genre, however, interjecting fictional details and dialogue when necessary to sustain the story's flow or to emphasize a point. The memoir is a precursor to his fiction, where O'Brien harnesses dichotomies—chaos breaking contemplative silence, death intruding upon the innocence of a young man's dreams—that create a jarring effect, negating the possibility of working within the comfort zone of absolutes. In addition, O'Brien applies his journalistic tendencies, recording various events with the distance necessary to give the reader a comprehensive look at war and its consequences. In other ways, however, the narrative is far from objective, the author's introspection rising to the surface—as in O'Brien's statement of a "thesis" that suggests anything but a factual memoir—at which times the book acts more as polemic than memoir. Philip Beidler regards the book as a tour de force of style, a work that "genuinely succeeds a good deal of the time in quite literally invent-ing its own context of vision, and in the process it makes Vietnam signify in ways that would set the example for many of the most important works to come" (*American Literature* 100). Finally, O'Brien implicitly asks, why can't the book serve both purposes equally well? It is that line of ques-tioning—the repeated articulation of the vision and its subsequent revi-sion—that will serve him well in the fiction.

The memoir begins in medias res, during a conversation between O'Brien and his comrade Barney as they hunker down to avoid enemy fire during O'Brien's third week in Vietnam. The surreal dialogue, which comes across more as two friends carrying on a discussion in the relative quiet of a café than as words exchanged in the chaos of battle, is a coun-

terpoint to the scene of war around them. The scene foreshadows the irony
and absurdity that figure so prominently in O'Brien's recollection of the
war. When the fighting has stopped, the company moves forward, driven
always by some ambiguous goal the men can never quite grasp. They
approach a village, and O'Brien and Barney argue over its name. Barney,
giving in to O'Brien's contention that the place is named St. Vith, re-
sponds, "What's the difference? You say St. Vith, I guess that's it. I'll never
remember" (5). In that simple exchange, the two outline the push and pull
of forces beyond their control as they struggle to maintain their sanity
from both imminent death (the war's action) and the stinging monotony
of daily life (the war's inaction). Barney's admission that the name of the
town is hardly important (he will forget the name as soon as it is spoken)
is the first in a series of scenes that explicate the immediate experience
but, in the long run, add up to nothing. When O'Brien leaves Vietnam
behind, and despite his promise to himself to savor the moment of departure, he decides that the wisest course of action is "You keep to yourself" (201). Names—of towns, of people, of objects—mean so much less
than the flash-impact on his memory of those images decades later.

O'Brien's participation in the war takes on a feeling of inevitability
when he explains the mind-set of a small Minnesota town accustomed to
sending its young men to war, despite the possibility that any or all of
them could return in body bags. In chapter 2, ironically titled "Pro Patria"
(literally "for country"), O'Brien describes the pressures that he felt to
fulfill, as he saw it, his obligation. His childhood is a Norman Rockwell
portrait of Middle America: Little League baseball, fireworks on the
Fourth of July, the high school band playing "Anchors Aweigh." As he
prepares to go to war, the dignitaries that arrive from surrounding towns
to wish the men luck blend with memories of the local fair and the ubiquitous patriotic parade.

Those images, were they written with sentimentality, could become
maudlin, undermining the narrative's objective of truth, either in its
"story" or "happening" forms. More than in the fiction, however, the
memoir allows O'Brien to draw on his objectivity to create an honest, at
times even confessional, narrative without risking a descent into melodrama. For instance, O'Brien admits succinctly in the first pages of *If I Die*,
"I was not soldier material, that was certain" (22), and after much internal
debate, he submits to the will of the government that insists he risk his
life in a war with which he does not agree. Much of the anger that O'Brien
feels toward his situation is vented in passive-aggressive rage. He describes scribbling obscene words on pieces of paper in his parents' base-

ment and vowing to himself to take no part in the war. He harbors delusions of grandeur, dreams of protesting the war and thumbing his nose at the Establishment. Finally, though, the signs are destroyed before anyone can see them, and the crayons that he uses to create his antiwar messages are placed back in the box he had used as a child not so many years before. He takes his place in line with the other recruits, and "at noon the next day our hands were in the air, even the tough guys" (21).

Above all, the war is an education for O'Brien: he learns the language of the soldier and of war; he acquires the skills necessary to move relatively unnoticed among his own comrades before being shipped to war; he learns that in order to survive, a soldier keeps his head down and his eyes open; he admits, finally, that the war has changed him irrevocably. The war is a complex, cloudy proposition, the outcomes of war much more clear-cut. "Now, war ended," O'Brien writes, "all I am left with are simple, unprofound scraps of truth" (23). O'Brien reaches a conclusion that the reader has had in mind all along: the author philosophizes too much and thinks too clearly to voluntarily offer himself up to a war like Vietnam. He is not a pacifist, as one might infer from the memoir; in the end, O'Brien simply cannot reconcile his return to the community should he decide to flee.

The journalistic quality of the statement—the reader can imagine O'Brien standing outside himself, distanced from the gravity of his own decision, yet complicit with O'Brien the soldier in any value judgments that may come out of the Vietnam experience—prompts Philip Beidler to focus on the scrapbook nature of the text: "Here is no plot, no 'growth of character' along some continuous line of evolution. Instead, the book is something like a series of linked epiphanies, a set of meanings both in themselves and in their various possibilities of significant relationship admittedly provisional at best" (*American Literature* 100). One of several "linked epiphanies" illustrates the author's matter-of-factness and his acquiescence to his fate as soldier. The first line of chapter 6, ironically titled "Escape," tells much not only about the soldiers' activities, but about O'Brien's attitude toward his training: "In advanced infantry training, the soldier learns new ways to kill" (50). He relates the story of his friend Erik Hansen (later, O'Brien would dedicate *Going after Cacciato* to him), who has enlisted for an extra year—two years total—in order to avoid infantry duty. O'Brien, on the other hand, takes his chances, believing that not only will he be spared the more dangerous detail, but that he will save himself a year's service. Ironically, O'Brien implies that such a gamble is part of the process. He is, of course, dead wrong. In a story that has become familiar in O'Brien's work through retelling, in many different forms, he recalls making preparations to desert. Instead, the "escape" is not to a place far away from the war, but rather from advanced infantry training directly into the war.

O'Brien's introduction to Vietnam is not as hostile as one might expect. In fact, his presence at first has a sense of normalcy about it that surprises the young soldier. He describes leading Vietnamese children in a sort of "traveling circus" (77), a procession of men and weapons and equipment that seems out of place in the quiet of the Vietnam countryside. The children, who sell Coca-Cola and dirty pictures to the men, also clean their weapons. The men play football and establish relationships and are easily lulled into a false sense of security. That tranquillity is broken by a description of Mad Mark, a platoon leader who carries a shotgun (outlawed in international conflict, O'Brien points out) and keeps the ear of a Viet Cong soldier as a talisman. The difficulty of O'Brien's role as "legs"—emphasizing that particular feature of the soldier dehumanizes him by ignoring the intellect entirely—is not limited to hazardous duty. His sensibility is assaulted by the men in his own army, particularly the ones who view their commitment to the military as morally superior to those "intellectuals" who find fault with the American presence in Southeast Asia.

The conflict between old guard and new guard is illustrated in O'Brien's relationship with Major Callicles, a 44-year-old career soldier given the unenviable task of escorting investigators to the scene of the My Lai massacre (see chapter 2 for historical background on the event). While O'Brien is appalled to discover such atrocities, Callicles is more matter-of-fact, seeing the event as a symptom of a culture gone bad, the action unfortunate but, perhaps, necessary. He begins a one-man crusade against what he perceives as the corruption of Americans coming in contact with Vietnam. O'Brien reports that Callicles, after being reprimanded by the battalion commander for his actions, including a meltdown that might have gotten several men killed, waited several nights before burning down a whorehouse. The major is handed the worst possible sentence for a man of his hard-bitten attitudes: Given two hours to vacate LZ Gator, he leaves in shame.

O'Brien's interaction with Callicles, and earlier with a chaplain who holds similar attitudes as the major, begins to define for the young soldier the culture of war and the military mind-set, against which he struggles throughout his writing career. Callicles acts as mentor to anyone willing to suffer his closed-minded views, and O'Brien ironically recounts the major's notion of courage, which Callicles defines with the abstractions that O'Brien finds so repugnant: "You know what courage is? I can tell you that. It's not standing around passively hoping for things to happen right; it's going out and being tough and sharp-thinkin' and making things happen right" (195).

In fact, O'Brien is likely the only soldier in his platoon who has spoken with "the enemy." In chapter 9, "Ambush," O'Brien writes one of his many digressions as a story of his studies in Prague, Czechoslovakia, in 1967, two years before he would be shipped to Vietnam. A Czech friend of O'Brien's offers to introduce him to his roommate, a North Vietnamese student who, O'Brien discovers at the end of their three-hour conversation, is also a lieutenant in the North Vietnamese army. Not surprisingly, the man, Li, finds American policies wrongheaded and ill-informed. He tells O'Brien that the Vietnamese were "defending Vietnam from American aggression" (93) and claims that the American notion of a divided Vietnam is far from the truth. The encounter serves as an important point of reference for O'Brien, who, even through that short conversation, understands the Vietnamese better than most of the soldiers who serve multiple tours of duty while learning little more than how to kill the enemy and keep their heads down well enough to survive.

The chapter details not only his interaction with Li, but also the dual nature of the ambush, which may be a military maneuver in earnest or, just as likely, an elaborate ruse that placates the soldiers' superiors into believing that important work is getting done. As with every other activity in Vietnam, the ambush has its own unique set of rules: O'Brien recalls how Alpha Company would draw a cordon and, with the maneuver directed by radio, the platoon would then engage the Viet Cong. Only once during his tour of duty does O'Brien actually "see the living enemy, the men intent on killing me" (95), and he listens to a conversation between a Captain Johansen and a lieutenant, who discuss the ambush and bemoan the fact that it was not more successful. O'Brien recalls, "They were talking these matters over, the officers pleased with their success and the rest of us relieved it was over, when my friend Chip and a squad leader named Tom were blown to pieces as they swept the village with the Third Platoon." It was, O'Brien reports with no little irony, "Alpha Company's most successful ambush" (96).

O'Brien's recollection of My Lai and its far-reaching consequences is tempered by an unfortunate reality: when pushed, even the pacifists, the ones who hate the war, have no alternative but to push back. In the ensuing maneuvers, the men are afraid to move for fear of triggering mines, and the nights take on an even more ominous blackness than before. That constant fear is transmuted into hatred for the faceless enemy, and O'Brien comes dangerously close to becoming that which he so vehemently despises.

O'Brien's homecoming will far transcend the war experience, though he levels an implicit criticism at the machinery of war when he wonders, as he boards a jet headed for the United States at the end of his tour of duty, "What kind of war is it that begins and ends this way, with a pretty girl, cushioned seats, and magazines?" (202). The Vietnam experience has profoundly changed O'Brien. That change is still more apparent when his plane flies over the United States border and above the familiar Minnesota landscapes, and the land strikes him as an "unknowing, uncaring, puri-fied, permanent stillness" (203). O'Brien could never say the same for himself, and the consequences of his cowardice in having gone to war will follow him as he attempts to exorcise the demons of war in his fiction. Reflecting upon his continued bitterness toward the war, O'Brien says, "The Midwest for me is not just a sweet background I naively grew up in full of innocence and romanticism. I have a real bitterness towards it that lasts to this day. . . . So when I write about the Midwest, I'm writing about it in part out of a sense of real rage and anger, justifiable rage and justi-fiable anger" (Shostak and Bourne 85).

CHARACTER DEVELOPMENT

Much of the memoir takes place not on the battlefields of Vietnam, but in the mind of the author, whose direct observations of the characters and situations that comprise his memories of war are bolstered by the au-thority of the first-person narrator. The relationship between Tim O'Brien the soldier and Tim O'Brien the author has been examined by more than one critic. Maria S. Bonn astutely situates the author's stance, writing, "O'Brien is very conscious of his position as an intermediary between those with personal knowledge of the war and those without. He is the one who has been there and back; he has lived to tell the tale. Yet at the end of this statement he denies the educational potential of such a posi-tion. He cannot advise or teach. All he can do is tell his war stories" (3). O'Brien's self-effacing attitude toward his own authority gives the memoir a written-about rather than an experienced quality that increases its value to the reader who would look to *If I Die* for contexts and narrative struc-tures that appear in O'Brien's fiction (see the section "The Memoir's In-fluence on O'Brien's Fiction," below). One of the most strident expressions of O'Brien's depth of hatred for his actions, and perhaps the most cogent example of the intersection of O'Brien the writer and O'Brien the soldier, comes after he arrives in Vietnam and witnesses the war firsthand: "I spent some time thinking about the things I would do after Vietnam—after the first sergeants and rifles were out of my life. I made a long list. I would write about the army. Expose the brutality and injustice and stupidity and arrogance of wars and men who fight in them" (90). Given his upbringing, O'Brien can hardly be prepared for what greets him. Despite his initial visceral response to his plight, his reaction to the fighting is often non-chalant enough to be remarkable, the young man's sensibility over-whelmed, it seems, to the point of abject acceptance of whatever fate might befall him.

The memoir's first chapter, "Days," relates the ennui of experiences out of time. The days run seamlessly into one another—the chapter's title implies their sameness, even though the period in question might be weeks or months rather than days—and the soldiers are forced to fall into the routine or to be lost. Even the men who live and die together are all the same, and O'Brien recalls, "You can go through a year in Vietnam and live with a platoon of sixty or seventy people, some going and some com-ing, and you can leave without knowing more than a dozen complete names, not that it matters" (79). O'Brien, too, is lulled into the routine. In describing an exchange between Bates and Barney, two fellow soldiers, O'Brien characterizes the war for men at the beginning of their tours of duty, brash and brave. After several encounters with the enemy, however, none of the men have the swagger of war-film stars; those who are not killed or wounded slip into an unnatural calm that signals an understand-ing of the graveness of their situation. Survival is primary, and fiery he-roics are left to the John Waynes of the world.

The most important relationship—and one of the few—that O'Brien establishes is with Erik, a like-minded intellectual who introduces O'Brien to the work of T. E. Lawrence (the man who would become known as Lawrence of Arabia) and discusses literature and soldiering with the re-luctant O'Brien. Although O'Brien claims that with Erik's offer of Law-rence's book *The Mint* "I became a soldier. . . . I took on a friend, betraying in a sense my wonderful suffering" (34), his role as soldier is superseded by that of, to his mind, the voice of reason that continues to question everything and everyone he knows. When the two are separated after boot-camp graduation, Erik writes long letters to O'Brien rationalizing their collective plight in terms of literature and philosophy. Erik's role is not unlike that of the "Evidence" chapters in *In the Lake of the Woods*, or Johnny Ever, the maniacal deejay-vision of David Todd in *July, July*. Erik acts as a stabilizing force in O'Brien's life in Vietnam. Drawing an appropriate connection between art and journalism, Erik reminds O'Brien that "unclothed, poetry is much like newspaper writing, an event of the mind, the advent of an idea—bam!—you record it like a spring flood or the latest quintuplets" (102). The letters he receives, steeped as they are in the poetry of Robert Frost, Robinson Jeffers, Ezra Pound, T. S. Eliot, and others, are one of the few intellectual touchstones for O'Brien, who suffers the ignorance of his comrades with increasing indulgence in order to blunt the absence of meaningful communication.

Erik, since taking on an additional year of military service for a promised job away from the front lines, has more time for introspection, and he shares those thoughts as detailed examinations of his own experience. Chapter 19, "Dulce et Decorum," is an ironic invocation of a line from Horace—"Dulce et decorum est, pro patria mori"—that the poet and war protestor Wilfred Owen used for the title of his most famous poem. Owen translated the lines in a letter to his mother as "It is sweet and meet to die for one's country." In an echo of Horace and Owen and a sentiment that O'Brien expresses repeatedly in his own work, Erik rails against the duplicity of the system. Only after a similar transfer to a safer position away from the villages of Quang Ngai does O'Brien fully appreciate how the fog of war affected him over the preceding months. When he receives one last letter from Erik, who prepares to leave Vietnam, the questions he addresses parallel O'Brien's thoughts throughout: "What difference then? What earthly change have centuries of suffering and joy wrought? Is it only that Christ is become a yellow-skinned harlot, a Sunday-morning short-time girl?" (181). The letters from Erik serve a dual purpose, corroborating O'Brien's own views on the war and life in general—the two rarely express significant differences of opinion on such matters—and articulating a position from which O'Brien, as the ostensible journalist acting in a soldierly role, must keep his distance in order to better report what he has witnessed.

Standing in sharp contrast to the thoughtful rhetoric of the war survivor are the more strident voices of those who see Vietnam as an opportunity to rid the world of communism and quell a youth movement toward amorality back home. Many of the soldiers with whom O'Brien shares duty are in this category, including Major Callicles, whose inability to solve problems manifests itself through violence. O'Brien engages a more formidable intellectual opponent, however, in the form of Edwards, the chaplain, a man of the cloth who also happens to agree with the goals of American involvement in Vietnam. Not coincidentally, the chaplain appears in the "Escape" chapter, his contentious relationship with O'Brien set against the young soldier's preparations to desert. O'Brien is ordered to visit Edwards after making a naive request to meet with the battalion commander to air his grievances.

His encounter with the sergeant is typical of O'Brien's run-ins with authority. Expressing little but disdain for O'Brien, the sergeant dresses him down with a profanity-laden diatribe suggesting O'Brien's difficulty in getting a fair hearing on his grievance. Edwards approaches O'Brien with a transparent camaraderie that immediately alienates the soldier. O'Brien, still determined to have his ideas heard, states succinctly his reasons for meeting with the chaplain. His problem, he tells Edwards, is "one of conscience and philosophy and intellect and emotion and fear and physical hurt and a desire to live chastened by a desire to be good" (54). The chaplain, hardening his tone toward the persistent soldier, condescends to O'Brien and admonishes him for his arrogance. The irony of Edwards's attitude is that O'Brien does, in fact, realize at least one truth far above his "puny intellect" (57): despite his best attempts, he is utterly unable to stop the war. The conflict between Edwards and O'Brien illustrates the contradictory roles that O'Brien the soldier and O'Brien the writer play in constructing the memoir.

THEMES

If I Die's most important themes are essential to the later fiction and, because of the memoir's more or less linear organization, easier to flesh out. As with any narrative concerned almost exclusively with war, O'Brien examines how comfortable images become harbingers: instead of indicating a time for rest and dreams, night becomes associated with death; rather than suggesting efficiency and progress, routine becomes a precursor to war; places that would otherwise invite familiarity and comfort instead harbor the enemy. All those themes are colored by O'Brien's war experiences, and he compares and contrasts the before and after as a way of articulating the extent to which his worldview has changed.

Even after weeks in basic training and the additional toughening they have undergone in advanced infantry training, the soldiers in O'Brien's platoon revert to childhood fearfulness when it comes to spending nights in enemy territory. One of the most stifling fears occurs in conjunction with Vietnam as an unfamiliar, and thus unwelcoming, place, particularly at night. He also records how, on his night walks, the landscape nearly overwhelms him with "the fear of getting lost, of becoming detached from the others, of spending the night alone in that frightening and haunted countryside. It was dark" (85). He makes much of the notion that the anticipation of war is worse than the war itself; during battle, at least, soldiers burn off nervous energy directed at an enemy outside their own minds. The visions that night engenders, however, are just as frightening as their combat experiences. The soldiers' superstitions and fears have the patina of folklore and magic. Those passages prefigure and serve a similar purpose as images that O'Brien would use to good effect in *Cacciato* a handful of years after *If I Die*.

The night/day dichotomy and the memoir's other themes are set against their binary opposites in the text, a notion that Andrew Martin explores through Michael Herr's *Dispatches*, in that "two wars actually took place in Vietnam: the real war, in which people died in the hundreds of thousands, and a make-believe war that was the product of political expediency and public relations" (88). For example, O'Brien juxtaposes the events of chapter 4, "Nights," with the earlier descriptions of monotonous waiting for action in "Days." With a pair of newly acquired night-vision goggles, O'Brien sees into and through the darkness with a clarity missing in his earlier experience. The goggles demystify the darkness, easing the soldiers' anxiety. The semblance of control that O'Brien has over the darkness, however, is short-lived. More than once, he finds himself wishing for the serenity of night, when the bittersweet ache of loneliness would tell him that he is no longer in Vietnam.

The brutal routine that characterizes the soldiers' activities is a symptom of the homogeneity O'Brien finds so disturbing in the U.S. military machine. Upon first arriving at basic training, O'Brien recognizes the malaise that would cast a shadow over his tour of duty, his relationship with Erik notwithstanding, until his discharge many months later. He bemoans the fact that "in that jungle of robots there could be no hope of finding friendship; no one could understand the brutality of the place" (33). O'Brien's first impression is not incorrect. The soldiers live alike; the soldiers die alike. Although O'Brien fights the sameness, intermittently attempting to establish meaningful communication with his fellow soldiers in order to convince himself that he is not part of the machine, he finally gives in to the uniformity of experience as a means of survival. After the first battle, the men undergo what has, for them, become a necessary routine: "Cordon, wait, sweep, search. The mechanics were simple and sterile" (5). The upshot for O'Brien of those battles and their routine is that, simply, "things happened, things came to an end. There was no sense of developing drama" (7).

The routine established in *If I Die* and reiterated many times in O'Brien's fiction suggests a rationale for the massacre at My Lai (itself an important event in *If I Die* and *In the Lake of the Woods,* in particular) and other atrocities that, but for the deferred guilt of some of the participants or firsthand observers, might never have been reported. In *A Rumor of War,* Philip Caputo hints at such an impulse in his own war experience. After being transferred closer to the action at his own request, he recalls, "My convictions about the war had eroded to nothing: I had no illusions, but I had volunteered for a line company anyway. There were a number of reasons, of which the paramount was boredom" (161). In "Escape," a detailed account of O'Brien's preparations for desertion as he trains for war in Fort Lewis, Washington, O'Brien sits next to an unassuming lieutenant on the Greyhound bus to Seattle. The lieutenant, sensing a kindred spirit in the young soldier, confides that he craves battle only "to try out all the stuff I've learned. I think I'm better than those dinks" (63).

As O'Brien discovers, however, the power of place is as important to the way the men react to their situation as their training or their uninformed preconceptions of war. Upon first reaching Vietnam, O'Brien describes the landings, the preparations for battle—including "now or never training" in which the men are taught to throw hand grenades and practice walking through minefields—and the daily activities of men on the ground. The place, with its "inky, mildew smell" (68), affects O'Brien immediately. The place names and the enemies attached to those names— St. Vith, Pinkville, My Lai, the 48th Battalion, the Viet Cong—are invoked both here and in the fiction, and O'Brien, fully aware of the significance of My Lai in any history of the war, plays on that image to illustrate the dangers inherent in Vietnam duty. Even before the world knew of My Lai, he writes, "frustration and anger built with each explosion and betrayal, one Oriental face began to look like any other, hostile and black, and Alpha Company was boiling with hate when it was pulled out of Pinkville" (113–14). Even though Alpha Company performs its job efficiently and professionally, for the most part, the idea that the land could ever be taken from the Vietnamese is absurd to O'Brien (he makes much of this notion through the character Van in *Going after Cacciato*), who understands that "it is not a war fought for territory, nor for pieces of land that will be won and held" (125). As soon as they leave an area, the land reverts back to the men who were there in the first place and who disappear back into the land like ghosts when chased.

One of the most enigmatic of the places that O'Brien sees while in Vietnam is remarkably similar to the milieu of Paul Berlin's imagination in

Cacciato. Chapter 18, "The Lagoon," describes a place at once idyllic and dangerous, a small village on the South China Sea where the inhabitants net shrimp and dry them on the beach, and the soldiers spend their days avoiding the Bouncing Betties and toe-poppers and grenades buried in the sand beyond the village. Although it affords the soldiers a sense of peace sorely lacking in their day-to-day routines, "it is not a village Gauguin would have painted; it is not a romantic place. . . . It is a war village, a refugee camp" (161). O'Brien's depth of hatred for Vietnam does not allow him to see the place as romantic, though other soldiers tend to view it as a welcome respite in the midst of chaos and violence. None of the lagoon's restorative powers can remain, however, and O'Brien ends the chapter with an anecdote about an American fire base near the lagoon. Attempting to calibrate its weapons, the fire base accidentally bombs the village, killing 13—including seven children, for whom O'Brien provides names and ages—and wounding more than 30 others. As a result of the miscalculation, the families of the deceased and injured are given solatium payments—20 dollars for each maiming and 33 dollars for each death.

Despite his best efforts at living on the land without being affected by it, O'Brien discovers that, when his time comes to muster out, he has assimilated many of the land's characteristics. He contrasts the landscapes of Vietnam and the Minnesota prairies with such ambivalence that the reader is forced to wonder what remains for O'Brien back home. Homecoming is not a celebration so much as an assurance only of a life less likely to end suddenly and tragically (see Norman Bowker's story "Speaking of Courage" in *The Things They Carried*). The psychological damage has been done. The town that compelled him to fight in Vietnam holds little promise for his future, as O'Brien makes clear in his first novel, *Northern Lights,* with the ambivalent homecoming of Harvey Perry. An earlier thought that O'Brien has while weighing the relative merits of a long life on the run or a short life in battle is indicative of his attitude upon his return home. In limbo between two life-changing events—desertion from the army or a year in Vietnam—one thought rises above the others: "There was just no place to be alone" (66).

THE MEMOIR'S INFLUENCE ON O'BRIEN'S FICTION

If I Die offers readers the opportunity to study the contexts and events that are integral to much of O'Brien's fiction. Despite the book's nebulous debt to its fictional episodes as O'Brien's imagination merges with the Vietnam experience, any reading of the memoir that fails to consider the book's influence on O'Brien's fiction would be incomplete. For the astute reader, many of the author's descriptions in his own first-person reaction to Vietnam and its consequences contain echoes of passages from later novels and stories.

One of the most common images in the fiction is that detailing the routine of war, which, according to O'Brien, "helped to make [the war] tolerable" (*If I Die* 44). The routines, Paul Berlin knows in *Cacciato*, are not negotiable, but rather determined by the standard operating procedures and the bureaucracy under which he fights for the length of his tour of duty. Although Berlin is part of the largest unit stationed in Vietnam, he has no idea how the bureaucracy works. Upon arriving in Vietnam, Berlin "was lost. He had never heard of I Corps, or the Americal, or Chu Lai. He did not know what a Combat Center was" (36). His experience is an indication of how indoctrination into the world of Vietnam profoundly changes a person; even more importantly, the confusion and disillusionment that Berlin feels at witnessing combat and killing spawns the fragmented narrative that follows.

Another apparent parallel—*If I Die* can certainly be seen as a precursor to *The Things They Carried*, and perhaps in part to *Cacciato*, in terms of the melding of journalistic and impressionistic styles—is O'Brien's use of various catalogs that situate the narrator as an objective recorder of events and, paradoxically, allow him more imaginative leeway. O'Brien accomplishes this through the use of simple lists: of physical objects in "The Things They Carried," of the names of the dead in *Cacciato*, and, notably in chapter 14 of *If I Die*, "Step Lightly," of the many different ways a man can die in Vietnam. The chapter's opening line, "The Bouncing Betty is feared most" (120), sets the tone for the litany of destruction that follows: the M-14 antipersonnel mine, the booby-trapped grenade, antitank mines, directional-fragmentation mines, and the CACK, a grenade held together by a rubber band and thrown into a vehicle's gas tank, where it will corrode and, eventually, detonate. Although O'Brien presumes to be objective in such lists, subtle subjective responses to the event form a counterpoint to otherwise static snapshot images. In describing the lethal effects of the Bouncing Betty, for instance, O'Brien writes that after stepping on the triggering mechanism, "the unlucky soldier will hear a muffled explosion; that's the initial charge sending the mine on its one-yard leap into the sky. The fellow takes another step and begins the next and his backside is bleeding and he's dead. We call it 'ol' step and a half'" (120).

Similar descriptions define O'Brien's fiction style. The title story of his collection *The Things They Carried* is one example. After building his story on the premise that the soldiers' identities are inextricable from their physical and psychological baggage, Lieutenant Jimmy Cross, charged with leading his men to safety, blames himself for allowing Ted Lavender to die from sniper fire while urinating. The sheer absurdity of the image and the cataloging of the objects draws attention away from the deadly serious lesson that Cross learns through the death of one of his own men. The scene is closely linked to the weapons scene in "Step Lightly," and in "Nights," O'Brien's synecdoche—the part of the soldier representing the whole, and in this case implying the great weight of responsibility on each individual—indicates the extent to which the soldiers are the sum total of the objects with which they are laden: "Let the war rest there atop the left leg: the rucksack, the radio, the hand grenades, the magazines of golden ammo, the rifle, the steel helmet, the jingling dogtags, the body's own fat and water and meat, the whole contingent of warring artifacts and flesh" (26). In the chapter "Under the Mountain," O'Brien foreshadows Jimmy Cross's guilty repudiation of his girlfriend after Lavender's death when he writes, "I thought about a girl. . . . I memorized. I memorized details of her smell. I memorized her letters, whole letters. Memorizing was a way to remember and a way to forget" (33).

Even O'Brien's failed attempt at deserting finds its way into the fiction. While in advanced infantry training at Fort Lewis, Washington, O'Brien, whose platoon has been assured that they are headed to Vietnam, despite hopeful rumors that London or Frankfurt may be in the cards, makes intricate plans to desert, reading articles that describe the best ways to get to Canada, checking airfares to Ireland, and itemizing expenses. Only after researching his options does he realize that the plan has merit. After a bus ride into Seattle with the required money, an "AWOL bag," and letters written to family members to detail his flight, he breaks down and cannot follow through with the plan. The trip enervates O'Brien, who can write only, "I was a coward. I was sick" (66). The amount of preparation borders on the absurd; the paranoia that O'Brien feels for his actions was a sure indication of his guilt were he to disappoint his townsmen by avoiding his duty. That image, in various incarnations, appears in all of O'Brien's novels: as O'Brien and other characters feel that to fulfill society's obligation is undoubtedly a more powerful motivating force than the threat of any legal action against draft evaders. Although the characters in question, with William Cowling in *The Nuclear Age* and Billy McMann in *July, July* the sole notable exceptions, enlist for military service that they will later regret, Baskir and Strauss point out that of more than 200,000 accused draft offenders, fewer than 4,000 ever spent time in prison, and only 250 ever spent more than two years behind bars (69).

Chapter 17 of *If I Die*, "July," also prefigures the later novel *July, July*, describing a particularly bloody battle in which the soldiers' leader, Captain Smith, garners a Purple Heart for a wound so small, O'Brien observes, that "it looked like a moth had done it" (151). If the chapter does not directly influence the similarly titled novel, O'Brien at the least reveals his disdain for Captain Smith by invoking the physically and spiritually damaged David Todd, a college baseball star who loses a leg in the war and returns to his 30th college reunion tormented by a survivor's guilt. At the same time that Captain Smith attempts to justify the Purple Heart, O'Brien once again employs a catalog—this time of the various wounds incurred by Smith's men—to underline the situation's absurdity. Smith, wanting nothing more than to prove his competence (an impossible task, O'Brien assures the reader), takes unnecessary risks with his men. He is relieved of his duties the following month.

One event toward the end of Smith's command illustrates the surreal mingling of war and fantasy that O'Brien hones to a fine point in *Cacciato*, *In the Lake of the Woods*, and *The Things They Carried*. Alpha Company, expecting to be engaged by the enemy, choppers onto a mountain where a monastery has remained unmolested for centuries. The expected battle in an area "as far from the war as you can get in Vietnam" (157) never materializes, although the men leave their mark on the monastery by detonating a Claymore mine and chipping stone from the Buddha.

The synthesis of realism and dreamlike flights of fancy creates a strong, flexible context for the stories and mirrors specifically the author's examination of his own participation in the war, and in general the individual's decision to participate in the war or not. H. Bruce Franklin points out that O'Brien's "confession—that cowardice kept him from making the moral choice of running away rather than becoming a killer—appears again and again in O'Brien's writings, sometimes elaborately sublimated, sometimes candidly blunt" (35). His characters, too, undergo varying degrees of introspection or self-recrimination, moving more or less linearly from acceptance to anger and, finally, a revisionist denial: from Harvey Perry, who accepts his fate without dwelling upon it in *Northern Lights*; to Paul Berlin in *Cacciato*, whose waking dreams transport him from the battlefield to the observation post to anyplace else; to a cast of narrators and characters in *The Things They Carried*, all of whom describe in detail the horror of the war; to the delamination of John Wade in *In the Lake of the Woods*; to Thomas Chippering in *Tomcat in Love*; to the 30-year retrospective of *July, July,* whose most powerful image is that of the desperately wounded David Todd lying on a riverbank fully expecting to die. Although such images at times border on propaganda—a term with which O'Brien would likely not take umbrage, as it implies a reasoned response to the status quo—the author voices his opinion with a conviction bolstered by his firsthand knowledge of war and a knack for recording poignant details through the filters of time and imagination.

ALTERNATIVE READING: NEW HISTORICISM

Given the focus in O'Brien's novels on historical events, a reading that takes into account the impact of history and culture on his characters' lives in the narrative present is reasonable. New historicism is a valuable way of exploring historical context in O'Brien's novels. The term denotes "an array of reading practices that investigate a series of issues that emerge when critics seek to chart the ways texts, in dialectical fashion, both represent a society's behavior patterns and perpetuate, shape, or alter that culture's dominant codes" (Cadzow, "New Historicism" 535). In addition, language, since it is a socially constructed system, can reveal much about the time in which a work is created; such a reading strategy, then, "initiates a reconsideration of the ways authors specifically and human agents generally interact with social and linguistic systems" (535). As in close textual readings—what is popularly known as New Criticism—the role of the author is limited in new-historical readings, which "reject both the autonomy and individual genius of the author and the autonomy of the literary work and see literary texts as absolutely inseparable from their historical context" (Bertens 176).

The Vietnam memoir, including the well-received *A Rumor of War* (Caputo), *Born on the Fourth of July* (Ron Kovic), and *Dispatches* (Herr), became something of a cottage industry in publishing in the decade following the cessation of American involvement in Vietnam in 1975 (O'Brien's memoir is unusual, having come before the war ended for tens of thousands of American soldiers). Tobey Herzog discusses the difficulties that O'Brien would face so soon after his war experience, positing that "Vietnam with its fragmentation, complexity, and illogic presents special problems for an author attempting to order the chaos in a meaningful way. . . . Not surprisingly, the author's difficulty in gaining control of literary materials mirrors the American soldier's problem of handling his Vietnam experiences by establishing meaning, order, and control in his life" (*"Going after Cacciato"* 88). Perhaps the most appropriate question that a reader might ask regarding O'Brien's first published book is, why was the memoir necessary in order to make the fiction possible?

Steven Kaplan, O'Brien's chronicler in *Understanding Tim O'Brien*, suggests that through the memoir form, "he attempts to purge himself of the influence of others by exposing and taking responsibility for his own actions during this critical period of his life. This book can thus be seen as something more than just a war memoir. It is the candid *confession* of a young man who committed what for him constituted self-betrayal" (22). O'Brien's repeated references to his decision to fight and the tortured second-guessing that followed validates that notion. The memoir, coming as it did just three years after O'Brien's return from Vietnam, provides a necessary transition for the author from wartime observation to fiction.

The role of *If I Die* as viable history has been called into question, and rightly so. Bonn points out that "throughout the memoir O'Brien repeatedly privileges the written text and the story; but throughout the memoir O'Brien also undermines that privilege, until it is ultimately unclear whether he embraces or rejects the power of the story and its storyteller" (3). Part of O'Brien's rationale for the book's split personality—the combination of nonfiction and fiction elements that works so effectively to present *a,* if not *the,* version of Vietnam—might have been his own childhood, having been raised, he writes, "out of one war and into another" (11) as the son of World War II veterans. The war in which they served, however, could hardly have been more different from O'Brien's war, and *If I Die* expresses the uncertainty of a young man entering an arena unfamiliar even to seasoned veterans.

The massacre at My Lai becomes an issue late in the memoir and only aggravates O'Brien's jaundiced view of the war. The author unequivocally states his opinion on the matter, describing how, because of the bloodlust of Lieutenant Calley, Paul Meadlo, and the other soldiers who preceded him into My Lai, Alpha Company will be hated—and likely marked—men. The reader should keep in mind that news of the massacre was fresh more than a year after the fact. The context within which O'Brien creates the memoir allows him to leverage the period's history in order to state clearly his own thoughts on the matter. As close as O'Brien comes to a thesis in any of his work is his detailed description of his inability to fight the weight of history and disrupt the inertia of families who have known each other for generations, towns that expect their citizens to "do their duty": "I would wish this book could take the form of a plea for everlasting peace," he writes, "a plea from one who knows, from one who's been there and returned, an old soldier looking back at a dying war" (*If I*

Die 22). The innocent sentiment illustrates O'Brien's passion for elucidating the war's wrongs, images of "everlasting peace" drawn from a portion of his psyche not atrophied by the war. For once, he ignores the questions of courage and heroism that haunt him throughout his time in Vietnam. After all, as Bonn points out, "war stories are only stories; they do not have any practical ramifications" (8). While the stories themselves are ineffectual at bringing about change, passionate statements of personal beliefs are something else entirely. O'Brien expresses a contagious optimism tempered with a realism born of experience. As he succinctly puts it, "Vietnam was under siege in pursuit of a pretty, tantalizing, promiscuous, particularly American brand of government and style" (*If I Die* 141–42). The author would spend much of the next 30 years exploring that thesis and articulating powerful arguments against the ubiquity of war.

Northern Lights
(1975)

> The notion of a Minnesota culture immediately strikes observers
> as counterfeit. Minnesota, never a natural or cultural unit, was born
> and nurtured by continuous artifice. At the time of its founding,
> Minnesota was a fanciful invention used to draw immigrants to the
> state with the enticement of all the land they wanted in a "bracing
> and invigorating climate."
> —Joseph Amato and Anthony Amato, "Minnesota, Real and
> Imagined: A View from the Countryside"

The Vietnam experience that O'Brien renders so vividly in *If I Die* is presented in a markedly different context in *Northern Lights,* the author's first
novel, which focuses attention on Vietnam while exploring the effects of
the war on nonparticipants. *Northern Lights* establishes themes that suffuse
O'Brien's fiction: alienation, fear, courage, and reconciliation. Setting the
novel in his native Minnesota, a landscape with which the author is intimately familiar, allows O'Brien to examine the horror of war through the
lens of the familiar.

Northern Lights received moderate critical acclaim for a first novel, in
particular for its richly drawn settings and the complex relationship between the brothers Paul and Harvey Perry. Robert H. Donahaugh writes,
"Northern Minnesota is the setting for a long, *Deliverance*-like novel of

two brothers who seem not to learn from ordeals. . . . The book is eminently readable, and the author has a sharp ear for dialogue. As an
adventure story, this is very good indeed" (1241). O'Brien, with the
advantage of two decades' hindsight, is perhaps the book's toughest critic,
taking it to task for its stylistic shortcomings and his own relative inex-
perience with fiction: "I was under two influences: one was Hemingway,
one was Faulkner. Overwriting is probably the chief flaw of the book. It's
maybe a hundred pages too long. Too much gratuitous repetition. I continue to use repetition in my work to this day, but not so that it's done
just for its own sake" (Naparsteck 2). In fact, the critics who applaud the
novel for its ambition also question O'Brien's ability to write compelling
father-son relationships, one of the novel's key themes and the catalyst,
finally, for Paul Perry's sea change after a grueling ordeal in the Minnesota
wilderness. O'Brien concurs, explaining, "I was trying to parody Hemingway. . . . I was just a beginner, and I was sort of having fun with it, so
I tried to spoof *The Sun Also Rises, A Farewell to Arms,* and I thought I did
a pretty neat job of doing the spoofs, but unfortunately good literature
should be more than just gamesmanship" (Naparsteck 3). O'Brien has
compared *Northern Lights* to Hemingway's first novel, *Torrents of Spring,*
in the sense that both are works of fiction by writers who had previously
published nonfiction.

Despite O'Brien's self-directed criticism, the novel is important in the
body of the author's fiction for the ways in which characters confront the
forces that threaten to annihilate them. The novel recalls the Naturalist
texts of the early twentieth century, particularly the work of Stephen
Crane and Frank Norris, in which characters respond to events outside
their control with the understanding that they are powerless in the face
of nature; nevertheless, they persevere. *Northern Lights*'s central event, a
simple cross-country journey during which the brothers become lost and
are presumed dead, unfolds slowly, allowing for the development of the
characters and playing on the repetition—the banality, even—of life-
threatening events that emphasize the smallness of man in nature. The
novel contains autobiographical overtones, recalling a story that O'Brien
would publish in his collection *The Things They Carried* more than a decade
later: one man's attempt at reconciling himself to the whims of society
and finally succumbing to that pressure, as O'Brien came to grips with
his conscription into the military and his overwhelming desire to escape
to the safety of Canada. That issue informs much of the action described
in *Northern Lights.*

The novel is divided into nine chapters, each one suggestive of man's incessant struggle with nature (nature in the sense of both wilderness and the human nature that figures prominently in the characters' actions and attitudes): "Heat Storm," "Elements," "Shelter," "Black Sun," "Blood Moon," "Shelter," "Elements," "Heat Storm," and "Blizzard." In the novel's table of contents, an arrowhead, symbolic both of the land on which the story takes place and the Arrowhead people who are native to northern Minnesota, is surrounded by the chapter titles. The repetition of chapter titles in three instances mirrors O'Brien's own repetition of key elements and phrases in the story, including the "sobbing" of the wilderness that accompanies the brothers' trek through the wilderness, and the constant presence of their father, who holds sway even after his death. In pitting two brothers against one another philosophically, O'Brien examines what it means to go to war without leaving the sanctuary—or, as Paul Perry notes, the stifling sameness—of familiar ground. The author also questions, as much through what is unspoken in the character of Harvey as through the sharp, insightful dialogue of the other characters, the motivation behind America's role in Vietnam. That sentiment acts as a point of reference in all of O'Brien's fiction and allows the reader to trace the evolution of a writer who gradually comes to terms with his role in the war through his attention to memory, history, and art.

PLOT DEVELOPMENT

Harvey Perry's return from Vietnam is the starting point for *Northern Lights* and the impetus for the plot that follows. Harvey's understated homecoming after losing an eye in battle and his steadfast refusal to discuss his part in the war suggest that he has been changed by the event, although his life takes on the veneer of someone to whom nothing important has happened, or ever will. The town is determined to honor their local hero by staging a series of parades and speeches; Harvey takes little interest in either (see a similar discussion of Norman Bowker's return in *The Things They Carried*). Harvey's older brother, Paul (referred to as "Perry" throughout, the use of the surname connecting him always to his domineering father), has stayed behind in Minnesota and continues a government job processing subsidy applications for the county farm extension. At the outset, Perry waits in the dark for his brother, pondering how the relationship between the two might have changed in Harvey's absence. On the morning of Harvey's arrival, Perry wakes in time to consider the events of his life, deciding that "all collapsed around the few images. But even the images offered no natural sequence. They were random and defiant, clarifying nothing" (7). Perry's confusion and his fragmented thoughts signal his inability to order his life, an issue that comes to the fore later when he is stranded in the wilderness with his brother.

Perry leaves his house and walks by memory to nearby Pliney's Pond, where his father had taught Harvey to swim and had forced the unwilling Perry to do the same. Perry muses as he sits at the water's edge that he could have followed in his father's footsteps, as a Lutheran preacher—he had worn his father's vestments as another young man might don a military uniform—but consciously decides against pursuing the life that made his father a bitter, lonely man. When Perry picks up his brother at the bus station the following morning, the two have much the same relationship upon Harvey's return as before his deployment. The only indication that Harvey has changed at all is the milky, blind eye to which Harvey draws attention by his very nonchalance. Harvey's part in the war notwithstanding, the brothers' relationship is still haunted by the different experiences they had years before with their father. Like his father before him, also a Lutheran minister, the elder Perry largely ignores the promise of an afterlife, instead preaching perseverance and the inevitability of misery in this life. In one of many flashbacks, Perry recalls hearing that "things would get worse, and his theme was apocalypse: forest fire, death in the snow, a new Ice Age. He was a preacher of the elements, more pagan than Christian, appealing to the only true emotion of his frontier congregation, which was fear" (71). That worldview is pervasive and oppressive. Perry describes the family's history in details that recall a similar take on life and death as in William Faulkner's *As I Lay Dying:* living is little more than a way of preparing for death. Reviewers have also compared the novel's stark realism to Hemingway's *The Sun Also Rises* and *In Our Time.*

The Perry brothers face much the same restlessness that any young people living in a familiar setting for too long are apt to feel, and Perry sees around him "a melancholia, seeded in the elements, but he had no idea where it started" (65). They wonder why they continue to live where they do, deciding that the weight of history and family conspire to keep them in the place, where, "like twin oxen struggling in different directions against the same old yoke, they could not talk, for there was only the long history: the town, the place, the forest and religion, partly a combination of human beings and events, partly a genetic fix, an alchemy of circumstance" (317). Perry's idea of what Vietnam must have been like for Harvey mirrors his own bleak understanding of northern Minnesota, the uncertainty of the war conflated with an equally uncertain future in a dead land.

Before Harvey's tour of duty in Vietnam, one of the few times that the outside world impinges upon the sameness of Sawmill Landing is illustrated by their father's obsession with the cold war and his insistence that the three of them have recourse should the Soviet Union decide to unleash Armageddon (see a discussion of William Cowling's similar obsession in *The Nuclear Age*). When the father is diagnosed with terminal cancer, Harvey digs the old man's bomb shelter while Perry stays inside and watches his father die from a distance. He keeps the television loud to avoid hearing the sounds of death and thinks, more to assuage his own guilt at his actions than out of any obligation to his father, that they should all be together one last time, comforting the old man into the grave and learning the history that connects past to present. The shelter serves more as a symbol of a country's paranoia and fatalism in a time of uncertainty than as protection against any outside enemy. The hole, which physically resembles the grave that the father will soon lie in, also serves as a silent reminder of how the brothers have become polarized through the machinations of their father. If Pliney's Pond represents the possibility of symbolic rebirth for Perry—water often connotes a purifying experience and is commonly invoked in Judeo-Christian religions, which Perry would understand intimately through his father, as a symbol of birth and rebirth—the shelter only emphasizes the spiritual death that has already claimed the father and awaits the brothers. The father's physical death cements his legacy of influence over Perry, who can only replay in his mind his interactions with his father and will never be given a chance to reconcile with him. That Harvey digs the shelter alone represents his continuing acquiescence to his father's wishes and prefigures his role as the sole member of the Perry family to participate in the war—and, in the absence of his father's oppressive authority, his confusion upon his return from the war.

Complicating matters in Perry's mind is his wife, Grace, a kind, understanding woman who wants to move forward with their relationship, begin a family, and enjoy life in the present. Harvey's unrequited love interest is Addie (another connection to Faulkner's *As I Lay Dying;* Addie Bundren is the family's long-suffering matriarch), a bare-footed free spirit whose romantic fantasies compel Harvey to propose to her even while she openly flaunts her relationship with another man. Her primary goal, seemingly, is to goad Harvey into rekindling the life that he sacrificed in Vietnam. Addie attempts to draw him out of his torpor, imploring him to discuss how he lost his eye and asking whether he was afraid of dying and whether he cried. Harvey insists that his experience and his wounding have not adversely affected him, though when inebriated, he manages only to mumble inarticulately about the war. Even sober, his words don't quite make sense: "Came home from . . . feeling like a bum. War and all. Wasn't so good you know. I told you something about it last night, didn't I?" (146). Harvey is unable to get any closer to the truth of his experience than a few fragmented sentences. The parallel between Harvey and Perry becomes clear in repeated references to both Harvey's Vietnam experience and Perry's continuing inner struggle against his father's influence.

Grace, although portrayed as understanding and supportive throughout the ordeal, wonders aloud one night in bed to a half-conscious Perry if the two of them might be happier when Harvey leaves their house, where he has been living since his return. Outwardly, Harvey is willing to move on with his life; in the light of day, however, the subject is rarely broached and fades into the story's background. Given the unwillingness (or inability) of the brothers to separate, the trek through the wilderness becomes inevitable, and the catharsis that both brothers feel, Harvey for surviving and Perry for having saved his brother, offers a necessary bit of closure on a psychological burden that hobbles the Perry family far more than Harvey's own battle wound ever could.

Perry and Harvey verbally shadowbox around Harvey's return from Vietnam, redefining their relationship in the wake of Harvey's wounding and the guilt that Perry feels for not having participated. As a way of testing the relationship, they enter a cross-country ski race in Grand Marais. While there, Harvey, upstaged in front of Addie by a young Olympic-caliber skier with whom Addie eventually begins a casual affair, hits upon the idea of skiing home, a trip that should take little more than a day. Against his better judgment, Perry agrees to the plan. At first, Harvey easily outdistances his older brother, though in short order Perry leads. When a blizzard unexpectedly strikes, Perry, who loses his glasses and doubts that he can make it home, becomes the hero that he thought he could never be by saving his brother's life. Harvey, known affectionately as "the Bull" for his strength and stubbornness, comes down with pneumonia, and Perry forges ahead under adverse conditions. Perry's awareness of his newfound focus and courage marks an ambivalent turning point for him, when "he realized that he was developing a new and not entirely desirable capacity for treating suffering with clinical dispatch, solving a crisis, moving himself to do what had to be done and nothing more or less, then moving on to the next thing" (244). On equal footing—Harvey blinded in one eye and deathly ill, Perry without the aid of his glasses and uncertain as to his ability to lead the two out of the wilderness—the competition between brothers reaches its climax.

In a last desperate attempt at saving his brother, Perry stumbles upon a cabin occupied only by a young woman, whose husband is away, and her daughter. The woman unashamedly permits Perry to bathe and rest before he skis to town to alert the authorities to Harvey's location. The events of the past weeks seem to signal a transformation of sorts for Perry, who, after losing his job and questioning his motives for staying in the home territory, "felt dangerous. . . . He felt like a tree, very tall and strong and deeply rooted and fatless, tough hard fibers that an electric saw could cut. Safe, now. Safe and sound" (303). Perry feels a certain amount of guilt for not immediately contacting a rescue party for Harvey, but, he rationalizes, circumstances prevent him from skiing the last six miles to town in his current condition. An underlying sexual tension between Perry and the woman suggests a dress rehearsal for his return to society as a different man.

Although Harvey is rescued and recovers from his illness, Perry, disillusioned by an antagonistic reception upon his return, feels a "wave of the old melancholia" (310). He slips too easily back into his old ways, and the expected transformation is delayed. Harvey begins to drink more frequently and Perry gains weight. Grace, upset by the events surrounding their absence—she had prepared to live her life without Perry—still serves as the cornerstone of their relationship; or, as Perry thinks, "she had patience" (317). Grace has always understood the subtle ebbs and flows of life in Minnesota better than Perry, and her attitude toward Perry's reappearance has a matter-of-factness to it that suggests her willingness to return quickly to the old life. Perry thinks, "It was as though nothing had changed or ever would change, and partly she was right. In the winter, in the blizzard, there had been no sudden revelation, and things were the same, no epiphany or sudden shining of light . . . , the old man was still down there alive in his grave, frozen and not dead . . . , everything the same" (317).

In Pliney's Pond, Perry eventually finds solace in a place where he had felt, for all his adult life, only dread and the crushing weight of his father's influence; his transformation, however, weighed against the reader's expectation of a profound change, is neither absolute nor startling. Rather, O'Brien implies, elements outside the brothers' control remain, tolerated but never mastered. Harvey, symbolically lost, if not still stranded in the physical wilderness, exhorts Perry to travel anywhere with him and repeats a curious desire to head back into the wilderness. Harvey's motives are unclear. He recalls that their father had told him stories about the amount of game and limitless clean water they might find in that idyllic place, where, ironically, Harvey and Perry might escape from the very problems that their father had engendered so many years before. Harvey is unable to escape the repetition of his father's pronouncements, and he confides in Perry, a rarity for the younger brother: "You ever get the feeling you're doing the same things over and over again? . . . The old man, all the outdoor crap. . . . But it's not the old man anymore, it's me," he tells Perry. "Now it's in me and I can't get it out. Doing crazy things. Over and over" (340).

Although some critics have seen the novel as the second in a trilogy of works that limn O'Brien's Vietnam experience—the memoir *If I Die* being the first and *Going after Cacciato* the third—a disclaimer on the book's copyright page proclaims, "With gratitude to the Arrowhead people, who will know perfectly well that there is no such town as Sawmill Landing, that Grand Marais doesn't sponsor ski races, that these characters are purely fictitious and that this is just a story." The statement's implication, and a notion that O'Brien has expressed publicly regarding the origin of the book, is that *Northern Lights* is to be taken separate from the others, inasmuch as any books connected by such strong common themes can be seen as distinctly different from one another.

CHARACTER DEVELOPMENT

Even though an ill-fated cross-country ski trip consumes nearly half the novel, *Northern Lights* is perhaps more aptly categorized as character- rather than plot-driven fiction, focusing on the relationships between brothers, a father and grandfather whose influence extends beyond life, a wife and a girlfriend who express discontent with their lives and find different solutions for their problems, and a town whose unbending ways and death grip on tradition threaten to destroy it. O'Brien rarely skirts the literary allusion in his fiction, and he admits that the protagonist of *Northern Lights* has his roots in classic literature: "Paul was chosen for Paul on the road to Damascus, the Damascus Lutheran Church [where the Perry family has preached over the years], all the imagery of the light through- out the book. The same thing with his middle name, Milton—you know, blindness" (Naparsteck 2). Perry's blindness is primarily figurative, his inability to break from the past a result of both his steadfast adherence to tradition and a myopic sense of his own self-worth. In considering his brother's return from Vietnam, Perry exhibits a touch of the paranoia and jealousy that keeps him from mending his relationship with Harvey. Regarding the nebulous military and social boundaries defined by the Vietnam War, Perry thinks, "No sides, no maps to chart progress on, no tides to imagine surging back and forth, no real battles or victories or defeats. In the tangled density of it all, Perry sometimes wondered if the whole show were a masquerade for Harvey to dress in khaki and display his bigballed outdoorsmanship, proving all over again how well he'd followed the old man into the woods" (21).

Perry's character is much more transparent than Harvey's, in part because a third-person narration articulates Perry's thoughts and most often leaves Harvey's unspoken. His passive-aggressive reaction to his brother's return from Vietnam is similar to an event later attributed to John Wade in the novel *In the Lake of the Woods* that illustrates the older brother's often misguided energies: Perry, overly disturbed by the insects that flourish in the summer, sprays insecticide "until the can was empty and light, then he listened, and the odor of poison buoyed him" (4). When John Wade pours boiling water on his houseplants in the later novel, the seemingly harmless, if slightly disturbing, act signals a psychological break around which the novel revolves. In both cases, the past profoundly affects the present.

In fact, the novel's backstory—a term generally used to denote important historical facts and relationships that impact the present—is at times more important than even the relationship between Perry and Harvey. Perry, estranged from his father because of the father's stark and unrelenting philosophies on life, lives in his younger brother's shadow. As Perry in *Northern Lights* and several characters in O'Brien's later fiction discover (particularly Thomas Chippering in *Tomcat in Love*), the world can be neatly categorized as a series of a "few sharp images" (7) and little more, and the available ways of remembering are inadequate for giving true meaning to their lives. Attempting to recall his own life's most important events, Perry realizes, "It was as though he'd lived thirty years for the sake of a half-dozen fast snapshots, everything else either forgotten or superfluous or lost in the shuffle" (7). Father Perry expresses a fondness for Harvey, schooling him in the outdoor life viewed as so essential a part of life in Minnesota and, during his last days, commissioning a bomb shelter from his death bed.

Unlike Perry, Harvey is an enigmatic character so involved in the action of life that his lack of introspection hinders any possibility of reconciliation. As transparent as Perry's thoughts and feelings are to the reader, Harvey is opaque. After all, Harvey is the Bull, and his refusal to discuss his experiences in Vietnam only deepens Perry's sense of inadequacy; more is made of Harvey's unwillingness to talk of the injury than the injury itself. Harvey's personality has changed significantly from the voluble young man who left only months before, however, inhibiting Perry's inability to sympathize as fully with Harvey as he might otherwise. O'Brien further exploits that tension by offering the reader ingress into Perry's thoughts while emphasizing Harvey's silence.

Harvey's relationship with Addie, a young girl whose romantic fantasies compel Harvey to ask her to marry him—even though they know little about one another and, O'Brien suggests, are ill-suited for a long-term relationship—is, like his random impulse at novel's end to travel back into the wilderness, an attempt at reconnecting to the present by grasping at any possibility. Even to Perry, who wants nothing more than to start anew, Harvey's ideas are ridiculous. The one emotion that Harvey fully explores is fear, as evidenced by his admission to his brother that, in Vietnam, "it wasn't the pain I was scared of. I think it was that I wanted to . . . react right when my legs got blown off or my chest got shot open or something, you understand, seeing the stuff inside and going crazy bananas. I used to worry some about that, but not a lot. I didn't want to bawl like a baby" (192). While Perry comes to terms with his past and can look toward a future with Grace, Harvey slips into the background, his final confession shackling him to, rather than freeing him from, the past and involving him in the cycle of sameness that haunts Perry for much of the novel: "You ever get the feeling you're doing the same things over and over again? . . . The old man, all the outdoor crap. . . . But it's not the old man anymore, it's me. Now it's in me and I can't get it out. Doing crazy things. Over and over" (340).

Lurking behind the shadow of his father is Perry's grandfather, also a preacher, a man whose words were used more to bludgeon the parish into acquiescence to the vagaries of the landscape and the difficulty of survival than as any comfort to the individual. Perry recalls that the man preached "no hope and offered none. Strokes of good fortune . . . are forever followed by bad fortune; summer to winter; birth to death; construction to destruction; the elements" (71). No wonder that Perry, even though he fights his forebears' influence, defines his own existence in the same terms: wilderness takes precedence over settlement; and the event that brings about the most profound transformation occurs during winter, a time of death.

Perry's wife, Grace, seems not to understand the complexity of the relationship between the Perry men, though she is patient and kind and loving; after Perry has taken his symbolic plunge into Pliney's Pond, Grace and Perry make love, intending to begin the family to which Paul has been previously unable to commit. While Grace is by no means like Addie, a classic beauty, she is comfortable in her own skin. She and Perry fell in love while in college. Perry's father, able to communicate only in the negative to his elder son, suggests to Perry that Grace "looks like somebody's mother" (98), an insult in the context of the nascent relationship between Perry and Grace, but in the end an important symbol for Grace's nurturing of Perry and their attempt at starting a family, the one act that might allow them to escape from the repetition and sterility of Sawmill Landing. Of Perry and Grace, Grace is the practical one, a schoolteacher who articulates what Perry only feels.

Addie, a woman in her early 20s who tries to bring Harvey out of his post-Vietnam shell and then breaks his heart, is not as developed a character as Grace, but serves an important role nonetheless, as the outsider who, by her very presence, emphasizes the restlessness of the protagonists. Harvey claims to love her, and even Perry has a crush on her, though he remains true to Grace. Joining Addie in a Minnesota version of the Greek chorus—traditionally, a group of actors who comment on the present action and often foreshadow later events—are the townsfolk, people with names like Bishop Markham, Jud Harmor, and Herb Wolff, who represent the culture's character: sturdy, steady people who would rather die on the plot of land that their family has lived on for generations than ever consider moving away. The inhabitants are salt-of-the-earth midwesterners who tenaciously cling to the history that has come down to them. They will remain, even though the emigration of the younger people to cities such as Minneapolis and Duluth slowly erodes the society. When Perry mentions early in the novel his thoughts about relocating, Jud Harmor berates him: "'Selling!' the old man bellowed. 'What happens when everybody sells? Tell me that? . . . Think you're a tourist? You think that? You think you can't just stick it out?'" (121). Later, having made his decision, Perry is certain that he is "selling the damned and cursed house, selling out of the great histories" (346).

THEMES

The primary theme in O'Brien's first novel would act as a touchstone in the subsequent fiction and cement O'Brien's reputation as a "Vietnam writer": the returning Vietnam veteran's attempts at reestablishing contact with the world he left behind and the interplay of past and present (in this instance, often in the context of religion) in shaping that attempt. Implicit in that return is an exploration of the underlying consequences, including alienation, fear, courage, reconciliation, the failure of communication, and the cycle of life. Also important is an examination of how the ones left behind, the noncombatants, deal with the repatriation of their family members. As Heberle points out, "O'Brien's first novel initially raises the subject of Vietnam only to focus on Paul Perry's relationships to others and his interior turmoil. What seems one of the earliest examples of an important subgenre of American Vietnam literature, the veteran's return from the war to the United States . . . deliberately scuttles that classification" (71). Though Perry loves his brother and anticipates Harvey's return, a vague uneasiness forces him to confront Pliney's Pond one more time before Harvey's arrival. Indeed, aside from Harvey's inarticulate and unreliable versions of his wounding, the novel downplays the trauma inherent in warfare almost to the point of its negation. Instead, the text concerns itself more with Perry's response to the events of his own life in the context of Harvey's return.

The disunion between the brothers is emphasized through point of view, which grants access to Perry's thoughts and language and imposes strict limits on Harvey's ability to discuss his experiences. When he fully understands the depth of their misunderstanding, Perry does his best to tease out the tangle of language that separates him from Harvey: "So, he thought, a historic discord, linguistics and tone, a cataclysmic blindness, a pathless thicket of twisted meanings and intentions and desires, a guttural and inarticulate melancholy, passion without vision, simple elements" (90). Later, as the brothers ski deeper into the wilderness and toward the near-tragedy that defines their lives, Perry recalls a similar experience with his father many years before and the connection that, at times, can transcend language, "A communication of spirits. Language an artifact. Language a way to ask for the garbage to be taken out. A communication of tacit compatibility of spirit" (194). Ineffectual language, utilitarian but hardly insightful, also characterizes the townspeople of Sawmill Landing. The small talk typifying their conversations acts as a code that only insiders might understand, full of euphemisms, veiled references, and half-articulated thoughts. Their language further insulates the small town from the rest of the world; its repetition and surface meaninglessness belies the importance of what remains unspoken. The communication between father Perry and his son Paul suffered a similar breakdown, the result being Perry's continued search for meaning in the relationship with his father and, by extension, a reappraisal of his marriage to Grace.

Language also helps to define religion in *Northern Lights,* as the words that render religion in a recognizable context are little more than symbols for the objects and concepts they represent, stripped of any meaning that the symbols might otherwise connote. Although religion is an important matter, the theme impacts the present primarily as an oppressive memory of the past, a brutish imposition of order upon a chaotic world. O'Brien's modernist influences are made apparent in his denial of religion to salve the wounds of the present. Although Perry had at one time considered joining his father and grandfather in the church, the thought is disingenuous at best: he realized early in his life that such a decision would be akin to Harvey's acquiescence to his father's insistence on self-reliance; to side with his father would mean never having the opportunity to live outside the elder Perry's sphere of influence. The natural religion Perry embraces, however, manifests itself when Perry, finding his way to Pliney's Pond for a final symbolic confrontation with his father, at first does not notice the northern lights shining above him. After he wades fearfully into the dark water, "he floated dead still as a waiting embryo. In an infant's unborn dream, the future was neither certain nor even coming, not even the future, and the past was swimming like so many chemicals around him" (348). Upon leaving the water, "he saw the great lights" (348). Religion, language, and nature, then, are twisted, Perry realizes, into an immutable knot.

Natural cycles are tied to tone, and the background hiss of nature devours everything else. As Perry and Harvey ready themselves for their journey, "It was a slow anesthetic lunch. Perry found himself happy in Addie's new pensiveness. And Grace was quiet, and the hotel seemed to cry with tinny echoes, and Perry for once felt they were all in it together, the same mood as on a dying January day" (160). Not long after, Perry alone begins to understand the soundtrack that underpins his mood and his actions: "Sobbing sounds: coffee into a cup, leaves into a bushel basket, feathers into a pillow, air into a vacuum. He listened. No certain sounds, vague and muffled and indistinct. No rustles or movements. A sobbing sound, many sobbing sounds. Inanimate and elemental, into him and out of him, some distant time, very distant" (165). The oneness, the sameness, that both Perry and Harvey feel in their interaction with nature, the past, and each other is articulated in Perry's sensation during the journey, at a point when he realizes that he may not survive, when "he felt grafted to the forest floor. A vast cold froze it all together. The black forest was fused to the black sky, the black sky to the clouds, the clouds to the snow, the snow to the fire, all to one" (175). O'Brien would use a similar image in *Going after Cacciato* and later novels and short stories to emphasize the futility of his characters' attempts at living apart from the land, the place where they are born and, O'Brien reminds us, the place where they inevitably die.

ALTERNATIVE READING: MYTH AND ARCHETYPAL CRITICISM

Myth criticism explores the archetypes, or common patterns, that organize a work of literature and connect that work with others of its type. Some well-known practitioners of myth and archetypal criticism are the psychologist C. G. Jung, popular scholar of mythology and comparative religion Joseph Campbell, literary critic Northrop Frye, and psychoanalyst James Hillman. Ernst Cassirer, the author of *Philosophy of Symbolic Forms,* contends that myth is an organizing principle that uses symbols to denote meaning. As Reeves points out, "by this Cassirer means to insist that myth is a fundamental 'symbolic form' that, like language, is a means of responding to, and hence creating, our world. But unlike language, or at least the language of philosophy, myth is nonintellectual, nondiscursive, typically imagistic. It is the primal, emotion-laden, unmediated 'language' of experience" (*Guide to Literary Theory and Criticism* 521). That analysis neatly describes the reactions of O'Brien's characters to the world around them. Also, the distinction between myth and language is significant in an analysis of *Northern Lights,* as the later fiction, particularly the comic novel *Tomcat in Love,* focuses more on language and its ability to convey meaning than on the symbols themselves.

The novel's most pervasive mythical image in *Northern Lights* is Pliney's Pond, where Perry was made to swim as a child and to which he returns at novel's end, without his glasses, in the same manner that he led Harvey to safety earlier, to symbolically cleanse himself of his father's influence over his life. When Perry returns to his house to make love to Grace—the name connotes kindness and compassion, and in religious symbology pertains to an elevated state, one closer to God—an act of redemption forestalled by his own failings, "he smelled the pond in his lungs. The old man's crazy illusions seemed dull and threadbare, as though their vitality and old importance had somehow flowed with the black bile into Pliney's Pond" (348). The significance of the pond at the outset and Perry's return at the conclusion signals a closing of the circle of time. After the symbolic death of spirit early in the novel as Perry contemplates his brother's return from Vietnam, the pond gives rise to his desire to begin a family with Grace; his immersion in the water of Pliney's Pond and his return to the house with "the pond in his lungs" further hints at his own child's imminent birth. The story's intertwined threads, Heberle points out, consciously mirror the seasons, the relationship between the two brothers "suggesting their being trapped by debilitating paternal influences and natural circumstances that only Paul can understand and try to overcome. Furthermore, the entire plot transpires within a precise seasonal cycle, beginning in July and ending almost exactly one year later" (82). It is a classic tale of the circular cycle of death, regeneration, and rebirth.

The snow that Perry and Harvey immerse themselves in on their journey serves a similar purgative purpose, although the cleansing power of the snow and its implication of restored purity and innocence is offset by its negative connotation, specifically death, terror, and the supernatural. Ironically, Perry associates the religion he learned as a child with all three of those negative connotations; indeed, Frye contends that the winter setting in general represents not only death, but irony and satire. Still, the journey is an opportunity for Perry to assert himself in the shadow of his younger brother, and in doing so to best his fear and the weight of history. On the mythic level, however, the vastness of the wilderness and the randomness through which Perry discovers his heroism also suggest the capriciousness of nature and its indifference to human suffering.

Mythology proposes that the earth itself most often performs the role of mother-goddess, and Steve Kaplan points out that "some of the ideas in this novel about Nordic attitudes toward life stem from Finnish mythology, and according to the Finnish saga known as *The Kalevala*, it was a woman, Ilmatar, who was responsible for the primary acts of creation. It is thus fitting that after Paul has come to terms with his father's myth of endurance and bullishness, he begins to accept more fully the feminine role in the creation and continuance of life" (*Understanding Tim O'Brien* 77). That revised role includes a disavowal of his father's influence and a renewed attention to Grace, who is solely responsible for "the creation and continuance of life." Perry's attitude is a marked contrast to an earlier flashback to the time of his father's death, when "the house was cold and womanless with its dark-stained pine timbers and hardwood floors and yellow-gauzed curtains without origin, no origin except what was locked in the old man's brain, unspoken origins and locked-up secrets and thermostats kept to sixty on January mornings" (209). Perry, motherless from childhood, hides inside the house, caught between his dying father and

Harvey, who digs the bomb shelter. Harvey, as in his youthful forays into the wilderness with his father, literally becomes one with the earth. Only in the aftermath of the journey, however, may Perry reconcile himself to his past and begin to appreciate Grace, herself a mother figure, "soft as the pond" (350). Perry performs one last symbolic act with Grace, closing his eyes on his brother as Harvey continues to rant about the wilderness and a life that continues to be defined by disorder and aimlessness.

5

Going after Cacciato (1978)

> What, then, must it have been like for the three million American troops who went to Vietnam between 1961 and 1972? . . . You can't help but wonder how many had ever been to a foreign country, much less a Third World nation about as different from the United States as any in the world and in which they arrived as soldiers.
> —Christian G. Appy, *Patriots: The Vietnam War Remembered from All Sides*

O'Brien was no stranger to the publishing business—he had written a well-received memoir and one of the first novels to detail a soldier's homecoming from Vietnam—when he embarked on what would become his breakout novel. Still, he could have been little prepared for the almost unanimous critical acclaim that greeted *Going after Cacciato*, a complex, brutally honest book published three years after the United States had formally ended its military operations in Vietnam. The novel would, for the first time, bring serious popular and critical attention to O'Brien's work. After winning the National Book Award for the novel in 1979, O'Brien would also become synonymous with the Vietnam War. That association must have pleased him, at least initially; many Vietnam veterans returned home to silence or, worse yet, openly hostile responses to their role in the war. O'Brien gave voice to their disillusionment. Since that time, however, as Vietnam has become an acceptable topic of discourse in main-stream fiction and film (in part, certainly, due to O'Brien's groundbreaking work), the author has spoken out against the reductive category "war writer," preferring instead to be seen as a writer of human drama who uses the war as a context because of its immediate impact both on the reader and the characters portrayed.

Richard Freedman was effusive in his praise for *Cacciato*, opening his assessment with a sentiment echoing O'Brien's own philosophy on the power of language to address important issues and to organize the war into a recognizable and manageable series of memories—and its inability to change the past: "It won't do the Vietnam dead much good to know that here is a novel that makes us think of Hemingway, but survivors should certainly take notice of this highly original work" (1). Finally, Freedman writes, "To call *Going After Cacciato* a novel about war, is like calling *Moby Dick* a novel about whales" (1). In an analysis of *The Things They Carried*, a decade before her strident pronouncement against O'Brien's *July, July* and more than a decade after the publication of *Cacciato*, Michiko Kakutani pays homage to the earlier work, writing, "Tim O'Brien's *Going After Cacciato* . . . was one of the few Vietnam novels to capture that war's hallucinatory mood, the oddly surreal atmosphere produced by jungle warfare, heavy drug use and the moral and political ambiguities of American involvement" ("Slogging Surreally" C21). Kakutani is not the only critic to have placed the novel solidly in the canon of war literature so soon after its publication. Literary critics had access to the myriad Vietnam films that began to hit the market in the 1980s, and they recognized the importance of literature that refused to reduce the war to the absolutes that O'Brien rails against in his fiction. Critics who viewed the Vietnam film genre in general as sensational and exploitative were better able to draw attention to the body of powerful, passionate literature that veterans created after a suitable period of rumination. Andrew Martin writes, "By the time *Going After Cacciato* appeared in 1978, the Vietnam War debate was changing dramatically, as such popular films as *Coming Home*, *The Deer Hunter*, and *Apocalypse Now* began to affect the way people thought about the war" (90). In fact, the novel's Cacciato chase sequences have a filmic quality that emphasizes the fictive aspects of that thread of protagonist Paul Berlin's story, while also scrutinizing the issues of control that Berlin so desperately seeks in ordering his Vietnam experience, "an act of remembering and imagining [that] leads to self-knowledge and a measure of self-control" (Herzog, "*Going after Cacciato*" 89).

Through *Cacciato*, O'Brien explores his guilt at being grouped by association with the Americans who perpetrated the massacre at My Lai (although mentioned elsewhere by name in O'Brien's fiction, the action remains nameless here), where O'Brien spent the majority of his time in-country. Benjamin Goluboff claims that only through the novel's realist context does the subsequent fanciful chase of the novel's title gain meaning. O'Brien emphasizes the legacy of hatred and violence that Calley and his men left behind, and Berlin's escapist fantasy has as much to do with how he views the remaining six months of his tour of duty as it does his desire to leave Vietnam for the paradisiacal streets of Paris in search of Cacciato: "Paul Berlin's Batangan Peninsula Observation Post stands not only on dangerous ground but also on terrain that recalls a shameful history," Goluboff writes. "The persistent return of O'Brien's narratives to Ba Lang An is a gesture of acknowledgment, perhaps of repentance for that history" (57).

In *Cacciato*, O'Brien eliminates the filter of time that allows him to gain objective distance from similar stories in *If I Die* and *The Things They Carried*. Berlin's point of view is immediate—that is, despite being delivered in the third person, his story is subjective and not overtly affected by the prejudices of an outside narrator—and skewed by his war experience. Reality reveals itself to Berlin only when he is ready to process it. His perception is keen, if not entirely cognizant of the "reality" of his situation, when he takes on that task. The three narratives woven around and through Berlin's Vietnam experience are simultaneously realistic and surreal, objective and impressionistic. The conflation of fact and fiction, integral to O'Brien's stories, is never more clear than in chapter 17, "Light at the End of the Tunnel to Paris": after cataloging the various images that greet him upon his arrival in Mandalay, riots of color and activity that Berlin views with stunned bemusement, he gives in to the vision, "and he believed what he saw" (116).

ON THE OBSERVATION POST

The "Observation Post" chapters, set in the apparent narrative present as Paul Berlin stands watch, keep the chase for Cacciato from spinning off into meaninglessness. The events that seem upon first glance to take place in an actual observation post occur instead during the short time that Berlin and his fellow soldiers engage the enemy in combat. While the first of the "Observation Post" chapters outlines Berlin's goals during his tour of duty—primary, of course, is his own survival—each subsequent chapter shows Berlin's movement deeper into his own fantasy until, in chapter 40, "By a Stretch of the Imagination," Berlin, having already imagined most of his trek to Paris, reminds himself that "this wasn't a madman's fantasy. Paul Berlin was awake and fully sane" (272). The scene is one of the few where reality meets imagination, and it prefigures a swiftly approaching conclusion.

In the second "Observation Post," which takes place just after midnight, Berlin remarks on the slow passage of time. His reaction to the watch echoes both *If I Die* and *Northern Lights* when he posits, "Maybe it was the time of night that created the distortions" (45). A description in the third of the chapters recalls O'Brien's lagoon from *If I Die,* an idyllic place set side-by-side with the presence of abject terror and death. Berlin's view of the sea, however, has a calming effect on him. Having at one point left the relative safety of the tower, he looks back only to find that the structure has taken on the form of a Tinker Toy standing alone in the middle of nowhere. The tower exists only to fuel Berlin's imagination and to allow him the perceived tranquillity that he needs to organize and articulate the Cacciato scenes. It is the single accessible transition from war that makes the flights of fancy possible.

Later, the observation post becomes a place to examine the meaning of courage, to test out new possibilities for Cacciato's escape to Paris, to discover something of Berlin's own history, and to explore the fundamental difference between illusion and reality. That Cacciato's disappearance causes so much consternation for the platoon is ironic, given his comrades' attitude toward him. Cacciato is described as "curiously unfinished," "open-faced and naïve and plump," and "lack[ing] the fine detail, the refinements and final touches, that maturity ordinarily marks on a boy of seventeen years. The result was blurred and uncolored and bland. You could look at him then look away and not remember what you'd seen" (8). As the men chase Cacciato, Berlin asks the mayor of Ovissil, Afghanistan, to read his history. Although the mayor refuses, suggesting that Berlin is too young to have a history, the observation post allows Berlin time to reflect on the events that brought him to the war: the Indian Guides in Wisconsin; Sunday School; the Des Moines River; Louise Wiertsma, who had almost been his girlfriend in high school. The events take on the fantastic qualities that drive the Cacciato thread and finally force Berlin to confront his own fear of reality. And finally, in response to the mayor of Ovissil, Berlin, secure in the observation post, knows "he had a history" (181). Similarly, Cacciato's history is such that none of the men take him seriously. Cacciato is less than fit to lead the men on a chase to Paris, his final destination, and his unclear visage prefigures the blurring of the boundaries between truth and fiction in the novel. That distinction is never more in question than on the observation post, where "the facts, even when beaded on a chain, still did not have real order. Events did not flow" (206). Cacciato's improbable success in leading his squad on a blind chase across much of Asia and Europe illustrates Berlin's rabid, if barely controlled, desire to survive the next six months, muster out of Vietnam, and return home with his health and sanity intact.

What begins as an absurd notion—that anyone, let alone Cacciato, could make it to Paris, free from the war, is certainly nothing short of absurd— assumes the veneer of possibility. Berlin takes solace on many occasions by invoking possibility as he and the others from Third Squad halfheart-edly pursue their comrade. While marching with the men assigned to track down Cacciato, Berlin considers "the pleasure of pretending it might go on forever" and thinks, "Was it really so impossible? Or was there a chance, even one in a million, that it might truly be done?" (16). As the journey comes to a close, Berlin realizes that the end of his shift on the observation post is approaching and that he must hurry in order to finish his story. Although Berlin, who embraces his dual role as arbiter of the Cacciato thread and unwilling witness to the inescapable realism of war, understands that Cacciato's flight is a figment of his imagination, Cacciato teases Berlin into believing that the chase could be real. As a result, Berlin places more credence on the chase and, for one of the few times in the novel, displays an ambition lacking until now. The scene sets up a con-frontation with Sarkin Aung Wan, Berlin's alter ego, as the three threads converge. In the last of the "Observation Post" chapters, Berlin describes the events as an intersection of the real and fiction, and "what remained were possibilities" (323).

Cacciato's leaving behind objects that hint at his rendezvous with free-dom in Paris connects the story threads. The objects—his armored vest and bayonet, an ammo belt, a leaking canteen, a bit of rope, candy wrap-pers, ration cans—all suggest that he is not only literally but symbolically leaving the war behind, ridding himself of the tools of war as he nears his final destination (see a similar discussion of the importance of objects in the title story of *The Things They Carried*). The objects are palpable sign-posts to what has become a parallel, albeit tentative, reality. The lieutenant in charge of reining in Cacciato finds a deeper, more mysterious meaning to the objects, muttering, "Why? Tell me why. . . . Why the clues? Why don't he just leave the trail? Lose us, leave us behind? Tell me why" (17). The answer is one that O'Brien would address more than a decade later in *The Things They Carried:* like the thread of Ariadne that Theseus follows through the labyrinth in order to kill the Minotaur of Greek myth, the objects exist for Berlin to find, so that he may convince himself, through the use of the observation post as a metaphorical vantage point from which he views and controls the novel's intertwined stories, of the "possibility" that his dreams might become reality.

PLOT DEVELOPMENT

O'Brien takes an epigraph from Siegfried Sassoon, a World War I poet who speaks to the experience of war for many writers, not just those focused on Vietnam, and the phrase resonates throughout the novel: "Soldiers are dreamers." Ten of the novel's 46 chapters are titled "The Observation Post" and set more or less in Paul Berlin's narrative present as he waits with his platoon for the rising of the sun during a six-hour sentinel shift. The epigraph, however, prefigures the novel's forward-looking chapters, which utilize magical realism (see discussion in chapter 2) to weave a tale of one man's experience in the war and his desire to leave that war behind. The novel comprises three different narratives: (1) Berlin's night in the observation post; (2) Berlin's recollection of the previous six months, during which he has arrived in Vietnam and witnessed the deaths of many of his comrades; and (3) Berlin's waking dream, the Cacciato thread, in which the Third Squad is dispatched to track down and apprehend the deserter Cacciato. The Cacciato thread contains 20 chapters; Berlin's reminiscence of his own experience in the six months leading up to his night in the observation post fills the remaining 16 chapters. The novel's three interwoven yet fragmented threads illustrate the necessity of imagination in wartime; or, as O'Brien points out repeatedly in his fiction, "true war stories" are never, in reality, "true." Chapters 1 and 46, both titled "Going after Cacciato," bring the narrative full circle and emphasize the novel's "as-told-to" quality.

Far from suggesting what is to come in the chase after Cacciato (the soldier's name is derived from the Italian *cacciare*, "the hunted"), the novel's opening lines throw the reader into the war with the journalistic intensity and ironic distance that drive the earlier memoir: "It was a bad time. Billy Boy Watkins was dead, and so was Frenchie Tucker. Billy Boy had died of fright, scared to death on the field of battle, and Frenchie Tucker had been shot through the nose" (1). Even when not describing death, Berlin clearly wishes he were elsewhere. Everything in Vietnam is corrupted by the weather (O'Brien points out in *If I Die* that it is the land, in fact, that is the true enemy, and the land in this case is what causes the men the greatest fear), a metaphor for the Vietnam experience itself, as their gear corrodes and their foxholes fill with water. The men refuse to enter the tunnels, which hide the enemy and represent their darkest fears. By October, "Cacciato left the war" (2).

The stark, violent images of war and the fits and starts with which the war moves provide a compelling reason for Berlin to create an alternative story space for himself by imagining Cacciato's desertion. Chapter 14, "Upon Almost Winning the Silver Star," reprises the novel's first lines, invoking the deaths of Tucker and Bernie Lynn and describing the reaction of the men to Lieutenant Sidney Martin's order that they go into the tunnels where the Viet Cong have established operations. Berlin and Bernie Lynn are the two candidates to go after Tucker's body; Berlin lacks courage. Lynn, swearing at the indecision of his comrades, crawls headfirst into the tunnel and is immediately attacked. He survives the initial shot to the throat, as chapter 9, "How Bernie Lynn Died after Frenchie Tucker," indicates. Berlin witnesses both deaths, Tucker dead instantly of a shot through the nose and Lynn hanging on for a short time while Doc Peret gives him M&M candies before he dies. The events only reinforce his determination to stay at the rear of the marching line and to do as little as possible, the best of a very limited number of possible worlds in Vietnam.

The introduction of characters who have already died in earlier chapters and the recollection of events not described until later echoes a similar shifting time element in Berlin's dream narrative. The seeming randomness of the war chapters, Steven Kaplan points out, also indicates the extent to which Berlin has accepted some aspects of his war experience and attempts to accept the others with varying degrees of success. "A reason the war chapters do not follow chronological order," Kaplan writes, "is that in them the reader is given only that information which Paul Berlin is willing to remember or confront at a given point on his trek to Paris" (*Understanding Tim O'Brien* 95). The Cacciato chapters feed on the war chapters, and the war chapters have a profound impact on the shape of Berlin's imaginary odyssey to Paris. In chapter 16, "Pickup Games," Frenchie Tucker is still alive, and the men slog through Song Tra Bong (an area that would also figure prominently in *The Things They Carried*), enduring the conditions and remarking on the elusiveness of the living enemy. The routine of the war, rather than wearing on the men as it has in other of O'Brien's stories, is here preferable to random attacks, making death on a regular schedule apparently more appealing than that unseen and unexpected.

The violence of the war, rendered in *Cacciato* at its most absurd, eventually supersedes the monotony of the days, its chaos only increasing the nagging possibility of swift death. Although they engage in only one significant firefight in Berlin's experience, they understand that disrupting the routine invites disaster. Despite their best attempts at bringing the war to the Viet Cong, they resign themselves to the fact that "they could not drive the enemy into showing himself, and the silence was exhausting" (105). The men suffer the maddening combination of boredom and fear because they must in order to survive. Those extreme measures hint at Berlin's break from reality in the observation post and in the chase that follows.

Although the Cacciato thread is clearly a product of Berlin's imagination, the chapters recounting Berlin's tour of duty balance tenuously between truth and fiction, a notion corroborated by the chapter titled "The Way It Mostly Was," a description of a hump through the mountains. What happens in Vietnam on a day-to-day basis and the ways in which those events are related will differ. The chapter begins with a wide-angle shot of the caravan—38 soldiers and a young guide trudging their way up a steep hillside—before focusing on Berlin, as usual the last in line. As Berlin climbs higher, he becomes less attuned to his surroundings, "slipping quietly outside of himself" (162). The scene hints at the "slippage" of reality in both the Cacciato thread and the "real war." The story's focus shifts from Berlin to Lieutenant Sidney Martin, who is defined by long passages that rationalize his role in the war and his ill treatment of the men under him. When the omniscient narrator shifts to Martin, the reader discovers what Berlin and the others could never know, that "he loved these men. Even those whose names he did not know, even Paul Berlin, who walked last in the column—he loved them all" (165). The relationship between Martin and his men comes to a head when they "frag" him, explode a grenade, burying and killing him in one of the tunnels that figure so prominently in the war chapters. The scene is important both as a gauge of Berlin's acceptance of his actions in the war and as a rationale for Cacciato's leaving the platoon. Cacciato is the single man among them who refuses to touch the grenade—a symbol of the men's solidarity against their leader—that seals Martin's fate.

A reader might logically assume that Cacciato himself would play a major role in the novel. Despite the novel's title and the character's brief introduction, however, Cacciato plays a relatively minor role, more central reflector—that is, allowing the other characters the opportunity to learn about themselves through his actions—than protagonist, more guide in the Dantean sense than the target of the Third Squad, to which Berlin is attached. The story is told through Berlin's observations and waking dreams in snapshot images both as the narrator witnesses the events and as Berlin imagines them, in an ambiguous future tense (that time period, though not explicit in the text, begins in late 1968 and runs through early 1969) in which he increasingly distances himself from the war. Of course, the truth of the events is unknowable, an aspect of O'Brien's memoir and fiction generally that has been studied in depth in critical articles. The chase of the novel's title is a figment of Paul Berlin's imagination, a richly detailed hallucination of the 8,600-mile trek that the soldier Cacciato has undertaken in order to escape the war. The Cacciato plotline contains near-misses, mysterious characters who appear and disappear seemingly at random, and, finally, a resolution of sorts. In "The Road to Paris," the men track Cacciato for six days through the jungle without sighting him. The descriptions, based wholly on Berlin's imagination, are grounded in reality not by the subject matter, but rather by foreshortened sentences, the objectively rendered images of the journalist hoping to capture what he has seen, if only to convince himself of its reality: "Once they skirted a deserted village. Once they crossed a frayed and spindly rope bridge. Once, in the heat of early afternoon, they passed through an ancient tribal cemetery. But there were no breaks in the ongoing rain forest. And there were no signs of Cacciato" (33).

Upon arriving at the Hotel Phoenix in Delhi, India, the group is regaled by the hostess, an Indian woman named Hamijolli Chand—"Jolly," for short—who rides an exercise bike behind the registration desk. When she discovers that they are Americans, she discusses her two years in Baltimore as a student at Johns Hopkins. Although the woman's husband finds America corrupt and contemptible, she deems the country "a land of genius and invention" (148). Television, an image hinting at the cinematic qualities of Berlin's own imaginative flight, is the invention that characterizes American ingenuity for Jolly. Her statement is an ironic invocation of the technology that brings the masses together, in her opinion, and allows for the sort of homogenous experience and thought that O'Brien so vehemently dismisses, beginning with the basic-training scenes in *If I Die*. Television's primary accomplishment, Jolly intones, is as "a means of keeping a complex country intact" (149). The scene is both an indictment of the mass images that presume to bring people together and an exploration of Berlin's own consciousness. "In imagining places he had never been, Paul creates an exotic, Americanized tour of the world that reflects popular stereotypes and Hollywood adventure films," Heberle writes, "leavened by his awareness of current events and foreign social circumstances" (131).

In chapter 6, "Detours on the Road to Paris," Berlin, unconsciously seeking the stability of a partner who understands his need for escape, meets Sarkin Aung Wan, a young girl, "part Chinese, part unknown" (53), who has just witnessed the senseless death of her water buffalo, Nguyen, at the hands of Stink Harris and his automatic rifle. Berlin is pleased that the woman will accompany them on their journey, and her presence draws him deeper into his own dream as she helps him to translate the experiences. Although Berlin has been constructing the dream story for perhaps an hour, judging by his shift on the observation post, he has begun to believe his own imagination. When Sarkin Aung Wan agrees to join the men in their search for Cacciato, Berlin "could not stop toying with the idea: a mix of new possibilities" (59). The chapter is a simple statement of the power of imagination.

Between the chapters "A Hole in the Road to Paris" and "Falling through a Hole in the Road to Paris," actions that are simultaneous with one another, O'Brien places a combat chapter, "Fire in the Hole," and the fourth "Observation Post." By separating the Cacciato chapters in midaction, O'Brien further emphasizes the imaginative qualities of Cacciato's journey and the subsequent chase. Berlin's presence in both the observation post and as part of his own vision divides the protagonist's consciousness, calling into question the boundaries between reality and fantasy. At the same time, in an echo of a similar scene from *If I Die*, we discover that Berlin "had seen what bombing could do. He had seen the dead. *But never had he seen the living enemy*" (85; italics mine). The soldiers of the Third Squad find themselves in a series of tunnels, which they navigate with the same care as on a regular patrol. Berlin, never far from Sarkin Aung Wan, witnesses a scene odd even by his standards of imaginary quests: a Vietnamese man wearing a military uniform and a pith helmet looks through a silver periscope, oblivious to the arrival of the Third Squad. Upon being startled by the lieutenant, the man, Li Van Hgoc (he insists that they refer to him as Van), jumps to his feet, pours brandy from a decanter, and suggests, "So now we shall talk of war, yes?" (84). The character is a reference, perhaps, to the North Vietnamese soldier Li, whom O'Brien meets as a student in Prague in *If I Die*. The character serves as an important conduit between the men and their war experience.

What follows is a litany of questions, some straightforward and some highly philosophical, that reveals the Third Squad's relative innocence in war and fear of the unknown and unseen enemy. The questions might also be those of O'Brien himself, who admits seeing the living enemy only once, and that briefly, during his own tour of duty. Van indulges the men, though they take little away from the meeting except enigmatic answers. The men, even when finally confronting the enemy, could never truly know the enemy. Nervous to get out of the tunnel, they bind Van to a chair and insist that he give them directions. His ill treatment at the hands of the men does not prevent him from telling his story, which is meant to provide a counterpoint to the young American's experiences: Van was accomplished in electronics before being drafted; despite his best attempts at evading the draft, Van has been forced to hide in the tunnels where the Third Squad finds him, "ruined by a war I never cared about, never even thought about" (96). The upshot of his story hits close to home for many of the men, whose second greatest fear—death being the first—is that their actions, no matter how heroic, are pointless.

In the course of their six-month journey, the men meet and interact with a number of interesting characters, including Van, Jolly, and Captain Rhallon, an Iranian soldier who reluctantly tells the men that they are to be beheaded for their cowardice and their desertion. Rhallon acts as the voice of conscience that will continue to haunt the men, should they survive. A savvy and experienced soldier, Rhallon nonetheless presents himself as a bureaucrat hamstrung by the very system he represents. Understanding the gravity of their situation, Doc Peret implores Rhallon, "Facts are one thing. . . . Interpretation is something else. Putting facts in the right framework." Rhallon's disturbingly abstract response urges them to "pray for comfort in the certainty of your innocence. In the purity of your own motives" (226), an admonition that recalls similar scenes questioning the soldiers' reasons for their involvement in the war. In this situation, however, the men are saddled with the responsibility for participating in the action. In a larger context, the scene is also an indictment of American involvement in Vietnam.

As the soldiers wait to be beheaded the following morning, their necks shaved in preparation, Cacciato appears at the window of the prison. He hands Berlin an M16 just before the door to their cell explodes from its hinges, and Berlin, free once again, runs for his life. Freshly alive, the group makes its way across Eastern Europe and finally into Paris, where they intend to confront Cacciato. The journey loses focus, however, when the men develop different ideas of what success in tracking Cacciato to Paris means. Their choices are to keep running or to return Cacciato to the war. Neither sounds agreeable to Berlin, who would rather stay in Paris and build a life with Sarkin Aung Wan. By happenstance, Berlin finds Cacciato, sitting alone on the bed of his *pension,* in his underwear, peeling carrots. The brief encounter, however, puts the men no closer to capturing Cacciato. Upon returning to the Third Squad, Berlin cannot tell the men any more about Cacciato's disappearance than they already knew. The novel ends when Sarkin, quoting from Yeats, challenges Berlin to bridge the chasm between his imagination and the brutal reality of the war. Berlin accedes. In the final chapter, "Going after Cacciato," the narrative comes full circle and finds Berlin engaged in battle. He has soiled his pants in the heat of combat and realizes that he will never exhibit the kind of courage—a loaded word in O'Brien's lexicon—that some of the other men possess. Perhaps that is his strength. Perhaps that is what makes Paul Berlin's story worth telling. That and the possibility that Cacciato might finally make it to Paris.

CHARACTER DEVELOPMENT

The first "Observation Post" chapter defines many of O'Brien's soldiers, including Paul Berlin, the accidental warrior, "whose only goal was to live long enough to establish goals worth living for still longer" (26). O'Brien uses a pointillist technique to develop the novel's characters, both real and imagined, in order to intertwine the various threads and make them inextricable from one another. As Heberle points out, "While Paul Berlin mimics O'Brien's own fictional sense-making, he does so as a trauma survivor, and his dream is an attempt to cope with his own psychic collapse" (122). Indeed, the need for Berlin to escape through imagination becomes clear early on when he illustrates a serious lack of ambition and a habit of soiling himself in combat.

In chapter 45, the last on the observation post, the men with Berlin begin to wake, and his dream dissipates with the sun's rising. He scrolls though the names of the dead—Billy Boy, Buff, Ready Mix, Rudy Chassler, Pederson, Sidney Martin, Frenchie Tucker, Bernie Lynn—and fully understands that "the facts are not disputed" (322). Only a character as seemingly obtuse as Cacciato—"dumb as milk" (120)—can show Berlin the trek's possibilities. Berlin comments repeatedly on the increasing likelihood of Cacciato's success as he nears Paris, and the repetition serves as a check against reality. While the reality of the war recedes, Cacciato's desertion takes on the patina of myth.

In "Prayers on the Road to Paris," Berlin recalls Cacciato's habit of carrying a photo album filled with "more than a hundred pictures that somehow stuck better to memory than Cacciato himself" (119). The scene poignantly reminds the reader of Cacciato's humanity and the soldier's simple, heartfelt longing for home. Berlin, once again attempting to summon Cacciato's physical characteristics from memory, suggests that Cacciato really is different from the rest of them. Although he can recall Cacciato in various poses that only emphasize the soldier's simplicity, "the images were fuzzy" (120). In the final "Observation Post," Berlin lists the facts of Cacciato's desertion, "that one day in the rain, during a bad time, the dummy had packed up and walked away, a poor kid who wanted to see Paris, no mysterious motives or ambitions" (323). Berlin's admission that men must complexify their stories in order to make them believable resonates throughout the novel. Still, the facts are these: Cacciato deserted, the men chased him and cornered him on a mountain, they shot flares into the air and rushed his position, they never saw him again. Berlin concludes that "What remained were possibilities" (323).

Another character who represents possibility for Berlin is Sarkin Aung Wan, Berlin's alter ego—literally "other I," or a psychological twin—and confidante. Despite her youth, Sarkin is many of the things that Paul Berlin is not: assertive, confident, savvy, and ambitious. Still, as a figment of Berlin's imagination, she is fettered by the same limitations that compel Berlin to create the Cacciato thread. On the road to Paris, Berlin becomes infatuated with his own creation, though he understands that she might disappear at any moment. In one respect, Sarkin performs much the same role as the objects that Cacciato intermittently leaves behind, signs that the men are on the right track, leading Berlin when his nerve flags and forcing him at the conclusion to confront his fears. When the group reaches Paris, Berlin and Sarkin hunt for apartments, a hint that the two might stay together when the mission ends. When their search for Cacciato takes a turn, however, the relationship ends. Berlin finds that "sleep was impossible" (309), surely an indication that the Cacciato thread itself is coming to an end in the observation post. Berlin, to his consternation, cannot "figure a happy ending" (309) to his imaginary tale.

The list of men who die in the war increases in length as the stories progress. That list includes Lieutenant Sidney Martin, who had read classical history and sees war primarily as "a means to an end, with a potential for both good and bad, but his interest was in effectiveness, not goodness" (163). The lieutenant is an intelligent, driven West Point graduate who studies languages, knows a great deal more than his men do about war

strategy and history, and desires only that his unit perform to their capabilities, even if that means hastening the deaths of several of his men.
Those reasons alone would be enough for his men to despise him, though
they are especially disdainful of his insistence that they dispatch the tunnels undercutting the Vietnamese countryside according to standard operating procedure. The lieutenant's fragging is only one catalyst for the
Cacciato thread that Berlin weaves, although the death—in essence, a
murder—grounds Berlin's guilt in the reality of the war.

The men who accompany Berlin in the search for Cacciato are developed in chapter 22, "Who They Were, or Claimed to Be," an analysis
especially of names and what they denote: "A few names were known in
full, some in part, some not at all. No one cared" (145). Primary among
the men of the Third Squad is their leader, Lieutenant Corson, the antithesis of Sidney Martin. Simply, "the men loved him" (144). It is with the
lieutenant that Sarkin leaves Paris after Berlin gives voice, at Sarkin's urging, to the fears that have haunted him throughout. In a soliloquy replete
with spotlights and microphone, Berlin addresses the audience and takes
responsibility for his actions: voluntarily enlisting in the army, accepting
a promotion, joining the pursuit of Cacciato, voting to continue the pursuit, making his way to Paris, and addressing the audience where he now
stands. Berlin has permitted himself to open up since the journey began—
six months in the Cacciato thread, six hours in the night on the observation
post, and perhaps as many minutes in heated battle—and he discusses for
the first time the depth of his fear, "a fear greater than the fear of war: the
consequences of abandoning his sworn military duty and his self-respect"
(Saltzman 36). The only fear greater than staying is running, the possibility
that he will lose the respect of everyone whom he has ever known. The
sentiment appears often in O'Brien's fiction.

THEMES

With *Cacciato*, O'Brien tackles the themes inherent to the study of war.
The novel's structure, specifically the chaos and the fragmentation of both
the war scenes and Berlin's trek after the elusive Cacciato, lends itself to
an exploration of the nature of truth and fiction (including the power of
the imagination), courage, and place. Like the soldier Tim O'Brien in *If I
Die*, Paul Berlin weaves both factual accounts and fictive responses to the
war into a novel that attempts to answer—even if those answers are far
from satisfactory—the questions that arise in all of O'Brien's work. As in
the later *The Things They Carried*, O'Brien emphasizes storytelling, an ac-

tivity that broaches the possibility, as Berlin would phrase it, of organizing thoughts and ordering chaos through the use of language and image.

Courage is a primary issue in *Cacciato*. In the chapter "Falling through a Hole in the Road to Paris," O'Brien challenges his protagonist's ability to continue the story; Berlin had already questioned his own courage in the face of failure and death in the fourth "Observation Post." The upshot of Berlin's nighttime philosophizing is a contradiction that informs many, if not all, of his actions: In short, "how to act wisely in spite of fear. Spiting the deep-running biles: That was true courage" (80). Berlin invokes the ideas of Doc Peret, the platoon's resident philosopher, who asserts that the center of courage is deep inside each person, a biological rather than psychological device that can be called upon in times of great stress. Courage is addressed at length by Berlin in a monologue at novel's end, though little seems to be resolved other than to illustrate Berlin's ability, finally, to admit what he has most feared during his tour of duty in Vietnam. Heberle points out that courage in the face of the great number of deaths that Berlin witnesses has lessened his ability to cope with further loss, and

> since these memories of others' deaths continually intrude upon Paul's quest after Cacciato, appearing in brief associations and fragments and out of sequence, he has difficulty integrating them with the rest of his dream. This apparent narrative confusion derives from unresolved trauma, and accordingly it becomes psychically important for Paul to give the traumatic fragments formal closure and meaningful arrangement. (137)

Only when Berlin expresses his fears openly, then, does the dream remain alive. The novel's last two words, "Maybe so" (336), are relevant not only in the context of Cacciato's quest, but Berlin's own quest, an echo of Jimmy Cross's repudiation of love in the later "The Things They Carried" to become a more attentive, responsible soldier, to handle himself in battle, and to survive.

Any resolution of the issues in question, however, hinges upon the characters' ability to distinguish truth from fiction, as when Doc Peret wonders about the disappearance of Cacciato, "What part was fact and what part was the extension of fact? . . . How did it end?" (27). Those questions force the reader to consider not only the stories' content, but also the ways in which fact and fiction obscure truth making: Doc Peret's use of M&Ms as medicine in "How Bernie Lynn Died after Frenchie Tucker," or Oscar Johnson's reinvention of himself from a mild-mannered kid from Maine to a savvy Detroit hustler. In war, nothing is as it seems. In a discussion of the novel's most salient aspects, Maria S. Bonn writes that, while the notion of courage in war arises repeatedly, *Cacciato* is "a return to a consideration of war stories. O'Brien again takes up the question of the relationship between fiction and experience, this time in a more explicit and self-conscious manner; and he attempts to discover the kind of stories that we must tell for them to have a real efficacy in our lives" (8). *Cacciato*'s basic framework resembles that of *If I Die. Cacciato,* however, rather than passing as memoir—Berlin's memories of the first six months in-country could perhaps be said to fulfill the criteria—uses the dual devices of memory and imagination to emphasize the novel's fictive aspects and the importance of "the narrative art itself" (Saltzman 38).

The novel's different threads take much of their meaning from that "narrative art." A series of arresting images in Berlin's waking dream describe the various cultures Cacciato might encounter on his way from Vietnam to Paris, "people whose eyes and skins would change in slow evolution and counterevolution westward, whole continents opening up like flowers, new tongues and new times and all roads connecting toward Paris" (23). Later, on Berlin's train ride through the mountains to Afghanistan, O'Brien's sentences move the action forward, toward Paris, leaving behind the fog of war. Such passages contrast sharply to the brutal brevity of the war scenes, as in the death of Frenchie Tucker: "They watched him go down [into the tunnel]. A great big cussing guy who had to wiggle his way in. Then they heard the shot" (89). Later, Doc Peret, who has the best grasp of any of the men on the war's psychological effects on its participants, posits, "The point is that war is war no matter how it's perceived. War has it own reality" (197). That perception of reality, both for the characters and for the reader, is a function not only of the novel's actions, but the way in which those actions are recounted.

Almost as important to Berlin's perception of the war as the way he processes the events around him is his notion of place. The only point of reference for Berlin of the unfamiliar is, of course, the familiar. As a young man, Berlin had gone on an Indian Guides journey with his father so that they could be "pals forever" (40), though Berlin's "sense of place had never been keen" (40). His sense of Vietnam's people is even less keen, though he has come, of necessity, to know the land around him better than most. The hostile land facilitates the fertile imagination that Berlin exhibits throughout; still, ironically, it is the land that Berlin must survive. On the observation post, he realizes that on the Des Moines River of his home, fall will have passed, and the seasons will have changed in their predictable pattern. Nothing in Vietnam reminds him of that place, and he is a stranger in Vietnam no matter how many times he attempts to engage the enemy or how he rationalizes his role as soldier in a war that will be better for his leaving it.

The Cacciato thread allows Berlin to escape Vietnam and to discover unfamiliar places. He draws mind-pictures of Mandalay as the group move toward it, and "he imagined it clearly: museums and golden statues, hansoms drawn by white stallions in braid, white-coated waiters serving fancy food, flowers everywhere, and a clean soft bed" (112). On the road to Paris, however, Berlin is reminded of his role in the war. When the group meets Li Van Hgoc, he admonishes them from his underground sanctuary that "the soldier is but the representative of the land. The land is your true enemy" (86). Not only does Van disabuse the men of the notion that they are fighting an enemy that they rarely see, but he insists that their true enemy is beneath their feet, immutable and indestructible. Once again, the men are at a loss to define the enemy. Even though they may escape the Viet Cong, they surely cannot escape the land, which carries the weight of history. None of the men are prepared to fight a human enemy, let alone a land imbued with thousands of years of memories.

ALTERNATIVE READING: DECONSTRUCTION

The term *deconstruction* came into vogue in the late 1960s with the work of French philosopher Jacques Derrida, who challenged, and in many instances outraged, fellow philosophers by asserting that language and meaning are fluid, not determined, and that texts can take on different meanings with subsequent readings. The movement was later joined by well-known scholars Geoffrey Hartman, J. Hillis Miller, Paul de Man, and Harold Bloom, who brought Derrida's work to literary criticism. The Yale critics, as they were known, for their common affiliation with that institution, speak of deconstruction generally in terms of a text's meaning as influenced both by its structure and language. Art Berman points out how a number of factors, including "the social and cultural movements of the 1960s and 1970s—the importation of French existentialism, the disaffection with science and technology, the reaction against the determinism of a psychological behaviorism, the search for personal freedom and political harmony" (225), influenced a movement away from traditional literary analyses, including New Criticism (the essays collected in this book are examples of such readings), and toward a reading that would take into account theories in other academic disciplines. Deconstruction is a sea change from the more stable, logical readings that earlier New Critics found so reassuring. Such a destabilized reading in *Cacciato*—the convoluted narrative structures defy explanation without proper context, and the fragmented stories call into question traditional notions of time and space—informs the ways in which the reader receives and interprets the story.

   Although the theory behind deconstruction is quite complex and often has little to do with many realist novels, the notion is particularly relevant to O'Brien's style and content in *Cacciato,* which combines both realist and fabulist modes. O'Brien's novel can benefit from such a reading, so long as we view the text as both the story of Cacciato and his march toward Paris and the equally compelling story of Paul Berlin, the unwilling soldier, and his desire to escape the war. O'Brien's ethereal language, which describes scenes not readily understood in a traditional context, follows the dicta of deconstruction: "Everything can be 'put in question,' that is, viewed as arbitrary, free-floating elements in a closed system of 'writing,' with the result that previously settled assumptions of stability and coherence, both in words and in things, become radically shaken, even, as a number of critics have claimed, to the point of nihilism" (Kneale, "Deconstruction" 187). The result is "a radically different understanding of textuality and the philosophy of language generally" (Kneale 191). The words on the page, then, become as important as the ideas they articulate. Instead of emphasizing character and plot, O'Brien mediates the stories through the filters of language and time and points of view different enough from reader expectations to draw attention not only to the story, but to its means of delivery.

   Cacciato defines the rules of engagement in the Vietnam War at the same time that it questions the "reality" of the war and the events surrounding one particular case involving an AWOL soldier. Everything that occurs when Cacciato's fellow soldiers trail him from the jungles of Vietnam to the streets of Paris, an ostensible journey of more than 8,000 miles, is told through the "fog of war." The "truth" that the text claims for the search is undermined by the observations of the central character, Paul Berlin. Even though "the facts were simple: They went after Cacciato, they chased him into the mountains, they tried hard. . . . That was the end of it. The last known fact. What remained were possibilities" (323), both Cacciato's fate and the text's essential "truth" are negotiable.

   O'Brien also asks the reader, in an echo of the premise put forward by

Samuel

poet ~~William~~ Taylor Coleridge nearly a century and a half before, to sus-
pend disbelief and read the story as though Berlin experiences the reality
formed wholly in the soldier's mind. As Berlin and his group fall through
a hole that opens underneath them on the road to Paris, the description
reminds one not so much of the early chase chapters—which, on a level
entirely removed from Berlin's hallucination on the observation post, are
plausible—as it does the tornado scene from *The Wizard of Oz* or Alice's
plummet into Wonderland: "So down and down, pinwheeling freestyle
through the dark. Time only to yell a warning, time to snatch for his
weapon and Sarkin Aung Wan's hand, and then he was falling. . . . Silly!
Something came plunging by—a peculiar living object, a man—and as it
descended he saw it was the old lieutenant spread out full-eagle like a
sky diver. Then a flurry of falling objects . . . " (82–83). O'Brien moves the
narrative more or less seamlessly from the real to the bizarre without
admitting the absurdity of Berlin's actions. Rather, Berlin focuses incessantly on the "possibilities" of both his own imagination and the events
that comprise the Cacciato chapters.

In chapter 27, "Flights of Imagination," O'Brien combines for the first
time Berlin's in-country experiences with the hunt for Cacciato. While
Sidney Martin, the lieutenant who later gets fragged by his own men,
insists that the platoon search discovered tunnels for Viet Cong, Berlin
remarks on the number of different ways they handled dead bodies. Perhaps it is the horror of that image, in part, that prompts Berlin's break
from reality. In a brief paragraph set off from the rest of the text, Berlin
returns to the Cacciato thread in a scene that recalls the group's subter-
ranean detour on the way to Paris: "Flee, fly, flown . . . down the granite
country, and up, and the train carried them through central Afghanistan"
(178). Once again, the descriptions in the Cacciato thread are earthier than
those of the war scenes, the redolence of a strange and wonderful foreign
country a counterpoint to the stench of rotting bodies. The scene intimates
the limitations of a simple soldier to accept the horror he sees in combat
and is a powerful argument for O'Brien's passion for storytelling: stories
exist for the telling, but we are hard-pressed to give them meaning without the proper context.

Of O'Brien's fiction, *Cacciato* is, along with *The Things They Carried*, his
most self-reflexive—a term in deconstruction that indicates the extent to
which an author refers to himself in order to become part of the text and
to invite the reader to do so as well. The novel's structure is undoubtedly
O'Brien's most difficult, and Herzog writes of the elements driving the
novel's expression as art that "O'Brien faces the problem of capturing the

special character of the Vietnam experience (episodic, confused, and illogical) within a fictional framework providing unity, coherence, perspective, and meaning" ("*Going after Cacciato*" 95). In *The Nuclear Age,* a novel published seven years after *Cacciato,* the author mingles the dream visions of William Cowling with a realist narrative. Still, it would be more than a decade before *The Things They Carried* would provide a companion text to O'Brien's award-winning novel of imagination, war, and possibility that focused nearly as much on language and the act of storytelling as on the stories themselves.

The Nuclear Age
(1985)

Although only 6 percent of all young men were needed to fight, the Vietnam draft cast the entire generation into a contest for individual survival. The draft was not, however, an arbitrary and omnipotent force, imposing itself like blind fate upon men who were powerless to resist.

   —Lawrence M. Baskir and William A. Strauss,
         Chance and Circumstance

Although critics nearly universally praised *Going after Cacciato* for its ability to capture the Vietnam experience in abstract, surreal terms, O'Brien's subsequent novel, *The Nuclear Age*, met with ambivalence. Critics generally admire the author's earnestness and ambition in attempting, through his protagonist William Cowling, to connect the events of youth and early adulthood—Vietnam, the rise of counterculture, the Bomb and the advent of the cold war, and other politically and historically charged events from the second half of the twentieth century—as a way of defining one man's life. One reviewer favorably compares O'Brien's style, a "mixture of bemusement and sarcasm," to that of Joseph Heller, Don DeLillo, and Aldous Huxley, and praises a tone that "is uncannily perfect in capturing the mood of young Americans in an era of possible Armageddon" (Lochte 16). Others see the novel as flawed because of its chaotic portrayal of the wait-and-see fatalism of the cold war. Grace Paley writes, "In the sections dealing with William's childhood there's a kind of gentle but rugged play with the American family—with the *idea* of the American family. Because Mr. O'Brien is truthful, not mean or vengeful, he is able to be pretty tough though kind" (7). Finally, though, "it seems as though Mr. O'Brien has become afraid of the political meaning of William's sensible madness" (7). Paley explores an issue important in any examination of O'Brien's work, namely his effort over the past three decades at rendering such highly charged stories essentially devoid of political overtones. The danger inherent in such a notion, of course, is that the events portrayed are inevitably viewed—by readers and writer alike—through a political lens, and the novels that arise from those portrayals are almost necessarily didactic. Also, Michiko Kakutani deems the novel derivative of Heller's *Catch-22* (curious, in light of Lochte's comments to the contrary) and O'Brien's own *Cacciato,* in its exploration of the boundaries between sanity and insanity, imagination and reality.

The novel's three sections, "Fission," "Fusion," and "Critical Mass," denote increasingly unstable and powerful nuclear reactions and signal the building tension and, in the novel's conclusion, the literal and figurative explosiveness of Cowling's precarious situation. The section headings refer to the threat of the cold war; the novel covers the four-decade period from Cowling's Montana childhood in the mid-1950s to the story's present, modern-day America in the mid-1990s. That arc of time and technology, reminiscent of a similar image in Thomas Pynchon's *Gravity's Rainbow,* informs Cowling's understanding of how profoundly disorganized his life has become: "Like hide-and-go-seek—the future curves toward the past, then folds back again, seamlessly, always expressing itself in the present tense" (98).

O'Brien himself admits that he felt the impact of *Cacciato* on his later writing, and consensus from reviewers suggests that *The Nuclear Age* suffers from the anxiety of the earlier novel's influence. O'Brien, who struggled for nearly eight years to finish the manuscript, which went through at least two wholesale revisions and a number of publishers, has called the burden of writing a follow-up to such a well-received novel an "appalling process" (Muro 85). Mark Muro, playing on a parallel to Herman Melville, one of O'Brien's most admired writers (not the least because, as O'Brien points out, Melville's famous novel *Moby-Dick* was savaged by reviewers upon its release), writes, "The portentous hole, one might say, becomes both O'Brien's and his protagonist's whale: just as in his predecessor, Melville, the leviathan's whiteness served at once as an object of all quixotic travail, an all-meaning symbol and as a shadowing forth of all 'the heatless voids and immensities of the universe' that 'stab us from behind with the thought of annihilation,' so too William's back-yard pit" (85).

Although often characterized as a dark comedy—O'Brien himself claims, "I was trying to write a funny book. I think it is funny" (Naparsteck 6)—even the novel's title implies imminent loss, or at the least a pervasive mind-numbing anxiety. The comedy, when it comes, induces uncomfortable, forced laughter rather than release. Even if Cowling manages to escape with his family intact, the family must live with the promise of annihilation, both from within and without. That unease cuts to the very heart of the fear engendered by the cold war. Instead of sustaining the magical realism that carries *Cacciato* (see chapter 2 for analysis; O'Brien has expressed a fascination with the work of Jorge Luis Borges, one of the early masters of that style, which is also employed by Gabriel García Márquez, Toni Morrison, Jorge Amado, and Isabel Allende, among other significant contemporary practitioners), O'Brien relies more on the staid realism of his first novel, *Northern Lights.*

The parallels between *The Nuclear Age* and *Northern Lights,* published more than a decade earlier, are clear: Cowling fears the cold war and desires to protect himself and his family in much the same way that Perry's father insists, even from his deathbed, on building a bomb shelter; perhaps more importantly, O'Brien illustrates in both novels how Vietnam experiences can perpetuate lifelong feelings of anxiety and paranoia—and this despite the fact that of O'Brien's male protagonists, only Perry and Cowling have not participated directly in Vietnam. Although *The Nuclear Age* does not end as tragically as it might, Cowling manages only the same sort of irresolute hope that Perry feels after his own transformation. Both protagonists are subject to the whims of events outside their control. Still, as Heberle points out, the good news in Cowling's case is that, with his acceptance of his situation, "the balanced repetition, calm tone, and quiet eloquence of this resolution, unprecedented in the rest of Cowling's narrative, registers stylistically a dissolving of traumatization and a willing submission to the uncertainties of the nuclear age" (163). As Cowling wonders, in a world where action takes precedence over thought, "what can one do but dig?" (123).

PLOT DEVELOPMENT

William Cowling, a 49-year-old accidental political-activist-cum-family-man, has been a victim of the cold war for nearly 40 years. For much of that time, he has lived on the run. Now, he tells his story: "I was a wanted man; I was hounded by Defense Intelligence and the FBI; I was almost shot to death at Sagua la Grande; I watched my friends die on national television; I was a mover in the deep underground; I could've been another Rubin or Hoffman; I could've been a superstar" (8). Instead of having become an infamous counterculture icon, Cowling stands in his backyard 25 years later, digging a hole that will one day become a fallout shelter. His wife, Bobbi, a stewardess-turned-poet, and a 12-year-old daughter, Melinda, question his sanity. Cowling continues his digging, and Bobbi threatens to leave him. Fearing for his family's safety and dreading being alone, Cowling locks the two in the house and prepares to finish the shelter.

When Bobbi decides that she and Melinda will not suffer Cowling's eccentricities any longer, Cowling, desperate to keep them with him, barricades them into the couple's bedroom. Even after incarcerating his family for nearly three weeks, Cowling can only remark on the ingenuity with which he has handled the situation, the way he has fashioned a small service hatch through which the family now communicates. Out of escape options, Bobbi and Melinda attempt to play on Cowling's guilt in order to gain their freedom. Bobbi composes more of her poems ("Bad poetics compounded by bad logic" [199], Cowling fumes), and Melinda wonders aloud about their fate should something happen to Cowling, if he were unable to release them from their prison. Cowling's notion of how close the world has come to nuclear holocaust is not to be swayed, however, and he continues digging. In order to transfer Bobbi and Melinda to the shelter, Cowling drugs them with Seconal. For a time, he seems intent upon ending their lives in order to save them by detonating an explosive charge in the bunker.

In alternating vignettes, the novel moves from past to present in a dizzying series of repetitions and narrative loops, the trademark of O'Brien's fragmented characters. The scenes in the present frame the novel's real "plot," while the past recollections offer some motivation for Cowling's odd behavior. The flashback chapters, which detail Cowling's obsession with nuclear war from an early age, including his preoccupation with a Ping-Pong table in his parents' basement, where he hid to avoid the inescapable blast, are based on autobiographical events, the result of the young Tim O'Brien having grown up in an America on edge from the constant threat—real and perceived—of mutual assured destruction:

> I was 10, 11, doing what was expected of me, watching the
> Bomb on TV, and one night I woke up in the middle of the

night. I remember just being incredibly scared, realizing "My God, the world can really go" and that that might affect me personally. Then I remember how I grabbed my pillow, gathered all my blankets and went down to the basement and hid under the Ping-Pong table. It was weird. I gathered boxes. I laid wood and stuff on top, old rugs all around. Whatever I could find. I put charcoal briquets on the table to absorb the radiation. I don't know. It was better than nothing. I remember filling Mason jars with water. . . . I was worried about water. (Muro 85)

O'Brien's actions as a young boy would be attributed almost verbatim to Cowling in *The Nuclear Age.* Unlike O'Brien, however, William Cowling grows up in the small town of Fort Derry, Montana, in the shadow of the missile silos that stand silent but ready to fulfill their terrible mission. One of young William's most persistent memories is of his father playing Custer in an annual re-creation of the Battle of the Bighorn. William's psychological makeup is molded in those mock battles; he is a product of a schizophrenic culture, one that demands death and destruction at the same time that it fears obliteration. William, like most children his age, is subject to the push and pull of those contradictory emotions. Even though he knows that his father, as the doomed general Custer, must die, he is fascinated by the violence of war. "I wanted to warn him, rescue him, but I also wanted slaughter," Cowling explains. "How do you explain it? Terror mixed with fascination: I craved bloodshed, yet I craved the miracle of a happy ending" (10–11).

William's parents find his fears to be unfounded; when those fears become persistent and worrisome, however, they try to assuage their son's anxiety. Finally, years later, exasperated at William's visions of the end of the world, they persuade him to see a counselor in Helena, Dr. Charles Adamson. William remains in contact with Adamson long after the end of their first sessions together; they grow close throughout those meetings, even though the doctor seems at first not to be interested in his young patient's problems, instead describing his own issues at length. William cannot decided whether Adamson is testing him, attempting to get the young man to open up to him, or if the doctor is genuinely insecure and unhappy. In fact, the relationship between William and Adamson is similarly nebulous throughout. One thing the two do seem to agree on is the sorry state of the world, and they spend their sessions talking about "how volatile and dangerous the world is, fragile as glass, no margin for error, and we agreed that the best strategy was to put a premium on avoiding unnecessary risks: stay alert, never take chances" (48–49). Recalling the relationship in the novel's present, Cowling muses, "A hard person to pin down. How much was acting, how much was real? Even now, in memory, it all blends together" (56).

Cowling's memories wander from the present to the Cuban missile crisis in 1962 and the escalation of war in the Gulf of Tonkin in 1964. He attends Peverson State College and is struck by the apathy of his generation toward what he perceives as widespread injustice. Because of his deep-seated fear of nuclear holocaust, Cowling is aware of the implications of history and holds great disdain for his fellow students, who sleepwalk through their lives with little concern for the future. He takes an interest in geology, believing rock to be more solid and enduring than the subjects of study in other disciplines. Geology provides a counterpoint to his continued interest in history and political science, which exemplify for Cowling "the certainty of absolute uncertainty" (68).

He prides himself on his imagination and his individuality, and when the war in Vietnam reaches critical mass, he pickets the college's cafeteria with a sign that reads "THE BOMBS ARE REAL" (74). Few students notice his protest. Eventually, after two months, Cowling attracts the attention of Ollie Winkler and Tina Roebuck, two peers who are even more outcasts than Cowling. Surprisingly, Sarah Strouch, who had gone to high school with Cowling and who was unapproachable because of their different attitudes and social status—Sarah was a cheerleader and Cowling an outsider—joins the group. With her personality and drive, she quickly becomes the group's leader, organizing rallies, teach-ins, and classroom boycotts and bringing a trendiness and passion to politics that had been lacking in the group before her involvement. It is Sarah who encourages the group to escalate their activities to include violence, if necessary, attendant with the continued bloodshed in Vietnam. Cowling immediately recognizes her commitment to the cause and in short order comes to understand that he no longer fits. Sarah, he knows, "was out to change the world. I was out to survive it. I couldn't summon the same moral resources" (163).

When Cowling receives his draft notice in the summer of 1968, he dodges, going underground with Sarah, Ollie, and Tina. The group travels to Key West, and from there they undertake paramilitary training in Cuba with two men, Nethro and Ebenezer Keezer, who are more serious about the group's work than any of the members, including Sarah. After describing in graphic detail the carnage of Vietnam that he has experienced firsthand, Keezer intones, "And you folks—you nice folks have not seen shit. Understand me? You have not _seen_ shit" (177). After flashing back to the Ping-Pong table of his youth, Cowling freezes up on the weapons range and then fails the final test, an assault on a beachhead position during which Cowling experiences live battle firsthand: "I lay flat and hugged my rifle. It was all I could do, hug and twitch. Gunfire swept the beach. This, I deduced, was how it was and had to be. If you're sane, if you're in command of the present tense, you dispense with scruples. You recognize the squirrel in your genes. You sprawl there and twitch and commit biology" (188). The rest of the group passes the test and begins its activities, a series of subversive actions that lands Sarah on the cover of _Newsweek_ as a wanted terrorist. For two years, Cowling upholds his commitment to the group by acting as a courier, traveling the country to deliver materiel and documents to his fellow insurgents.

Despite their love for one another, Cowling and Sarah are doomed in their relationship because of their different attitudes toward the war. While Cowling understands that self-preservation is his primary impulse, Sarah's idealism leads her to believe that she can change the world. She begins an affair with Ned Rafferty, a latecomer to the group who joins only out of his desire to be with her. According to Cowling, the two "made a splendid match" (219); Sarah's relationship with Ned, however, is also doomed to failure. As a last defiant act against the revolutionary values that have become increasingly alien to Cowling, he and Ned destroy a cache of weapons that are to be used in a raid. The action, more than any other in Cowling's life, gives him a tentative sense of closure. After years of living as a wanted man, he concludes, "For me, at least, the war was over" (260). The story moves rapidly through the eight years or so that follow his leaving the group. Though he participated in the group's activities, Cowling avoids jail time. A decade later, he completes a master's degree in geology. In an overarching irony, Cowling, now a geologist, discovers a deposit of uranium, an essential ingredient in the atomic bombs he has feared since childhood and the same bombs that the group had risked their lives to protest. As a result of Cowling's trust in the solidness of rock, the friends are now worth $25 million.

Cowling, unencumbered by his past, begins to look for Bobbi. While tracking her, he learns much about her that threatens to destroy his illusion of her. He follows her to New York, where she was enrolled in a creative-writing program at Columbia, and from there to Germany, where she lived with her husband, Scholheimer, a noted translator. He returns to the United States when he discovers that the mercurial Bobbi has left her German husband and returned to graduate school in Minnesota. Though she still loves Cowling and begs him to elope with her to Rio, Sarah helps Cowling find Bobbi, an action that encapsulates the complexity and contradictions of Cowling's life: "In part, [finding Bobbi] was a problem in detection, teasing out clues, but there were also the complications of language and uncertainty and Sarah" (275). Cowling's whirlwind courtship of Bobbi is similar to the blur of events that connect him from the "era of Vietnamization" to his newly discovered wealth: he buys a limo to take Bobbi from Minnesota to Helena, Montana; they are married and honeymoon in the Sweetheart Mountains; in 1983, they have a daughter. Though Cowling fears that Bobbi will disappear from his life, he confides his fears in her. When Bobbi does leave for two weeks—significantly, Cowling notes, taking her diaphragm with her—the relationship changes. Cowling, always one to fear the worst, "expected to find a last poem nailed to my heart" (288). It is during this time of uncertainty that he devises a desperate plan to keep the family intact. For the first time, a voice emerges from the hole, encouraging Cowling to dig quickly.

In the end, as Cowling prepares to explode a bomb in the hole, killing his family and himself, he comes face to face with Melinda, who for the first time fully understands what her father plans to do. In that instant, Cowling articulates the fears of the cold war: "We share the knowledge that there is no mercy between fathers and daughters. We will kill for our children. Our children will kill for us. We will kill for families. And above all we will kill for love, as men have always killed" (308). Cowling, held in awe by the bravery of his daughter as she confronts him, concludes that "if you're sane, the world cannot end, the dead do not die, the bombs are not real" (310). The admission negates his childhood fears and his protests against the war. Only through such an epiphany is he able to reconcile his current life with the past that has haunted him for 40 years. In a final statement that implies his acceptance of faith over science, the unseen over the real, Cowling posits the possibility, slim as it is, that humankind can survive even the threat of the nuclear age: "I will hold to a steadfast orthodoxy, confident to the end that E will somehow not quite equal mc^2, that it's a cunning metaphor, that the terminal equation will somehow not quite balance" (312).

CHARACTER DEVELOPMENT

William Cowling is one of O'Brien's most complex characters, a man whose actions, based solely on his responses to his memories, are disconnected from reality. The reason for the character's complexity may have little to do with the individual, however, and more to do with the time in which he lives. Cowling, O'Brien suggests, is a cold-war everyman, a representative type who plays out Americans' worst fears on a surreal stage of his own making. James Marcus, understanding O'Brien's unwillingness to resolve the intricacies of his novels with facile endings, concludes that "O'Brien raises a complicated and essential question: Where is the boundary between a personal, homemade neurosis and the epidemic madness of the age?" (450). Read as a mirror of the society of which he is a product, Cowling reflects the fragmentation and alienation that characterize the cold war, Vietnam, and myriad other events that are the focus of his obsession with history and his own past. Cowling's primary action in the present—the hole that he digs in order, he believes, to save his family—is futile, an indication of Cowling's dwindling capacity to relate to reality. His action, pointless by its very nature—the result of the digging is nothing more than a negative space—is also a metaphor for society's response to the increased likelihood of nuclear war. Compounding young William's fears about nuclear annihilation is the difficulty of any adolescent to find his way in the world. When his parents fail to understand their son's concerns, Cowling insists that he loves his father, even if he "hated the whole grown-up world with its secret codes and secret meanings" (28). Later, in describing his high-school days and his relapse into loneliness after almost a decade as an integral part of the antiwar group, Cowling recalls simply, "The problem was this: I didn't *fit*" (34).

O'Brien also blurs the line between dreams and reality, further compounding the reader's sense that Cowling will not be redeemed until he understands the difference between the two. Cowling's attempt at maintaining his tenuous grasp on sanity and making sense of his childhood in the context of his adult life is embodied in Bobbi. Even after he discovers that she has left New York for Germany to be with her translator husband, Cowling senses that she is his only hope for the future. "If you're crazy, I now understood, you don't feel grief or sadness," he postulates. "You just can't find the future. . . . If you're crazy it's the end of the world" (232–33).

In many ways, Sarah Strouch is a stronger character, more focused on the goal. Not unlike Mary Anne Bell in "Sweetheart of the Song Tra Bong" from *The Things They Carried*, Sarah becomes a willing pawn of the insurrection, and her fervent involvement in the movement is juxtaposed to the more visceral fear that haunts Cowling throughout his life. While anxiety and inaction characterize Cowling's life, Sarah defines herself through her actions. Although Sarah attempts to maintain her humanity through her relationship with Cowling, her willingness to acquiesce to the demands of the movement implies a power at work in society that supersedes the wants and needs of the individual. Even Cowling, who has escaped being co-opted by society, finds himself terrified at the prospects that await him in the future. His own history is a series of fits and starts, his indecisiveness at the prospect of making a wrong decision nearly pathological.

If Cowling is a complex character, Sarah is an enigma. From the time the two attend high school together, Cowling has admired Sarah from a distance. She is the popular cheerleader, he the outsider who talks to her only with difficulty. They find common ground for a time in their devotion to the cause, and simple adolescent differences melt away, replaced by the intricacies of adulthood. By the time Sarah dies after a long career as a counterinsurgent, Cowling and Sarah are platonic twin souls reunited in a relationship as incongruous as it is passionate. Despite having a romantic side that complements the steely exterior, Sarah sums up the contradictions of their relationship when she tells Cowling, "I love you, you know that, but sometimes—lots of times—I can't help wondering about your backbone. All that bullshit about a dangerous world. The bombs are real, la-di-dah, but you don't ever do anything, just crawl under your Ping-Pong table. That jellyfish attitude, I despise it. Despise, that's the only word. I love you, but the despising makes it hard" (172–73). After surviving for years on the run, Sarah dies of encephalitis. The disease is a physical manifestation of the problems that Cowling has faced throughout his life. When she arrives at Cowling's home for a last Christmas visit, he notices that Sarah's disease has gotten worse, and "tiny black veins snaked across the surface of the blister. Her speech faltered. She had trouble coordinating past with present" (292). Little more than a month later, she dies at Cowling's home. When the group's remaining members die in a shootout in the tropics, Cowling suffers a breakdown followed by a trial separation from Bobbi.

The friends who fall victim to their idealism are recognizable as types for the romantic insurgents cut in the mold of Che Guevara, a Cuban revolutionary who was executed by Bolivian soldiers in October 1967. The act established Guevara as a martyr, a symbol for right, and Ned, Ollie, Tina, and Sarah are pleased to be associated with such a sanctified figure. Cowling, considering the group's genesis, wonders, "When I look back on that period, it's clear that my motives were not strictly political. . . . Granted, the war was part of it, I had ideals and convictions, but for me the imperative went deeper. . . . It occurred to me, even at the time, that our political lives could not be separated from the matrix of life in general" (80). Clearly, Cowling's motivation for joining the group stems from his earlier role as outsider, a part that he plays well, but not nearly so well as the others he has recruited to join him. When the group takes over the individuals' identities, Cowling's usefulness comes to an end. He is once again relegated to the margins, while his friends become infamous by acting out on what Cowling has come to think of as their distorted politics.

Cowling, placed outside the fray by his cowardice, saves his own life by realizing what others have not: "All those complexities and ambiguities, issues of history, issues of law and principle—they've vanished. A stack of tired old platitudes: The war could've been won, the war was ill conceived, the war was an aberration, the war was hell" (130). In the present, with everyone from his past gone, he waits in the shelter to destroy himself and his family. When Melinda wakes from the sedative that Cowling has administered, she realizes what he is about to do. Cowling relents, and, despite his belief that all has come to naught, he vows to live in the present with as much hope as he can muster. His response is an eloquent, understated microcosm of cold-war America.

THEMES

Of the several important thematic threads that tie *The Nuclear Age* together, none facilitates an understanding of Cowling's character and the novel's historical context better than the notion of, as Kakutani puts it, "what it means to be sane in an insane world" ("Prophet of Doom" 12). The weight of history crushes Cowling, and major historical events are a blur, a symptom of the protagonist's displacement from society; or, as Herbele puts it, "Cowling's derangement, marked both literally and figuratively by hyperarousal, is reflected not only by the rhetorical instability of his account but also by the wildly miscellaneous character of its narrative materials, which flip-flop from historical events to cataclysmic visions, from past recollections to present imaginings, from comedy to tragedy" (152). Despite the difficulty that he has at times in expressing himself and organizing his thoughts—hence the litany of questions he repeats as he comes closer to destruction—Cowling makes one of his most cogent statements by reducing the zeitgeist of the time to a single sentence: "It was the era of Vietnamization" (222).

What is significant about his recollection of his past is not the events themselves, which rate little more than an afterthought, but rather the often insignificant details that accrete to construct his present. Cowling comments on "how you couldn't nail down the instant of turn or change but how small actions kept leading to larger actions, then the inevitable reactions" (224), and it is the past that inevitably manufactures present reality and hastens Cowling's alienation from society and his family. When viewed as a problem of organization, then, rather than as a psychological flaw on Cowling's part, the question of Cowling's deteriorating mental state takes on added significance. As O'Brien tells Martin Naparsteck, "this guy in *The Nuclear Age* had the courage to do what I didn't and a lot of other people didn't, which is to risk embarrassment and censure and endure humiliation about walking away from the war. . . . despite his service in a kind of Waspism and his wimpy attitude toward the war, [he] manages to do for the most part what he thinks is right. . . . To me, he's the only hero I've written" (5).

Simultaneous to Cowling's psychological unraveling is a decreasing capacity for language, a sign in O'Brien's work of a character on the verge of a breakdown. Cowling's relationship with his wife, Bobbi, seems to be built upon little more than his own misguided romanticism and a poem that she offered him on their first meeting. The very language that she uses to draw Cowling into a relationship, however, later becomes a weapon that she uses to indict Cowling's digging. "My wife is meticulous about such things; she's a poet, the creative type; she believes in clean metaphors and clean language, tidiness of structure, things neatly in place," Cowling bemoans. "Holes aren't clean. Safety can be very messy" (6). In the same way that Cowling protested the war by picketing outside his college cafeteria with a sign reading simply, "THE BOMBS ARE REAL," Bobbi's capacity to define the problems in her relationship with Cowling are more sophisticated, each successive poem an ironic and scathing appraisal of Cowling's increasing delamination. In a poem titled "The Balance of Power," Bobbi writes, *"Here, now, is the long thin wire / from Sun to Bedlam, / as the drumbeat ends / and families pray: / Be quick! Be agile! / The balance of power, / our own, / the world's / grows ever fragile"* (65). The implication of Bobbi's poetry in exploring Cowling's increasingly disjointed ranting is that Cowling has become so unstable that their common language no longer effectively communicates meaning. Later, he laments, "The world . . . is drugged on metaphor, the opiate of our age. Nobody's scared. Nobody's digging. They dress up reality in rhymes and paint on the cosmetics and call it by fancy names" (124).

Perhaps Cowling's most unusual trait, though, is his fondness for making phone calls with no one on the other end, a series of one-sided conversations that allow him to communicate, ironically, with no one in particular: "It might sound strange, but those fake phone calls produced some of the most intelligent conversations I'd ever had" (37). He has long conversations with his former counselor, Dr. Adamson, a kindred spirit who understands what it means to be thrust into the margins and to rely on imagination as a way of maintaining one's sanity, even though Cowling understands too well the limitations of imagination, and "it occurred to me that the events of imagination are never easily translated into the much less pliant terms of the real world. Too damned inflexible" (227). Dreams and imagination mingle; reality bumps against the inevitability of nuclear holocaust and the destruction of Cowling's family. Like the chain reaction that creates a nuclear explosion, atoms smashing one on the other until the world is obliterated, Cowling cannot prevent the chain of events from his life playing itself on an infinite loop in his mind. "Like my father, like all of them, [Sarah] died and dies and keeps on dying, again and again," Cowling laments, "as if repetition might disclose a new combination of possibilities" (305). In his moments of greatest desperation, Cowling muses that "the hole is what we have when imagination fails" (306). Those are the moments when mindless repetition overtakes reality. Still, Cowling manages to discover possibility, a notion that flies in the face of everything he has come, by force of habit, to believe. "I will find forgetfulness," he declares. "Happily, without hesitation, I will take my place in the procession from church to grave, believing what cannot be believed, that all things are renewable, that the human spirit is undefeated and infinite, always" (312).

ALTERNATIVE READING: NEW HISTORICISM

Because of its focus on the arc of history that Cowling moves through on his way, finally, to a tentative understanding of the world he lives in, *The Nuclear Age* lends itself to a new-historical reading (see the "Alternative Reading" section of chapter 3 for a discussion of new historicism). The novel's setting—1995, though the novel was published in 1985—presumes to show a world in chaos, and the fact that O'Brien assumed, as did much of America, that the cold war would still be waged a decade after the book's publication indicates the extent to which animosity between the United States and the Soviet Union affected Americans' attitudes. The novel's speculative nature suggests George Orwell's *1984*, both novels rendering bleak futures and exploring many of the same dystopian themes: Cowling, like Winston Smith, struggles against a faceless enemy;

both protagonists understand the futility of meaningful human relationships in the face of socially imposed constraints; and while Smith's history—and finally his life—is relegated to society's "memory hole," wiped out and therefore forgotten, Cowling's history is threatened by a similar erasure when he posits, "the dead, perhaps, live in memory, but when memory goes, so go the dead. . . . There is no remembering when there is no one to remember. Hence, no history, hence no future" (241).

More important than the narrative present, however, is the past, whose events threaten to damage Cowling in a way that even the present cannot. Events familiar to readers of O'Brien's generation—tests of the Emergency Broadcast System, school drills, the threat of ICBMs raining down upon the country, photographs of bomb tests in *Life* magazine—draw connections between the Sputnik panic of the late 1950s and the present in which Cowling lives, four decades removed from his first intimations of disaster. Although Cowling's participation in paramilitary activities in the late 1960s nearly costs him his life, he looks back on those events with a nostalgia that emphasizes his present impotence. Now, Cowling asks a series of questions that indicates the depth of his confusion: "What happened? Who remembers the convoluted arguments that kept us awake until five in the morning? Was it a civil war? Was Ho Chi Minh a tyrant, and if so, was his tyranny preferable to that of Diem and Ky and Thieu? What about containment and dominoes and self-determination? Whose interests were at stake? Did interests matter?" (130).

Significantly, the outcome for Cowling's friends and compatriots who insist on fighting the war in their own way as their only recourse to "certain blood for uncertain reasons" (140) is to become part of history. In that way, their collective fate differs hardly at all from that of soldiers Curt Lemon, Ted Lavender, the fictional Tim O'Brien, or any other of O'Brien's many characters who, willingly or otherwise, struggle to survive. Cowling, however, as the single character in *The Nuclear Age* who has witnessed history from the advent of the cold war to what he sees as its inevitable conclusion, symbolizes the conscience of the American public. As with the paranoia and fear of the time—both in the presumed cold war of Cowling's present in 1995 and of the Vietnam era—the protagonist's actions and attitudes and his constant reassessment of his own mental health are a litmus test for current events. "Ask this question: Am I crazy? And then listen, listen hard, because you'll get one hell of an answer," Cowling intones in an opening monologue. "If you hold your breath, if you have the courage, you'll hear the soft drip of a meltdown, the ping-ping-ping of submarine sonar, the half-life of your own heart" (7).

For many readers, O'Brien's heightened sense of doom does not resonate. The terror that Americans felt at what they believed to be the imminent destruction of civilization at the hands of the Soviet Union has
been replaced by other, likely even more insidious, possibilities. O'Brien's
novel does, however, universalize the author's own fear, and articulates
his concern for the future, his definition of courage, and the need for social
responsibility. Vietnam and the cold war are isolated historical events with
far-reaching effects on society and man's inherent inhumanity toward
man. Michiko Kakutani finds distracting the catalog of historical events
that serve as points of reference for Cowling. Those points, however, are
often the only truly memorable events in a past that becomes increasingly
hazy for Cowling, even if Kakutani sees them as devoid of meaning when
"history and the consequences of the 60's are telescoped into little
newsreel-like paragraphs, full of names (Kennedy, Johnson, Nixon) and
events (the assassinations, the moratoriums, the sit-ins) and freeze-dried
statistics" ("Prophet of Doom" 12). To reject O'Brien's use of history as an
organizing strategy in *The Nuclear Age* is to dismiss the effect that the
shortening of time and memory has on Cowling. He continues to question
his past even after he realizes that, because of his past, death has become
a welcome option. His final query is the most important: "The question
is simple. In this age, at this late hour, how do I make a happy ending?"
(297). As Cowling discovers, even in the afterglow of his decision to spare
his family and himself and to make the best of what he is offered, history
conspires against him.

7

The Things They Carried
(1990)

> Someone has just saved my life. My rifle is gone and I don't feel
> like finding it or picking it up ever again. The only thing I can think
> of, the only thing that crosses my mind, is living. There seems to
> be nothing in the world more important than that.
> —Ron Kovic, *Born on the Fourth of July*

"My goal was to write something utterly convincing but without any rules
as to what's real and what's made up. . . . In this new book I force myself
to try to invent a form. I had never invented form before," O'Brien tells
Michael Coffey about the genesis of *The Things They Carried*. "Even in
Cacciato, which people found inventive, the form came through my reading of writers like Faulkner and Joyce, whereas this feels to me as if something has been invented" (60). Five years after the mixed critical reception
of *The Nuclear Age*, O'Brien returned with an effort that would rival the
award-winning *Going after Cacciato* in both critical reception and stylistic
ambition. Michiko Kakutani, who also favorably reviewed *Cacciato*, saw
TTTC as a companion text to the earlier novel and writes, "In prose that
combines the sharp, unsentimental rhythms of Hemingway with gentler,
more lyrical descriptions, Mr. O'Brien gives the reader a shockingly visceral sense of what it felt like to tramp through a booby-trapped jungle"
("Slogging Surreally" C21). Kakutani further praises O'Brien for his am-

bition in attempting to convey the horror of war and the power of storytelling. She concludes, "Mr. O'Brien has written a vital, important book—a book that matters not only to the reader interested in Vietnam, but to anyone interested in the craft of writing as well" (C21). Gail Caldwell concurs, writing that the book "leaves third-degree burns" and commenting on "its rhythmic brilliance and its exquisite rendering of memory. . . . This is prose headed for the nerve center of what was Vietnam" ("Staying True" 69).

The vignettes and stories in *TTTC* are linked by the presence of Tim O'Brien, a 43-year-old writer who discusses his need for storytelling and guides the reader through the text, serving as a bridge from story to story and from reader to experience. That combination of story and experience involves author, characters, and reader in a complex relationship questioning, with a rigor missing from *If I Die,* the truth-making mechanisms at a writer's disposal. O'Brien validates the lives of men like Norman Bowker, Jimmy Cross, Curt Lemon, Kiowa, and the others—the men who, even if they survive the war (of the four listed, Lemon and Kiowa do not), have no voice, no way of telling their own stories.

Perhaps more than any other of the author's work, *TTTC* is a damning, persistent antiwar statement made more effective through O'Brien's use of both war and postwar milieus, none more powerful or poignant than the renewal of a friendship with Norman Bowker and that comrade's death three years later by his own hand. Such scenes call into question American involvement in the war and demystify the process of making war, questioning how one might reconcile an active role as a soldier with a life entirely separate from that experience. *TTTC* ably dissects that warmaking impulse because it is not confined by the realist tradition of the memoir. In her analysis of both *If I Die* and *TTTC,* Marilyn Wesley posits that the memoir's realism is not as constructive a commentary on the war as *TTTC* precisely because the book's "formal realism and traditional narrative tropes . . . transform his memoir into the conventional account of a young soldier within the military tradition" (5). *TTTC* faces no such conflict, however, as O'Brien takes license to mingle fact and fiction (not unlike similar scenes in *Cacciato*) and "exploits conflicting codes of violence to get at the disparate 'truths' about Vietnam which involve the depiction of process rather than action" (5). Part of the problem with the Vietnam War, O'Brien tells interviewer Twister Marquiss, is that "these men are not the fearless, mythic cowboys America had come to embrace; they are real men, fighting for causes they can never fully comprehend, and the fear of death haunts them" (10). O'Brien has ruminated on his subject for much of his writing career. In "On the Rainy River," a story told on many occasions to illustrate his anguish over choosing duty at the expense of his own freedom, he writes, echoing a phrase from the earlier novel *The Nuclear Age,* that "certain blood was being shed for uncertain reasons" (40).

TELLING A TRUE WAR STORY

"My own experience [in Vietnam] has virtually nothing to do with the content of the book," O'Brien says. "Every now and then I would draw on my memories or attitudes about Vietnam, but of the whole time I spent there I remember maybe a week's worth of stuff. By and large, in the composition of the book, my attention was on trying to get a feeling of utter authenticity, which meant paying attention to language" (Coffey 60). Of course, the essential truth of O'Brien's experiences is irrelevant to telling a "true" story; or, as Daniel Robinson points out, "a true war story, then, may not have a point, and it certainly does not exist in the narrative vacuum of beginning-middle-end, but it functions at a level of truth beyond that found in the story's words" (262).

Perhaps the most analyzed story in the collection, rivaling even "The Things They Carried" because of its role as a linguistic Rosetta Stone, an interpretive key, to O'Brien's context and style and his thoughts on the writing process, is "How to Tell a True War Story." The story, according to O'Brien, is "the heart of the book—about telling stories, about repetition, and that blur between memory and imagination, how it doesn't matter. And yet as I was writing, my name appeared, and this stomach thing happened, somewhere between the bowels and the heart. You pay attention to that" (Caldwell, "Staying True" 69). The aesthetic statement encapsulated in "How to Tell a True War Story" expresses O'Brien's philosophy of writing and remembering, and grounds much of the author's fiction. Although "How to Tell a True War Story" relates a tale of surreal goings-on in the Vietnam jungle, the story acts principally as a primer on the art of storytelling. O'Brien's definition of a "true war story" accretes slowly as the story unfolds: he first contends, "This is true" (67); describes how "a true war story is never moral" (68); asserts, "True war stories do not generalize. They do not indulge in abstraction or analysis" (78); posits, "You can tell a true war story if it embarrasses you" (69); and realizes that "if there's a moral at all, it's like the thread that makes the cloth. You can't tease it out" (77). Finally, as he looks back on the war long since ended, he realizes that "you can tell a true war story by the way it never seems to end" (76). The word "tell," then, denotes both the act of relating the story (for instance, "How to Tell a True War Story") and the ability to discern a true war story from other stories ("being able to tell the difference").

The first lines of "Sweetheart of the Song Tra Bong" provide context for the collection as a whole and emphasize its overall construction: "Vietnam was full of strange stories, some improbable, some well beyond that, but the stories that will last forever are those that swirl back and forth across the border between trivia and bedlam, the mad and the mundane" (89). Although critics argue the proper classification of the work, treating it as either a collection of stories or a novel, the characters who inhabit *TTTC* are defined by their common experience. O'Brien's repeated themes underscore the war experience; several characters also make multiple appearances. The story "Love," for instance, is connected to "The Things They Carried" by Jimmy Cross's visit to O'Brien more than 20 years after their tour of duty has ended. Even in retrospect, from a great story-distance, O'Brien's sharp descriptions allow the characters and themes to come to the fore. "By focusing on character—the individual coming in close contact with what death looks like—and allowing the surrounding scenes and events to take secondary importance," Robinson writes, "O'Brien increases the absurdity and horror. His plots are determined not by incident and event, but by the changing moral attitudes and development of his characters" (262). Still, the stories' fragmented structure and the random displacement of time never allow the stories to coalesce into a seamless whole.

O'Brien analyzes the storytelling capabilities of some of his old comrades, including Rat Kiley, Mitchell Sanders, and others, who understand as well as O'Brien how important such simple acts can be to surviving the war. Kiley delivers stories in fits and starts, intrudes into his own retellings, and offer personal opinions. Sanders takes Kiley to task for ruining the stories with unnecessary details and tangents. In fact, the men who are poor storytellers or not actively engaged in making images—Norman Bowker, for instance—are the ones for whom life goes poorly both during and after the war. Although O'Brien shares complex ideas of what a story should be and how it should be crafted, the closest that anyone in O'Brien's work comes to succinctly and cogently defining the ways in which soldiers perceive the world is Captain Rhallon in *Cacciato*, when he posits as many different stories of war as there are soldiers engaged in the war. That notion is similar to O'Brien's theory in *TTTC* that "in any war story, but especially a true one, it's difficult to separate what happened from what seemed to happen. What seems to happen becomes its own happening and has to be told that way" (71).

The chapter "Notes" is a long digression on the act of writing and explains, in part, O'Brien's need for remembering and writing. O'Brien relates that the story "Speaking of Courage" was written after Norman Bowker hanged himself in a YMCA locker room in Iowa. In a long letter to O'Brien, Bowker discusses his definition of courage and the "whiner-vets" (156) who insist on parades and community recognition as recompense for their participation in Vietnam. The question implicit in O'Brien's renewed contact with Bowker is one that resonates whenever a soldier returns home to find a country that has not changed with him, a country that cannot accept the man it sent to war to protect its interests: Now that I've done my duty, how can I best go on with my life? Bowker's letter to O'Brien disturbs the author, who relates that his own readjustment was a relatively easy one, which he credits to his ability to tell stories. O'Brien, determined to tell Bowker's story both in his old friend's honor and in order to retain a sense of control over his own memories of the war, begins to draft the piece. When the writing goes too well, O'Brien realizes that successful remembering comes with an associated cost, a fear, as the author describes it, of facing the past head-on.

O'Brien's failure in the initial retelling and his later success is an important point of contact for the author, who understands that to succeed in telling a true war story, a writer plumbs the depths of his fear, his hatred, his anger, and comes away utterly transformed by the experience. When his young friend Linda dies in "The Lives of the Dead," O'Brien, a child himself at the time, connects that childhood tragedy with every event and every person that follows. He sees the soldiers who were killed in Vietnam—Kiowa, Curt Lemon, and the others—and imagines himself as a young boy, skating with his beloved Linda. His skating becomes a metaphor for the passage of time, the figure eights connecting past and present (and, when seen from above, tracing the symbol for eternity), his naive conception of time and mortality still admirably untainted, his imagination remarkably keen. The development of his imagination is the beginning of the telling of stories, which also becomes a lifeline, a way of coping with Vietnam.

The issues broached in *If I Die,* the essential notion of truth and fiction and the conflation of the identities of Tim O'Brien the soldier and the writer, are no less valid here. When Linda returns briefly from the dead to meet with Timmy in his imagination, she describes death as "like being inside a book that nobody's reading" (245). The exuberance of O'Brien's childhood imagination is short-lived. In the space of a decade after the event that he recalls so readily, he and the others would fight and die in the jungles of Vietnam, making stories not as entertainment, but as a way of surviving events for which they find themselves eminently unfit. Because of his experience in Vietnam, however, O'Brien understands that, while many of his stories are patently false and in no way connected to reality (or "reality," as he might put it), "stories can save us" (225). The dead mingle with the living, "and in this way memory and imagination and language combine to make spirits in the head. There is an illusion of aliveness" (230). Memory supersedes reality, and when O'Brien the writer, like the soldiers of his most famous story, carries with him the weight of the dead, his only recourse is to write their lives, to tell their stories in their absence.

"THE THINGS THEY CARRIED"

Of "The Things They Carried," the much anthologized title story, O'Brien says, "If I die, and God says, 'You got one piece of work we'll let you keep,' that's the piece" (Coffey 60). The story first appeared in *Esquire* in 1986 and quickly became O'Brien's masterpiece, not the least for its evocation of the physical and psychological burden that men in war must carry. The platoon's leader is Jimmy Cross, a young lieutenant pining for the company of his girlfriend, Martha, an English major at Mount Sebastian College and a devotee of the writers Chaucer and Virginia Woolf. Cross carries a photograph of Martha and her letters with him. The image bridges the gap between memories of home and the war's brutal reality. Letters and photographs are not the only objects, however, that move with the men as they seek the enemy. O'Brien makes clear several times in the story that their burden changes, shifts like the packs on their backs, some objects or memories sloughed off for other, more important objects that will, in theory, increase the men's likelihood of survival. First of all, writes O'Brien, "the things they carried were largely determined by necessity" (2). The catalog of objects that follows (weapons, knives, dog tags, C rations, the baggage of men at war) only obfuscates the more important burden, the great psychological weight of their experiences and memories. The image is particularly ironic, given the disparate nature of the two. That both are necessary indicates the lengths to which the men in the platoon must go in order to remain connected to the world they left behind. The plethora of detail in the story illustrates the narrator's desire to convince the reader of the story's truth. Such detailed descriptions also suggest an unwillingness on the writer's part to get too close to his memories, preferring the journalistic style over a more intimate, subjective portrayal of the events.

The objective scenes in "TTTC" are reminiscent of similar scenes in *If I Die* and *Cacciato*. The watershed event in "TTTC" is the death of Ted Lavender, one of Cross's men killed by a sniper's bullet while urinating. Lee Strunk, who by dint of a lottery system has been given the dangerous task of crawling into a tunnel to clear it, returns unharmed. Lavender dies. Lavender's death is as swift as it is unceremonious. The distance that the narrator achieves from the event through such a description—Kiowa's assertion that the death was "not like the movies" (6) suggests both the men's closeness to the war and the banal, oddly ironic ways that men in war sometimes die—inoculates the narrator from becoming maudlin or melodramatic. More important for Jimmy Cross is the simple fact of Lavender's death, an either/or proposition (that is, either his men survive or they die) that haunts him throughout the war. His soldier has died, and he was powerless to make it otherwise.

The religious imagery connected with Jimmy Cross is apparent in his initials and his surname, the cross that the lieutenant bears in his love for Martha, which he blames for Lavender's death. Twister Marquiss draws a less biblical parallel with the character of Jimmy Cross, writing, "Cross' name indicates not only his burden but also his Protestant work ethic" (9). The day after Lavender's death, Cross destroys the letters and the photographs, hoping that the symbolic purging will allow him to better protect his men. He pledges not to think about Martha.

The physical objects that figure so prominently for the men early in the story slowly evolve to become much more abstract and complicated: they symbolize war, its survival, the survivor's guilt, and vague definitions of courage and duty. Even though the men understand that "imagination was a killer" (11), they carry objects "determined to some extent by superstition" (13), share the "weight of memory" (14), and most importantly carry "the emotional baggage of men who might die" (21). As the story progresses, the men's burden moves increasingly away from the physical and toward the metaphysical, abstract, and intangible notions that keep the men tenuously grounded in an even more tenuous reality. Jimmy Cross falls victim to this evolution, thinking so much about Martha and her incidental connection to Lavender's death that the weight of memory and guilt overwhelms him.

Finally, he decides that the emotional part of him is as dead as Ted Lavender. The reader never questions Cross's goodness, his affection for his men, or his suitability to be a dutiful soldier. He becomes much like *Cacciato*'s Sidney Martin, the lieutenant so obsessed with standard operating procedure that the soldiers under his command ensure his death in the tunnels that they had searched against their will. Cross's final pronouncement on the matter: "He would dispense with love; it was not now a factor" (26). That Jimmy Cross feels compelled to buy into the culture of war and subjugates his humanity to the rules of engagement is a subtle, powerful antiwar statement. Cross erects a boundary between his humanity and his experience, the sole stay against the uncertainty and chaos of war, where life and death are determined by chance and subject to the whims of fate.

PLOT DEVELOPMENT

The soldiers' common experiences connect "The Things They Carried" to the stories that follow. The narrator details his obsession with storytelling in several vignettes that give the collection a "written-about" quality articulating the extent to which O'Brien's fascination with language and storytelling is set against more traditional fiction. "What sticks to memory, often," the narrator writes, "are those odd little fragments that have no beginning and no end" (36), and he offers many of those odds and ends, strewn among the longer stories that have come to him from the ashes of the war. Upon Jimmy Cross's return to relative normalcy in the United States, many years after the end of his tour of duty in Vietnam, he visits Tim O'Brien at the author's home in Massachusetts. The two enjoy discussing their common experiences and comment on "all the things we still carried through our lives" (27). O'Brien, cognizant of Cross's continued love for Martha and the guilt that he still carries with him over Lavender's death, gathers the courage to ask Cross about Martha. His response says much about stories in general: "You writer types . . . , you've got long memories" (28). Cross, to O'Brien's surprise, shows him a photograph of Martha, the one described in "The Things They Carried" as a shot of a slight, lithe schoolgirl concentrating on a volleyball shot. In the present, Cross relates how he met with Martha at their 10-year reunion (the timing of which is exactly that of *July, July*, in which the college friends from the class of '69 return to catch up on old times, though neither Cross nor Martha appear explicitly in that book). She became a missionary after college, traveling in Ethiopia, Guatemala, and Mexico. While she and Cross renew their friendship at the reunion, and Cross admits to Martha that he still loves her, she becomes defensive.

He wonders what may have happened to her since they last saw one another, and her enigmatic response makes sense to Cross only in an abstract way that forces him always, more than a decade later, to consider the erosion of the relationship: "She didn't understand how men could do those things. What things? he asked, and Martha said, The things men do. Then he nodded. It began to form" (29).

For O'Brien, Cross's gesture—showing his friend, without shame, a replacement for the photograph he had burned years before in Vietnam so that he might be a better soldier to his men—indicates the depths of love, a subject O'Brien explores in its different forms throughout *TTTC*. The process of telling stories is, for O'Brien, often as much a matter of confession as a way of organizing the past. For instance, in "On the Rainy River," he begins with, "This is one story I've never told before" (39). The admission heightens the importance for a writer, or anyone struggling to make sense of memory and to make right what is utterly, absurdly wrong, of establishing the relationships that make storytelling possible in the first place. The story has become familiar by now: O'Brien considers dodging the draft; spends hot summer days in a pig-processing factory in Worthington, Minnesota; contemplates the war and his imminent participation; and unburdens himself, not unlike his friend Jimmy Cross in the photograph-burning incident, when he writes, "Most of this I've told before, or at least hinted at, but what I have never told is the full truth" (46). He commits what he perceives as a profound act of cowardice by joining the fight.

The confusion of young men introduced into a war where the enemy is often equated with the spirit world for their ability to appear and disappear at will manifests itself in "Enemies," a story about a blood feud between Lee Strunk and Dave Jensen. The conflict elevates O'Brien's own unease at slogging through the Vietnamese jungle, where "the distinction between good guys and bad guys disappeared" (63). Strunk and Jensen eventually find a way to trust one another, reaching a point at which they agree that, in the event of a "wheelchair wound," should one or the other be grievously injured and his quality of life compromised, the healthy man would find a way to end the other's life. When Strunk steps on a land mine, he decides that he does not want to die, instead begging Jensen not to fulfill his side of the bargain. Jensen promises not to kill Strunk. When he hears news that the dust-off chopper that took Strunk was brought down over Chu Lai, however, Strunk's death "seemed to relieve Dave Jensen of an enormous weight" (66). The story is an example of what O'Brien has described as "trying to write about truly incredible things and make them credible. Almost always, the events of fiction are incredible. But why tell stories about the ordinary? I wanted in this book to write about storytelling—about rendering the incredible credible, and the frustration of doing it" (Caldwell, "Staying True" 69). Strunk and Jensen need each other so profoundly that even their mutual hatred becomes a sort of love for one another, the promised coup de grace a violent but honorable way of fulfilling an obligation to duty and comrades. The story is also an example of the brutal paradox of Vietnam.

Although many of the stories utilize a third-person omniscient voice that underscores the collection's fictional aspects, O'Brien appears as the first-person narrator in others, including "The Man I Killed," an intense, introspective look at the death of a Vietnamese soldier, ostensibly by O'Brien's own hand. This story and others form a contradictory association between the violence of death and an idyllic passage reminiscent of Virginia Woolf's impressionist short story "Kew Gardens" (in "The Things They Carried," the reader is apprised of Martha's affection for Woolf's prose, and she would certainly know the story): As O'Brien's victim lay in the road, "the butterfly was making its way along the young man's forehead, which was spotted with small dark freckles. The nose was undamaged. The skin on the right cheek was smooth and fine-grained and hairless" (127). Additionally, in the vignette "Good Form," O'Brien admits that the story related in "The Man I Killed" is apocryphal. O'Brien patrolled in the area at the time of the young man's death, though "I did not kill him. But I was present, you see, and my presence was guilt enough. . . . I blamed myself. And rightly so, because I was present" (179). The repetition of the phrase "I was present" indicates O'Brien's deep-seated guilt over the mere fact of his participation in the war. Such images are common in O'Brien's fiction, and the more spectacular and grisly the event, the harder O'Brien struggles to make sense of the image through description. Curt Lemon's death in "How to Tell a True War Story" describes a similar disconnect between language and action. The scene is nearly poetic in its rendering, the young soldier as much the protagonist of a Greek tragedy as a mass of flesh and blood blown unceremoniously into a tree.

A similar fate greets the men who fight in "In the Field." While in "Sweetheart of the Song Tra Bong" Mary Anne Bell finds herself unable or unwilling to resist the pull of the land that erases her identity and drives a wedge into her relationship with her boyfriend, Mark Fossie, Jimmy Cross must lead his men across a field that has been flooded by the Song Tra Bong River. Cross, obsessed with the safety of his men after Lavender's death, notices one of his young soldiers, face caked with mud, and "the filth seemed to erase identities, transforming the men into identical copies of a single soldier, which was exactly how Jimmy Cross had been trained to treat them, as interchangeable units of command" (163). As he decides where his men will make camp for the night, Cross ruminates on Kiowa's death in the field, his body sucked into the vacuum of a mortar crater, and recalls the violence and chaos of the previous evening's battle. Cross avers that his letter to Kiowa's father would be impersonal; he must maintain dispassion as a leader of men, a notion that O'Brien explores further in "Field Trip," a story focusing on the author's return to Vietnam with his fictional daughter, "where I looked for signs of forgiveness or personal grace or whatever else the land might offer" (181). The field remains, but in a form much different from what O'Brien remembers, smaller now, and full of light. The air is soundless, the ghosts are missing, and the farmers who now tend the field go back to work after stealing a curious glance in his direction. The war is absent, except in O'Brien's memory.

The real war, or at least the war that O'Brien recreates in *TTTC*, comes to an unceremonious end for the writer when he is wounded in the buttocks and reassigned to duty on a helipad as a supply loader, a job that he despises even worse than infantry, because his comrades "were soldiers, I wasn't" (198). His disillusionment with the war comes to a head in his relationship with Bobby Jorgensen, the medic who nearly cost O'Brien his life and the person O'Brien blames for the gangrenous wound that forced him, for all his hatred of the war, to be separated from the action. The breaking point for O'Brien is as random as his misplaced hatred for Bobby Jorgensen. Those emotions indicate the difficulty of identifying the true enemy, focusing one's energies on survival, and making sense of a senseless war.

"The Lives of the Dead," which catalogs the friends and comrades he has lost over the years, comes closest to fully articulating the connection between war and the present. An important and incongruous image is the death of a Vietnamese farmer in an air strike, retaliation for an earlier sniping. As if both to mock the man's memory and to wrap their minds around the unnecessary atrocity, the men treat the death as an opportunity for celebration, with the dead man as the guest of honor, including toasts to the man and his family. The writer's principal interest in the final story, however, is not the soldiers who gave and took lives in Vietnam, but the young girl Linda, who succumbs to cancer when both she and O'Brien are nine years old, barely sentient enough to understand the gravity of death. In describing an encounter at the ticket booth of the local movie theater, O'Brien remembers how they would practice their love by avoiding each other's glances and "by the fact of not looking at each other, and not talking, we understood with a clarity beyond language that we were sharing something huge and permanent" (230). Despite their youth, however, O'Brien looks back upon that relationship more than three decades later as one of the most intense he has ever experienced. For the last time, the author mingles notions of love and war, death and life, recalling times when he would mingle reality and dreams to make the pain of losing Linda bearable. A discussion of the possibilities that await both innocent and experienced storytellers recalls Paul Berlin's repeated notion in *Cacciato* of the unlikelihood that they will reach Paris, where they can symbolically leave the war with their lives intact. The certitude of their journey's success is based not on its reality, however, but on the power of imagination and passion and their ability to believe, if only for a time, that the impossible has somehow cracked wide open to reveal promise.

CHARACTER DEVELOPMENT

In *TTTC*, O'Brien uses the war as the context for his interpersonal relationships—with both the living and the dead—and those relationships form the foundation for the collection's stories. In "Spin," a story that, in part, recalls in brief vignettes a handful of odd and uncharacteristically light moments from the war, O'Brien offers a short biography of himself as a way of defining his role as writer. The things O'Brien remembers—the image is too similar to the things the men carry to be coincidence—are the snapshot images that fill his stories: the deaths of Curt Lemon and Kiowa; Norman Bowker and Henry Dobbins playing checkers in a foxhole as they wait to engage the enemy; hiring an old Vietnamese man to guide them through the minefields of the Batangan Peninsula; the maddening boredom of the war interspersed with periods of intense fighting. O'Brien reshapes the images to reconcile them with his writerly present, "a kind of rehappening" (32). That the work of the writer is a "rehappening" implies that the events, in some form, must have occurred once. The statement also implies the presence of a witness to war, even if the stories take precedence over the reality of the war. O'Brien discusses how time has passed for him and understands "that in the important ways I haven't changed at all" (236). "The Lives of the Dead" allows O'Brien to resolve an otherwise loosely organized compilation using his recollection of his first love Linda as the anchor image. An important dichotomy for the

writer is the relation between the physical and the psychological; he recognizes that, while the body remains viable for only a brief period, the
spirit remains.

Although O'Brien's admission in the book's conclusion is a bittersweet
rendering of his experience, the earlier story "Sweetheart of the Song Tra
Bong" details a loss of innocence, a passage heightened by the fact that
the soldier is a young woman named Mary Anne Bell. The girlfriend of
Mark Fossie, an infantryman who offhandedly invites her to join him in
Vietnam, Mary Anne travels to Southeast Asia from the United States to
be with her beau. The improbably strong relationship and its gradual,
inevitable collapse emphasizes the depths to which Mary Anne falls during her indoctrination into the war. She and Fossie have known each other
long enough to become comfortable, the continuation of the relationship
a given. They will marry, have three blond children, and live the American
Dream. Marilyn Wesley, in her analysis of "Sweetheart," asserts that the
introduction of Mary Anne Bell into an otherwise traditional war story
transforms "the archetypal tale of a young man's initiation into the male
mystery of violence into the story of a young girl on a whimsical visit . . .
which opens [the story] to fresh interpretation" (11). What transpires is
nothing less than Mary Anne's mutation from a 17-year-old coed wearing
pink culottes to a war-hardened veteran sporting a necklace made of human tongues and patrolling with a platoon of shady Green Berets. The
wilderness, far from intimidating Mary Anne in the same way that it
repels the other American soldiers, instead enchants her. Rat Kiley, who
narrates the story under O'Brien's own narration, relates how quickly she
was taken under the jungle's spell. Later, when she has become fully ac-
culturated to the war, she remarks to Fossie, "You're in a place . . . where
you don't belong" (111). The statement is symbolic of her profound transformation in Vietnam and an ironic invocation of the attitudes of O'Brien's
soldiers as a whole: None of them belong, even if Mary Anne desires to
remain in Vietnam. No one is surprised when Mary Anne melts into the
mountains and does not return. Although the men understand that she
has been fully subsumed by her surroundings, "a couple of times they
almost saw her sliding through the shadows. Not quite, but almost. She
had crossed to the other side. She was part of the land" (116).

The character who more than any other represents a balance between
O'Brien and Mary Anne Bell is Jimmy Cross, who understands the depth
of depravity that the war engenders, yet does his best to reestablish a life
apart from the war. Cross's essential humanity sets him apart from many
of O'Brien's characters, some of whom are so scarred by the war that the

machination of their fate has been set in motion long before their deaths, caused as surely by the war as if, like Curt Lemon, they had tripped a land mine. A passage describing Cross's response to Kiowa's death illustrates his humanity and also connects Cross to O'Brien, who returned from a round of golf one summer day to news that he had been drafted. Cross's mind wanders to the municipal course where he played, and he debates with himself what club he should choose for a shot over water. His thoughts snap immediately back to Vietnam, where, he knows, the stakes are infinitely higher.

The incongruity between the decisions of a free-and-easy everyday life and life-and-death decisions in war pervades *TTTC* and calls into question the war's morality. The question is explored nowhere more poignantly than in the lives and sudden deaths of men like Curt Lemon and Lee Strunk, and in scenes conveying the ironic tragedy of the war: Dave Jensen's relief at not having to kill his comrade; O'Brien's disdain at his separation from his fellow soldiers, despite having nearly died on the front lines; a young Vietnamese, tormented by the burning of her village and the deaths of her family, making gestures that are construed by the men as dancing; a butterfly on a dead man's nose. The collection's ensemble characters, despite the brevity with which most of them inhabit the text, are integral to the overall effect of O'Brien's fiction, not the least for their role as latter-day heroes who exhibit flaws that would have been unconscionable to their predecessors: "Unlike the inspiring and yet coolly unrealistic cowboys, soldiers, and celebrated heroes of our childhood dreams and movies, taking fire—actually taking rounds intended to kill us, to kill the trembling flicker of perception that stands between us and dusty death—gives us vision about our vulnerability in crisis" (Horner 266).

THEMES

The Things They Carried deals primarily with themes tracing the movement from innocence to experience, the pathology of courage, and the passage from loss to redemption—none of them unfamiliar to readers of O'Brien's work, though in the case of *TTTC*, those themes are viewed exclusively through the filter of memory as O'Brien considers how best to reshape his past and that of his comrades. The return of his friends Cross and Bowker prompts O'Brien to consider even more seriously what he has known all along: Stories have real redemptive power, if not to change the world, at least to make sense of the past. O'Brien connects his war experience with the childhood memory of Linda's death in an overt symbol of the interconnectedness that the storyteller sees in every event, in every relationship, in every story.

The title story indicates how the vagaries of war dictate the men's lives, a notion that runs counter to everything they have been taught as Americans. The war forces them into "a kind of inertia, a kind of emptiness, a dullness of desire and intellect and conscience and hope and human sensibility" (15) and breaks them physically and psychologically with the efficiency of a machine. Nowhere in O'Brien's fiction do his characters return to their previous lives unscathed. The notion is true many times over in *TTTC*: Norman Bowker and Jimmy Cross are the most obvious examples, men with pasts so incompatible with their postwar lives that they hold onto the faintest hope for better lives. In war, they are unthinking, unfeeling automatons; once home, however, the men pursue their own self-destruction as a matter of course, fueled by the emotions brought to the surface by war: anger, fear, guilt, ennui, love, hate, giddiness, doubt, awe. The war experience is made worse by its ability to change a man immediately, to place him in a role where he acts as he thinks he ought, often at his own peril, as O'Brien relates in "The Ghost Soldiers": "It's like you're in a movie. There's a camera on you, so you begin acting, you're somebody else" (207). The passage from innocence to experience, then, is rarely a conscious decision.

One of the most insidious consequences of having such a decision made for a soldier is that he must, assuming he survives his tour of duty, return home. In "Speaking of Courage," O'Brien describes Norman Bowker's repatriation, a parallel to Harvey Perry's experience in *Northern Lights*. The townspeople who sent Bowker to Vietnam are oblivious to what he has suffered and continues to suffer; though he tends not to bemoan the absence of parades in his honor, the inhabitants willfully ignore what he and the other returning soldiers have endured on their behalf. The town, in short, "had no memory, therefore no guilt" (143). Because the story takes place after Bowker's return, aside from a digression that reveals how Bowker nearly won the Silver Star, the title refers ironically not to the courage he must have possessed in the war, but rather that which he displays while attempting to order his life in a society indifferent to his struggle. As a way of marking time, he repeatedly drives a loop around the local lake, remembering old girlfriends, hoping one day to track down high-school buddies who have moved to Des Moines or Sioux City, flashing back to Kiowa's death in the shit field, wanting to tell his stories to his father, who watches baseball on television as if to deny that his son had ever been gone. O'Brien succinctly sums up Bowker's dilemma: "The war was over and there was no place in particular to go" (137).

As Bowker's story implies, an adjunct of experience is courage, though the two are at times mutually exclusive; or, as Horner puts it, "so ambiguous is the truth about courage, so intense and forgivable are the inconsistencies and contradictions of real men in crisis, a classic honor code . . . deconstructs its own pressures in the hideous violence of war" (265–66). O'Brien, anxious over the decision he must make regarding his own imminent military conscription, writes, "it was my view then, and still is, that you don't make war without knowing why" (40). The draft notice in his pocket means that he has become the property of the government of the United States of America. The military, he finds out quickly, owns him for more than just a tour of duty. O'Brien fights to the best of his ability, or at least well enough to survive with relatively minor wounds, but his decision to do so is based on the simple thought that "I would kill and maybe die—because I was embarrassed not to" (59). Indeed, the old fears expressed in previous works—the certain knowledge that he would be a social pariah if he were to dodge the draft and the notion that people who have little idea of the horror of fighting a war for unjust reasons control his life—are present in *TTTC*, most notably in "On the Rainy River." In an analysis of what it means to possess courage, he posits a definition similar to that of Paul Berlin in *Cacciato*, who assumes that the core of courage comes from a biological process, from the very tissues urging him to move in battle or run when necessary.

The matter of reconciling loss with redemption requires as much courage in his postwar life as O'Brien could ever muster in his tour of duty. "The Lives of the Dead" chronicles that reconciliation in O'Brien's case, and his other characters undergo similar epiphanies. A significant step in the process for O'Brien is his empathizing with the Vietnamese soldier he claims to have shot in "The Man I Killed." Although he later admits, in keeping with the essential "unknowable" and mutable nature of memory, that he participated in the man's death only as an observer, the story transmutes the author's desperate need for courage into horror at his action and, finally, redemption, since the man's story lives on in O'Brien's words. O'Brien empathizes with the man, his sworn enemy, to the point of presuming to know his history and his thoughts: The man, he knew, would have been a soldier for a single day before being killed by O'Brien. Having gone to university with a young wife, he would have enlisted with the 48th Vietcong Battalion. Further, in a creative move that places O'Brien's consciousness inside his victim's head, he understands how the man "would have been taught that to defend the land was a man's highest duty and highest privilege. He had accepted this. It was never open to question. Secretly, though, it also frightened him" (125). Significantly, the man's thoughts are identical to O'Brien's own. The facts of the man's life become apparent to O'Brien only when the two soldiers are connected by death, as if by killing the physical body of the Vietnamese, his spirit is offered up to O'Brien, who then tells the man's story as a way of keeping him alive.

The subject is explored fully in the collection's final chapter, the appropriately titled "The Lives of the Dead," which describes the process of annihilation that precedes any refashioning of the memories into a coherent "story-truth." O'Brien recalls that, in the same way he mingled his own thoughts with those of the dead soldier in "The Man I Killed," the soldiers in general

> had ways of making the dead seem not quite so dead. Shaking hands, that was one way. By slighting death, by acting, we pretended it was not the terrible thing it was. By our language, which was both hard and wistful, we transformed the bodies into piles of waste. Thus, when someone got killed, as Curt Lemon did, his body was not really a body, but rather one small bit of waste in the midst of a much wider wastage. (238)

Many times throughout the collection, and in his body of fiction as a whole, O'Brien uses such images to explore the indignities of war. In an important sense, those images remind us how far above the din stories rise to redeem wasted lives.

ALTERNATIVE READING: READER-RESPONSE

Reader-response criticism was organized as an interpretive strategy in the 1930s by Louise Rosenblatt, whose *Literature as Exploration* (1938) became a groundbreaking work in the discipline. As its name indicates, reader-response allows the reader to participate in the act of interpretation by bringing his or her own experiences to the fore and grounding those experiences in the text. The resultant dialogue between reader and writer leads to a better understanding for the reader not only of the text at hand, but of the novel's dominant issues in the context of the reader's life. R. Baird Shuman points out that reader-response "posits that all readers, by bringing their individual backgrounds and value systems to their reading, create their own texts as they shape their personal, highly individual

transactions with the texts they are reading" (30). Three decades after
Rosenblatt's study, theorists Stanley Fish and Wolfgang Iser published
research that redefined the nature of reading and the role of the reader.
Not surprisingly, the resurgence of reader-response criticism in the 1960s
had a social component, since "society has become so global, so transna-
tional that all national boundaries as we have known them are being challenged" (Shuman 30). In addition to being influenced by the advent of
true globalism, and the Internet linking the world of information in ways
we could not have imagined even 20 years ago, reader-response criticism
takes into account other approaches, including feminist, new-historicist,
psychoanalytic, and postcolonial criticism, among others.

Because of the fragmentary nature of *TTTC* and the importance that
O'Brien places on his own responses to the war experience, the text lends
itself to such an analysis, inviting readers to consider their own circumstances, war-related or not, and subsequently base their interpretation of
the text on analogous events in their own lives. In fact, Norman Bowker's
correspondence with the writer in "Notes" serves as an example of
O'Brien's own reader-response when he uses Bowker's letter as the basis
for the story "Speaking of Courage." Bowker and O'Brien served together
in Vietnam, and Bowker is familiar with O'Brien's work since then. When
Bowker suggests that O'Brien write a story about a man who returns from
Vietnam and finds himself able only to drift, he admits that the story is
autobiographical and that "I'd write it myself except I can't ever find any
words, if you know what I mean, and I can't figure out what exactly to
say" (157).

Reader-response is also closely related to the highly subjective manner
in which O'Brien tells his own stories. He explains the genesis of the character Tim O'Brien in *TTTC* and discusses the various connections one
might make between the war and events that seem, upon first glance, to
be unrelated to war:

> A month into the writing of the book . . . , I found my name
> appearing. I was typing, and I remember thinking, this will be
> fun, I'll do it for an hour, and then go back to a made-up first-
> person narrator of another name. . . .
> I'm not a totally intuitive writer; I know what I'm doing.
> But—what a joy. What a joy just to feel something like that
> while you're writing, to feel the return to your heart. It doesn't
> happen to many writers, and it hasn't happened in my life,
> ever, writing. So that hour was an important hour for me in

my life—not just in my writing career, but in my life, as a human being. Where I felt the remembering of Vietnam—not just Vietnam, but my writing memory as well—intersecting with my life in a way that meant I was home. (Caldwell, "Staying True" 69)

In "Notes," he articulates a similar notion, and his admission that his interpretation of the events is only one of many (echoing Captain Rhallon's soliloquy in *Cacciato,* that for every soldier there is a different and unique reality) facilitates a like fashioning and refashioning of reality by the reader.

Steven Kaplan invokes Iser when he suggests that the collection's success is not based on the complexity of O'Brien's stories, but rather their uncanny ability to resonate with readers, most of whom have never experienced war. He writes, "The stories in this book are not somehow truer than the thing that actually happened in Vietnam because they contain some higher, metaphysical truth. . . . Rather, what makes these stories true is the impact they have as the events within them come alive for a reader" (*Understanding Tim O'Brien* 177). Catherine Calloway, discussing "How to Tell a True War Story," writes, "By defining a war story so broadly, O'Brien writes more stories, interspersing the definitions with examples from the war to illustrate them. What is particularly significant about the examples is that they are given in segments, a technique that actively engages the readers in the process of textual creation" ("How to Tell" 253). The notion is not unlike O'Brien's own belief that, far from being a "Vietnam writer," he tells stories using the Vietnam War as context. By making the distinction, O'Brien hints at the stories' universal appeal, and thus their openness to different, but equally valid, readings.

Implicit in reader-response criticism is the idea that the reader will tease apart the text to discover themes, historical backgrounds, plot points, and other contextual, stylistic, and structural devices connecting writer and reader. In *TTTC,* O'Brien relates how he regularly checks and rechecks his motivations for writing; he reveals those reasons so that the reader may better understand not only the war, but the nature of storytelling. Even under dire circumstances, a soldier preparing to engage the enemy on what may be the last day of his life, O'Brien understands the larger implications of the stories he tells, writing "and in the end, of course, a true war story is never about war. . . . It's about love and memory" (85). In "Good Form," one of several chapters that demystify the writing process, O'Brien illustrates the extent to which he will go to hide the "meaning" of his stories in order to open them to interpretation by the reader:

> [Storytelling]'s not a game. It's a form. Right here, now, as I
> invent myself, I'm thinking about all I want to tell you about
> why this book is written as it is. . . .
>
>   I want you to feel what I felt. I want you to know why story-
> truth is truer sometimes than happening-truth. (179)

Significantly, "story-truth" has little to do with the reality of the war, as
O'Brien freely admits all along. Instead, the onus is on the reader to de-
termine the value of the work in her own life, to make sense of the connections arising from intense conflict. In debunking his own version of
"The Man I Killed," O'Brien further separates his stories from reality,
opening the text even wider for examination: "But listen," he confides
after divulging the essential fiction of his story. "Even *that* story is made
up" (179).

In the Lake of the Woods
(1994)

> Any military commander who is honest with himself will admit that he has made mistakes in the application of military power. He's killed people, unnecessarily. His own troops or other troops. Through mistakes, through errors of judgment. . . . The conventional wisdom is, "Don't make the same mistake twice. Learn from your mistakes."
>
> —Robert S. McNamara, *The Fog of War*

The follow-up to the critically acclaimed *The Things They Carried* more closely resembles *Northern Lights* and *The Nuclear Age* in its exploration of Vietnam's influence on the protagonists, even if the book's plot, a psychological mystery, often echoes the flights of fancy of Paul Berlin in *Going after Cacciato* or the complex structure of *TTTC*. The novel was chosen as one of the best books of 1994 by the *New York Times,* and reviewer Michiko Kakutani, who favorably reviewed both *TTTC* and *Cacciato,* praised *Lake* for "prose that combines the sharp, unsentimental rhythms of Hemingway with gentler, more lyrical descriptions" and concluded that "Mr. O'Brien gives the reader a shockingly visceral sense of what it felt like to tramp through a booby-trapped jungle. A vital, important book" ("A Novel" C31). Verlyn Klinkenborg, comparing John Wade's inability to come to terms with his role in Vietnam to O'Brien's inspired exploration of storytelling in *TTTC*'s "How to Tell a True War Story," sees *Lake* as the more somber fiction, one that examines "the moral effects of suppressing a true war story, of not even trying to make things present, a novel about the unforgivable uses of history, about what happens when you try to pretend that history no longer exists" (33).

The novel's structure places the reader in the position of a jury member asked to analyze, organize, and make sense of the known information. O'Brien's ability to work within the case's contradictions leads, finally, to an ambiguous outcome. The narrator, whom the author has compared to Joseph Conrad's Marlow in *Heart of Darkness,* a storyteller himself uncertain of the truth of his story, makes clear that the answer will never be known absolutely. Rather, the reader is left to weigh the possibilities. "This book is about uncertainty," O'Brien says. "This book adheres to the principle that much of what is important in the world can never be known. That's what disturbs people. *In the Lake of the Woods* suggests that the 'truth' of our lives is always fragile, always elusive, always beyond the absolute" ("An Interview with Tim O'Brien"). The novel's appeal derives not from the reader's satisfaction at solving the mystery, but from an accumulation of detail leading to a better understanding of Wade's character and the rationale for his decisions, including those made in Vietnam, whose legacy haunts him more than two decades after his return. As Pico Iyer points out, the novel's sense of mystery is heightened by O'Brien's prose, which "always hovers on the edge of dream, and his specialty is that twilight zone of chimeras and fears and fantasies where nobody knows what's true and what is not" (74).

PLOT DEVELOPMENT

Lake is a mystery told in snapshot images by a journalist attempting to uncover the truth behind the disappearance of a politician's wife. The novel's chapters shift freely through time, describing protagonist John Wade's actions in Vietnam as they relate to his present, beginning immediately after an election loss in 1986. Aside from the plot, which spans 8 of the book's 31 chapters and traces the plight of Wade, an erstwhile politician, and his missing wife, Kathy, O'Brien uses chapters titled "Evidence" and "Hypothesis" to situate point of view outside the primary story, allowing readers the opportunity to analyze the story's facts from a more objective perspective. The "Evidence" chapters, which "broaden the book's focus and prevent us from dismissing the horrors described in the novel as pure make-believe or peculiar only to the war in Vietnam"

(Iyer 74), contain interviews with Wade's mother; his sister-in-law, Patricia Hood; his campaign manager, Tony Carbo; and a host of other characters, including fellow soldiers, who piece together Wade's life from his childhood to the present. Snippets of testimony from the Lieutenant Calley/ My Lai war-crimes trial (see chapter 2 for a discussion of the event; chapter 21 of *Lake*, "The Nature of the Spirit," also relates salient details of the massacre); quotations from literary sources as diverse as Sigmund Freud, Fyodor Dostoyevsky, and Ambrose Bierce; and scholarly sources that define and describe in clinical detail Wade's problems also help to round out his character, even if they do little to solve the mystery of Kathy's disappearance.

John Wade has been a political star in the making since his return from service in Vietnam in the late 1960s. After serving six years in state politics, he is primed for a run at the U.S. Senate. Wade, whose political savvy is exceeded only by his appeal to voters as a war hero and genuinely good man, still heeds a lesson that has been with him since childhood: "Compromise . . . was the motor that made government move, and while an idealist in many ways—a Humphrey progressive, a believer in the fundamental human equities—he found his greatest pleasure in the daily routine of legislative politics, the give and take, the maneuvering" (154). The irony of Wade's political views is particularly pointed, given the charges leveled against him during his campaign.

Though at one time just before the 1986 election an overwhelming favorite to become Washington's next big star, Wade has just lost the primary in a landslide, having watched a nearly 20-point lead dissolve into a 40-point deficit in the space of six weeks. His once promising career in a shambles, he takes a break from the world of politics for a time, joining Kathy, director of admissions at the University of Minnesota, on a getaway to Lake of the Woods, Minnesota, as remote and desolate a place as the couple can find to ease the pain of Wade's humiliation. Although the two are not as close as they once were—in fact, since their college courtship and subsequent marriage, things have only stagnated—there is a sense that the relationship, if not Wade's political career, can be salvaged. Wade's desperation is apparent in the small details: he makes a rash promise to whisk Kathy away to Italy after their lives have returned to normal; he also suggests having children, a reference to his having encouraged her to get an abortion four years before in order to keep his political career on track.

Her taciturn husband gives away little of himself, a fact that Kathy has come to accept. Wade cannot conceive of allowing his wife to know his

thoughts and his Vietnam experiences, even though violent nightmares
frequently spill into Wade's everyday world. Kathy has suspected since
his return from the war more than a decade before that her husband hides
a secret. In fact, early in their marriage, Wade expressed concern that the
facts of his past might come to light, and he decides "to be vigilant. He
would guard his advantage. The secrets would remain secret—the things
he's seen, the things he'd done. He would repair what he could, he would
endure, he would go from year to year without letting on that there were
tricks" (46). His involvement in the war has never come up in conversation, and Kathy respects her husband's privacy. As it happens, she has a
secret of her own, an affair three years before with a Canadian dentist (the
same character, Harmon Osterberg, would return in the later *July, July*).
Wade's experience remains unknown until newspaper articles suggest his
involvement in the My Lai massacre, an action made famous by the trial
in which Lieutenant William Calley was questioned by legislators on his
unit's conduct in the slaughter of as many as 500 Vietnamese civilians.
The reports are the primary reason for the unceremonious end to his career, and the reader discovers through the narrator's research that Wade
was responsible for the deaths of an old Vietnamese man and one of his
fellow soldiers, who surprised Wade in a bunker.

Wade's precipitous fall is made all the more striking by his apparent
clear path to success in Washington. He is a respected combat veteran,
having returned to the United States in November 1969; lieutenant gov-
ernor of Minnesota at 37; and a highly sought-after candidate for Senate
at 40. In one day, the dream is erased and Wade's ghosts are set loose.
Even the solitude of the couple's retreat cannot repress the demons he has
fought for more than a decade, as "he felt crazy sometimes. Real depravity.
Late at night an electric sizzle came into his blood, a tight pumped-up
killing rage, and he couldn't keep it in and he couldn't let it out. He
wanted to hurt things. Grab a knife and start cutting and slashing and
never stop. All those years" (5).

When Wade discovers Kathy gone from the cottage and the motorboat
missing from the dock, he seeks help from the Rasmussens, the cabin's
owners and his supporters in the recent failed campaign. He is drunk at
the time and suspicions fall squarely on his shoulders in a good-cop–bad-
cop routine featuring a disgruntled ex-Marine and Vietnam vet who has
read the allegations of Wade's misdeeds in Vietnam and is sure of Wade's
complicity in his wife's death. The police questioning mirrors both the
accusations of impropriety that ruined his political career and his own

introspection. Wade's inability to communicate—the irony that a successful politician should have such a problem is stifling—carries over into other parts of his life and becomes an ever larger problem when meeting with the police. While answering their queries, "sorrow was also a problem. He couldn't feel much, just a shadowy uneasiness about his own conduct or misconduct. The interrogation bothered him. Important lines of inquiry, he realized, had not been pursued" (133). Wade's only supporter is Rasmussen, whose practical, analytical mind does not allow him to pass judgment on Wade too quickly; still, he asks Wade if he had any part in his wife's disappearance, and Wade answers as honestly as he can that he did not. Rasmussen aids in the search for Kathy, though neither man, after a time, is confident of her return. In an increasing cycle of accusation, guilt, and hopelessness, Wade maps out a strategy for his own exit, what amounts to a fatal plunge into the wilderness on the border of Minnesota and Canada. Desperate to discover the truth but powerless to do so, he carries on a conversation with the ether before throwing the radio, his only means of communicating with the outside world, into the water and heading into uncharted territory.

The narrator, who has researched the case thoroughly for years without finding a clue to support either Kathy's willing departure or Wade's guilt in her disappearance, calls into question the nature of truth. The question underpins the novel, and the narrator makes clear that the case will never be satisfactorily resolved. The ultimate irony of the situation is that the reader, given the information, has as good a sense of the "truth" of the events surrounding Wade's life as Wade himself. The act of reading and analyzing the story as an exercise in understanding human nature is one of the novel's primary ends, and, as Mark Heberle points out, O'Brien's attention to structural and stylistic details is as important an aspect of the novel as the plot, since "the narrative's discursive ambiguity is reflected by the variety of imperfectly realized nonfictional and fictional forms that *Lake* employs: biography, history, psychology, mystery/psychological thriller, detective story/criminal investigation, war story, political novel, romantic tragedy" (223). O'Brien displays a knack for sustaining heightened suspense in a novel whose mystery will never be solved, an accomplishment, Heberle continues, that "transform[s] the passive act of reading into an unstable investigative activity by the reader . . . and instead of simply following someone else's narrative, we are forced to construct our own as we move from one hypothetical scene to another and consider the evidence" (223).

CHARACTER DEVELOPMENT

Despite his indoctrination into the horrors of Vietnam, John Wade is not immune to the irony of warfare. He discovers quickly the ways in which the innocuous magic tricks he had learned as a child seeking to win his father's approval translate to the life-and-death struggle he faces in the war when, "with the South China Sea at his back, Sorcerer performed card tricks and rope tricks. He pulled a lighted cigar from his ear. He transformed a pear into an orange. He displayed an ordinary military radio and whispered a few words and made their village disappear" (65). The name is apt, as Wade has always expressed an interest in magic. He considers himself something of a loner and sees the name "as a special badge, an emblem of belonging and brotherhood, something to take pride in" (37). The darker side of the allusion, however, is that Wade will stop at nothing to alter the truth and to perform whatever magic he can in order to make reality conform to his fantasies and his ambitions. The tricks that once entertained and distracted now give him power over human life and are indistinguishable from the atrocities of war. Wade realizes, on one level, that the persona he has assumed will follow him for the rest of his life. Like the soldier Tim O'Brien in *If I Die*, however, he is powerless to stop the visions from visiting him and influencing his decisions.

Wade, who claims to have served in Vietnam only for love, instead becomes indoctrinated into the ethos of the jungle, even justifying indiscriminate killing:

> Sorcerer was in his element. It was a place with secret trapdoors and tunnels and underground chambers populated by various spooks and goblins, a place where magic was everyone's hobby and where elaborate props were always on hand—exploding boxes and secret chemicals and numerous devices of levitation—you could *fly* here, you could make *other* people fly—a place where the air itself was both reality and illusion, where anything might instantly become anything else. (72–73)

In fact, after a particularly disturbing incident in which he shoots PFC Weatherby, a fellow soldier who surprises him after a bloody confrontation, Wade relies on a coping strategy learned as a boy, when his alcoholic father would chide him for being overweight and practicing magic tricks instead of playing baseball: "Erase the bad stuff. Draw in pretty new pictures" (135). The strategy works so well that when Wade confidently alters company documents implicating him in the unsavory side of war, "memory itself would be erased" (272). Still, his time in Vietnam and his rela-tionship with his father, the fundamental issues haunting Wade, bubble to the surface and manifest themselves in his present life, as he knew they must. Instead of fighting the inevitable, Wade begins a life in politics as a way of lessening his guilt and finding the love he so desperately seeks.

Wade's relationship with his father is integral in forming his attitudes as an adult. Seemingly nothing that the young boy did could satisfy his father, who teased the boy endlessly despite his son's unconditional love. When Wade is 14, his father commits suicide, hanging himself in the fam-ily's garage and denying the boy the closure that he may have gotten had they reconciled. Wade blames himself for the relationship's failure and imagines searching for the man, spending hours "looking for his father, opening closets, scanning the carpets and sidewalks and lawns as if in search of a lost nickel" (15). In his mind, he carries on the conversations with his father that he could never have when the man was alive.

The seven "Evidence" chapters offer the reader a better understanding of both Wade and Kathy than the plot chapters that comprise the novel's present. Lack of communication, a primary obstacle to Wade's relation-ship with his father, also haunts his marriage to Kathy. Similarly, the failed relationship between Wade and his father, and the young Wade's subse-quent experiences in Vietnam, preclude a healthy relationship with Kathy. Kathy is a more complex character than she at first appears. She is savvy enough to realize that Wade is spying on her upon his return from the war, though the behavior is not obtrusive enough for her to end the re-lationship. An employee of Kathy's, stating for the record her thoughts in one of the "Evidence" chapters, suggests that "Kathy *knew* he had these secrets, things he wouldn't talk about. She *knew* about the spying. Maybe I'm wrong but it was like she needed to be part of it. That whole sick act of his" (97). Much of what we know about Kathy comes from the narra-tor's interview with Kathy's sister, Patricia Hood.

Also in the "Evidence" chapters, Tony Carbo, Wade's campaign man-ager, is perhaps second in importance only to Wade's own mother, who recalls her son's relationship with his father and provides insight into Wade's psychological makeup. Carbo describes repeatedly how he asked Wade if anything could derail the campaign only to be stonewalled by Wade, who was hopeful, despite years of inner torment to the contrary, that the cover-up of his involvement in war atrocities years before would not be made public. A recurrent voice in the "Evidence" chapters, acting as a Greek chorus—traditionally, a group of actors who comment on the present action and often foreshadow later events—from Wade's Vietnam days, is that of Richard Thinbill, a fellow soldier whose one salient detail of his Vietnam experience is the buzzing of thousands of flies on dead bodies. David J. Piwinski points out that Thinbill's brief, repeated references add important background to the story, as "the novel's narrative sections describing John Wade's involvement in the My Lai massacre are permeated with references to flies, which, in suggesting the symbolic presence of Beelzebub, imbue these scenes with an intensified aura of evil" (199). Court transcripts from the Calley trial serve to reinforce the notion that Wade and his fellow soldiers fought against a psychological malaise perhaps even more insidious than a tangible enemy while in Vietnam. Still, the narrator carefully maintains the semblance of objectivity throughout. The narrator's primary role is to report the facts as they are known, warning at the same time that "evidence is not truth. It is only evident. In any case, Kathy Wade is forever missing, and if you require solutions, you will have to look beyond these pages" (30). The narrator purports to seek the truth, but as with other of O'Brien's narratives, the quest is derailed by the contradictory nature of the stories themselves. In short, none of the characters are what they seem.

THEMES

One of *Lake*'s major themes is the lingering effect of war on its combatants, and the novel's other themes—the nature of relationships, trust, and love; the importance of communication; and a study of geographic and psychic wilderness—fall in line behind Wade's experiences in Vietnam and his relationship with his father. The narrator implies that Wade is a victim of circumstance, forced from early childhood to alter his reality in order to maintain some sense of order in his life; as such, he is a character deserving of some sympathy. His campaign manager, Tony Carbo, surmises that Wade entered the political arena to atone for past wrongs. The intrusive narrator, the biographer/historian who organizes the narrative's information and offers his own opinions in the "Hypothesis" chapters, corroborates Carbo's ideas. In fact, the question of responsibility in the face of organized, state-sanctioned violence is one of the larger issues with which the novel wrestles. In keeping with the book's purported purpose of examining objectively the case at hand, however, no judgment is made. Rather, O'Brien leaves the decision to the reader.

The author uses Wade's Vietnam experience as a sharp dividing line between his childhood and his political career, though the memories of Vietnam persist, even if Wade is unable to conjure them at will. As he sits in repose after several hours at My Lai, he knows that his actions will come to the fore, regardless of how carefully he protects his secret: "For a while Sorcerer let himself glide away. All he could do was close his eyes and kneel there and wait for whatever was wrong with the world to right itself. At one point it occurred to him that the weight of this day would ultimately prove too much, that sooner or later he would have to lighten the load" (110). In this way, Wade is not unlike William Cowling in *The Nuclear Age* or even Thomas Chippering in *Tomcat in Love,* though the three novels use variations in tone and structure to achieve their effect. *Lake,* for example, has little of the humor of *Tomcat,* and relies less on the arc of history than *The Nuclear Age,* preferring instead to focus on the one event that has shaped Wade's life more than any other. In tone, *Lake* approaches the somber realities of *Northern Lights,* a novel written almost two decades before.

Wade spends much of his adult life haphazardly attempting to establish bonds of trust with his closest friends and, especially, Kathy, but his inability to unburden himself of his secret precludes his ever attaining that goal. Most of Wade's attention as a child is focused on his relationship with his father, and his mother, though important in filling out the details of Wade's childhood in her interviews with the narrator, plays a subordinate role. Wade has been conditioned since childhood not to trust anyone—his father psychologically abuses the impressionable Johnny repeatedly before committing suicide—and the self-reliance necessitated by that relationship spills over into his war experience, when he assumes an alter ego in order to cope. The chain of events leading from Wade's failed upbringing to Vietnam to politics suggests that Wade is misguided even in attempting to atone for the perceived sins of his childhood, as he never fully understands his reasons for entering politics in the first place. Tony Carbo, Wade's campaign manager and closest confidante, corroborates that view, telling the narrator, "In retrospect, knowing what I know now, I guess he wanted to make up for what happened during the war. . . . Doesn't say anything about the Vietnam shit—not to his wife or me or anybody. And then after a while he *can't* say anything" (199).

The relationship between Wade and Kathy, revealed gradually through exposition and the testimony of friends and family in the "Evidence" chapters, describes their difficulties from the outset. Wade suspects that she has been seeing someone during his absence in Vietnam, and he spies on her after his return, keeping an eye on her dorm, aware of her every movement. Wade's actions force Kathy to consider what their future relationship might be like. After coming to terms with his duplicity, Kathy marries Wade. Despite his transformation in Vietnam, Wade still loves Kathy. That love is never in question in the narrator's re-creation of Wade's story, a fact making the indeterminate conclusion all the more poignant and mystifying. The reader, given the known facts about Wade and his past, can hardly believe that he might have killed his wife and tucked the act away in some inaccessible corner of his mind; nor is it likely, given what the story reveals about Kathy—her brief affair notwithstanding—that she would leave Wade at his lowest point to fend for himself. The nature of love is, according to O'Brien, the central issue of the story, although he hints at its complexity and elusiveness, recalling, "I began *In the Lake of the Woods* with the scene on the porch. An image of two very unhappy people, lost in the fog, lost in a deep spiritual and psychological way. As a writer, I had to discover bit by bit the causes of their immense despair, just as the reader does" ("An Interview with Tim O'Brien").

With love betrayed comes despair, and the lack of communication between Wade and Kathy undoubtedly opens the chasm. In one of the "Hypothesis" chapters, the narrator astutely posits "one of the problems—they never talked anymore. They never communicated, they never made love. They'd tried once, on their second night, but it had been an embarrassment for both of them, and now it seemed they were always guarding their bodies, always careful, touching only for comfort and closeness" (114). After a week at their cabin in a postelection torpor, during which time Wade and Kathy attempt to piece their lives back together, Kathy disappears. An 18-day search of more than 800 square miles of Minnesota and Canadian wilderness has the police no closer to finding her. Although images rise to the surface in the haunting guise of nightmares and nagging back-of-the-mind hallucinations, Wade suffers a total absence of cogent recollection of the night's events, leaving him to question his own stability. "These were not memories. These were sub-memories," he muses. "Images from a place beneath the waking world, deeper than dream, a place where logic dissolved" (134). He vaguely recalls pouring boiling water on the houseplants, and he bemusedly throws them away before Kathy can discover his strange action.

Wilderness provides a metaphor for the disintegration of Wade's political career—and the theme of treks into the wilderness in Vietnam and Minnesota, and figuratively into his own mind—and connects Wade to Kathy in such a way as to delve deep into his memories. After Wade loses the primary, the couple retreat to the wilderness to mend their strained relationship. In a way, however, their retreat is as much about discovering an entity even larger and more immutable than their own problems:

"Everywhere, for many thousand square miles, the wilderness was all one thing, like a great curving mirror, infinitely blue and beautiful, always the same. Which was what they had come for. They needed the solitude. They needed the repetition, the dense hypnotic drone of woods and water, but above all they needed to be together" (1). Even though Wade retreats to the wilderness out of necessity, however, nothing good can come of it. Instead of the soothing, healing aspects of nature that he had hoped to find, Wade's troubled psyche is triggered by "the steady hum of lake and woods" (7), an image nearly identical to the "sobbing" wilderness that accompanies the Perry brothers on their cross-country ski trek in *Northern Lights*. After Kathy's disappearance, Wade "would remember this with perfect clarity, as it if were still happening. He would remember a breathing sound inside the fog. He would remember the feel of her hand against his forehead, its warmth, how purely alive it was" (7). Still, he would never remember the circumstances under which Kathy left. The truth would be as elusive, and no doubt as disturbing, as Wade's memories.

ALTERNATIVE PERSPECTIVE: PSYCHOANALYTIC CRITICISM

Psychoanalytic theory is generally associated with the work of German psychologist Sigmund Freud (1856–1939), who developed the concepts of psychoanalysis to diagnose his patients' problems by framing their issues in terms of past experience, particularly that of childhood. Despite having lost some prominence as a theory of psychology, Freud's work has been extraordinarily influential in informing the literary criticism of the last century. In fact, Freud himself made headway into literary theory with his studies of Shakespeare and Dostoyevsky, in addition to an essay titled "Creative Writers and Day-Dreaming," all published during the first quarter of the last century. Other well-known practitioners of Freud's theories include Marie Bonaparte, Otto Rank, and Ernest Jones, and later Jacques Lacan, Julia Kristeva, Helene Cixous, and Luce Irigaray, who brought their own work, particularly in feminist criticism and deconstruction, to bear on their textual interpretations. Applied to contemporary literature, psychoanalytic theory has come to denote the connection between a character's internal motivations—often seen as the accumulation of events throughout that character's life—and that person's actions in the present.

John Wade's history lends itself to such an analysis. Not only has Wade been shunned and psychologically abused by his own father, but he feels compelled to atone for that failed relationship by participating in a war for which he is, at least at the outset, wholly unprepared. He compensates for his inadequacies and anxiety by falling back on the magic tricks he had learned as a child; by doing so, he never fully escapes his childhood. Wade's interest in magic illustrates the extent to which he is willing to defer reality, or at the least to fashion his own version of the world. The coping strategies he learned in Vietnam carry over to the present, where, after Kathy's mysterious disappearance, Wade considers that "the thing about facts . . . was that they came in sizes. You had to try them on for proper fit. A case in point: his own responsibility. Right now he couldn't help feeling the burn of guilt. All that empty time. The convenience of a faulty memory" (192). Even though Wade understands his guilt, his conscience will not allow him to discover the reason, although in a chapter titled "The Nature of Politics," the narrator reports, "In certain private moments, without ever pondering it too deeply, he was struck by the dim notion of politics as a medium of apology, a way of salvaging something in himself and in the world" (155). Much of the blame for such a disconnect between reality and memory and the unremitting guilt that can be assuaged only through public service, the narrator implies, may be placed on his early family life and, of course, his war experience. Although Wade's mother has apparently supported him—it is through her interview with the novel's narrator that much of Wade's childhood is revealed, including a violent response to his father's suicide—the death of his father and his initial inability to cope with his father's absence is symbolic of the separation from reality that Wade undergoes when he joins the war. He would struggle his entire adult life to mend that chasm.

None of the characters who comment on Wade's past life in the "Evidence" chapters seem to fully comprehend him. Wade often has difficulty piecing together the events of his own life, as illustrated by his inability, finally, to discover exactly what happened to Kathy on the night of her disappearance, and a passage in an "Evidence" chapter from Dostoyevsky's *Notes from Underground* hints at the extent to which Wade has pushed his past into his unconscious:

> Every man has some reminiscences which he would not tell to everyone, but only to his friends. He has others which he would not reveal to his friends, but only to himself, and that in secret. But finally there are still others which a man is even afraid to tell himself, and every decent man has a considerable number of such things stored away . . . Man is bound to lie about himself. (148)

The connection between his current life and the life he left behind in Vietnam—O'Brien makes clear that the reader should see the two intertwined at the same time that the Vietnam Wade and the reformed Wade struggle for their own expressions of identity—is only one significant example of how the past resurfaces in the present. Such secrets inevitably influence actions and attitudes in the present, and Wade is helpless to counter the rush of unbidden memories confusing and angering him, as "in the months and years ahead, John Wade would remember Thuan Yen the way chemical nightmares are remembered, impossible combinations, impossible events, and over time the impossibility itself would become the richest and deepest and most profound memory" (111).

The guilt he carries with him (an extension of the themes of "The Things They Carried," published in the eponymous collection just four years before) cannot be exorcised. The narrator drives the point home by quoting scholarly sources in the "Evidence" chapters, one of which, J. Glenn Gray's *The Warriors,* pinpoints the center of Wade's torment: "Suddenly the soldier feels himself abandoned and cast off from all security. Conscience has isolated him, and its voice is a warning. If you do this, you will not be at peace with me in the future. You can do it, but you ought not. You must act as a man and not as an instrument of another's will" (144). The statement is relevant to Wade's service and actions in Vietnam and to his relationship with his father, both of which continue to profoundly color his decision making in the present, including his choice to cover up his involvement in My Lai.

The dichotomy of reality and illusion so important to Wade as he tries to maintain his sanity in Vietnam manifests itself in his attempt at maintaining a relationship with Kathy at the same time that he must kill or be killed. He recalls nights with Kathy before the war. The narrator then points up the incongruities of Wade's double life as soldier and lover, recalling "first . . . there was Vietnam, where John Wade killed people, and where he composed long letters full of observations about the nature of their love. He did not tell her about the killing" (61). That Wade persuades an individual as strong as Kathy to bend to his will and have an abortion in order to keep his political career on track is a testament to the power of his role as Sorcerer. In a sense, the killing Wade does in Vietnam has continued, and his control over Kathy, despite her own notion that she has power over her own life, is only an indication of his need for order and stability and his desire to achieve those goals. When Wade accompanies Kathy to the doctor to have the abortion performed, the waiting room conjures all of the images he had hoped to keep at bay through the action—himself as a small child performing magic tricks, the young man back from Vietnam spying on his girlfriend, the politician with the deformed psyche—and "for a second it occurred to him that his own stability was at issue" (159).

In the end, the reality of Wade's world butts up against the illusion, and he is powerless to fight it. To now, he has managed to bury his past in his unconscious, where it lurks as an out-of-focus memory, though the news of his involvement in war atrocities changes that. His only recourse to the events of the previous week is to set off into the wilderness, where he will find Kathy or offer himself up to nature. The novel's narrator, wanting to add his own conclusion to the matter despite, as he has attested several times, his inability to bring closure to the case, transforms the case of John and Kathy Wade into a story affecting not only the principals, but anyone who would consider the nature of their relationships with others:

> John Wade—he's beyond knowing. He's an other. For all my years of struggle with this depressing record, for all the travel and interviews and musty libraries, the man's soul remains for me an absolute and impenetrable unknown, a nametag drifting willy-nilly on oceans of hapless fact. . . . Our lovers, our husbands, our wives, our fathers, our gods—they are all beyond us. (103)

Attempts at knowing the unknowable would become an important touchstone for O'Brien's later characters.

Tomcat in Love
(1998)

The war against Vietnam is only the ghastliest manifestation of
what I'd call imperial provincialism, which afflicts America's whole
culture—aware only of its own history, insensible to everything
which isn't part of the local atmosphere.
—Stephen Vizinczey, 1968

O'Brien's Vietnam context takes on a new aspect in *Tomcat in Love*, the
author's first comic novel. The departure was a welcome one for O'Brien,
who maintains that he was not forsaking the themes treated in earlier
novels, but rather finding a different way to explore those themes. O'Brien
tells Karen Rosica, "though I am known as a 'Vietnam writer'—whatever
that may be—I have always pegged myself more as a 'love writer,' and
in that regard *Tomcat in Love* is no departure at all. I am still circling, after
nearly thirty years, the same old obsessions." Despite having followed a
comic impulse, albeit a much darker one, in the earlier *The Nuclear Age*,
O'Brien succeeds in writing *Tomcat*'s comedy only after the wrenching
uncertainty and psychological tension of *In the Lake of the Woods*. "I had
always thought of myself as a pretty affable guy. I thought I was fun to
be around. I liked to joke, but I'd never in my work made any effort to be
comedic. It was not part of my professional life," O'Brien tells Tom Walker.
"I think life made me do it. It was time to look at the world as to love and

loss, grief and betrayal" (G3). For O'Brien, *Tomcat* arises as an evolutionary inevitability in his fiction, the comic novel coming from a sense that the author had sufficiently articulated the important issues with unsettling poignancy in the earlier works. And although the novel is an obvious shift from the tone of the previous works, O'Brien says, "My raw materials remain pretty much the same: the things we will do to win love, the things we will do to keep love, the things we will do to love ourselves" ("Tim O'Brien: Past Interview").

The narrative's comic tone, heavy with irony, double entendre, and mis-interpretation, only superficially conceals the serious topics that O'Brien explored in his earlier fiction. The Vietnam War acts as one such touch-stone, calling into question Chippering's identity (both to himself and others) and his notion of reality. Chippering's fate rests on his ability to flesh out the facts of his own life and to reconcile those facts with his past. O'Brien treads a tenuous line between comedy and tragedy, and he takes chances in this complex novel that finds him at the height of his creative powers. Of the complementary comic overtones and serious undertones, Heberle writes, "Although the war is uncovered as a traumatic experience for Chippering, his own self-representation, his unreliability as a narrator, and even the pervasiveness of his traumatization subvert the conventional solemnity of the subject" (259). Chippering's fight is one for order, truth be damned. Throughout our lives, he contends, "we are betrayed by im-probabilities" (69).

PLOT DEVELOPMENT

In *Tomcat*, reality and imagination are often indistinguishable, made more so by the unreliable ranting of the novel's protagonist, Thomas Chip-pering. Chippering is a self-conscious and pathologically unstable narra-tor who, on the topic of human experience, muses, "It often amazes me how little we retain of the critical events in our lives. A snapshot here. An echo there" (105). The novel's comic effect is heightened by the irony of Chippering's own contradictory life and loves, and even the epigraph— "the art of losing's not hard to master / though it may look like (*Write* it!) like disaster"—taken from Elizabeth Bishop's poem "The Art of Losing," hints at the story that follows: artful disaster. The lines refer to the novel's central relationship between Chippering and his childhood sweetheart, Lorna Sue. Bishop's words gain significance as the story progresses in light of Chippering's profound inability to maintain his romantic rela-tionships.

Each of the novel's 37 chapters offers a "snapshot" view of Chippering's fragmented life, the pieces forming a whole detailing the depth of his obsessions. Chippering himself also intrudes into his own story in asides intended solely for his women readers—women who themselves have been betrayed by their lovers. Footnotes provide a quasi-scholarly commentary on Chippering's story and add to the novel's humor. By implying that the text is somehow based on scholarly research and detailed explanation (see the "Evidence" chapters in *Lake*), O'Brien further blurs the novel's fictive qualities and presumes an authority that mirrors Chippering's own supercilious attitudes.

The novel's time line works much as that in *The Nuclear Age,* shifting repeatedly from present to past and back again, using digression both as a way of connecting past to present and as an avenue for Chippering's rationalization of present actions in terms of the past. With much verbal throat clearing, Chippering intently squares the ledger for past misdeeds, though he is capable of doing so only in the most abstract terms: "Here I must digress—a tactical transgression, perhaps, but I urge forbearance. The shortest distance between two points may well be a straight line, but one must remember that efficiency is not the only narrative virtue," he says. "Texture is another. Accuracy still another. Our universe does not operate on purely linear principles" (56). Chippering's philosophy parallels similar passages from William Cowling in *The Nuclear Age;* Chippering, to his credit, however, never considers murdering his own family.

The novel opens with Thomas Chippering—linguist ("seven-time nominee for the Hubert H. Humphrey Prize for teaching excellence" [199]), narcissist, self-described war hero, cuckold—recounting in self-flattering terms his many loves and his attempt at avenging a disastrous divorce from Lorna Sue Zylstra. The event around which the novel revolves occurs on a sweltering morning in 1952 in Minnesota when the young Chippering and his friend Herbie Zylstra, Lorna Sue's brother, build an airplane out of two plywood boards. Their attentions shift, and he and Herbie discover Lorna Sue in her parents' attic. Chippering's memory of the event four decades later is photographic, and he recalls, "I am almost certain that both Lorna Sue and I understood deep in our bones that significant events were now in motion" (5–6). What begins as a harmless project becomes a bizarre rite of passage when they nail Lorna Sue to the boards, which they have fashioned into a cross. Despite the crucifixion—in fact, Chippering discovers, perhaps in part *because* of it—Chippering and Lorna Sue are inseparable. They make love for the first time at age 16, marry a decade later, and remain together for two decades until Lorna

Sue meets a real-estate tycoon while vacationing with Chippering in Tampa. The end of their marriage is the end of life as he knows it. Still, the image of Lorna Sue on the cross burns indelibly in his mind.

Aside from the disastrous conclusion to his marriage, Chippering is estranged from Herbie, whom Chippering believes may have all his life harbored incestuous fantasies for Lorna Sue. In adulthood, Chippering despises Herbie as much as he had once loved him as a child, blaming the rift solely on his erstwhile friend, who "seemed possessed by a sullen, brooding jealousy, as if I had stolen his sister from him or somehow defiled her" (10). When Chippering's relationship with Herbie unravels, little common ground remains between the two: Chippering comes to believe that Herbie probably started a church fire in 1957, a crime for which Chippering himself was under suspicion (in fact, he thinks, the whole Zylstra family idolizes Lorna Sue in an unhealthy manner, and their attitude toward her must have been the catalyst for Herbie's arson); similarly, many years later, Chippering blames Herbie for the dissolution of his marriage when Herbie discovers a deception on Chippering's part, a pile of uncashed checks to a nonexistent therapist and a "love ledger" detailing Chippering's voyeuristic habits. Chippering claims pointedly, "Herbie killed my marriage. He murdered love. Intentionally. Systematically. He found the weakness in me, and he showed it to Lorna Sue" (11).

After fulminating over his options, Chippering decides that revenge is the best course: he will travel to Tampa and win back Lorna Sue at any cost. Chippering proudly reminds the reader that he is, after all, a trained soldier and linguist who "can kill with words, or otherwise" (27). During Chippering's ill-advised quest for revenge, the novel's comedic potential is realized in the many events that contradict Chippering's own sense of control. He is tied up by two young women disgusted by his advances; compelled to relate his Vietnam experiences, including his romance with a young Vietnamese gardener, to the janitor who releases him from his bondage; spanked in front of one of his university classes by Herbie and Lorna Sue's tycoon husband while Lorna Sue looks on; and accused of corrupting the morals of his young pupils when he teaches *Macbeth* to a preschool class where he takes a job to support himself. Later, he makes a scene as the host of a children's television show when he violently wrests control of the show from its producers and kidnaps some of the children. The net effect of the fragmented stories flowing from Chippering seemingly without his conscious consent is, in the fragmented style of *The Things They Carried* and *If I Die*, a collection of stories that describe the protagonist's world not as it is, but rather as he perceives it.

Significantly, the past intrudes upon the present when Chippering returns to his childhood home and begins an affair with Mrs. Kooshof, a woman living alone in the house. When Chippering suffers a breakdown in the house's backyard, Mrs. Kooshof (Chippering insists on the formal address, even after they have become intimate) invites him in. They become a couple, and for a time, Mrs. Kooshof serves as a distraction, keeping Chippering's thoughts of Lorna Sue at bay. He eventually hits upon using his new love interest as an accomplice in his plan for vengeance. Two subplots are important for understanding Chippering's character, and he reveals them to Mrs. Kooshof in the course of their first conversations. One concerns a threat that Chippering receives from a group of Green Berets with whom he had an unpleasant encounter in Vietnam. The men left Chippering to get lost in the Vietnam wilderness, and he recalls the event in flashbacks that, at least in part, explain his actions in the present. After wandering aimlessly for two days, Chippering realizes that what he had construed as a joke was in earnest, his life in danger. His overriding thought during that time acts as a metaphor for the novel as a whole: commenting on the sameness of his surroundings, he laments that "everything was a mirror to everything else" (144), just as his life has become a reflection of his own desires, a two-dimensional world without substance. Later, when he falls in love with a prostitute whom the men continue to mistreat, Chippering calls an air strike in on their position, nearly killing them, and rearranges the events so that he is awarded the Silver Star for valor. In the present, while Chippering plans the details of his vengeance on Lorna Sue, he sees one of the Green Berets waiting on the steps outside his classroom. The specter of Vietnam haunts Chippering until the novel's conclusion.

The seriousness of his Vietnam experience is illustrated in a chapter titled "Lost," when Chippering's attempt at wooing a bartender and her friend becomes a recollection revealing the extent to which Chippering is afflicted by his past: "Lost, I told them. Lost as lost gets. Abandoned in those mountains, no compass, no north or south, just the dense green jungle blurring into deeper jungle, and for two days I followed a narrow dirt trail that led nowhere. Here was a place where even lost gets lost. . . . And none of it seemed real" (144). Ironically, Chippering's admission constitutes one of the few times in the novel that the reader may take his words at face value.

Another subplot details Chippering's dismissal from his university position over a sexual-harassment case, which Chippering attempts to cover up by agreeing to write his manipulative victim's senior thesis. The young woman, Toni, calls Chippering at home and Mrs. Kooshof answers, setting off one of many confrontations between the two over Chippering's ambitious amorous adventures. Chippering claims innocence on the grounds of Toni's interest in literature, in the process revealing the reason for his continued difficulty with relationships. Chippering contends, "I saw no reason to reject the poor girl, whose heart and soul were engaged. . . . The idea was to defuse things. To objectify our master-student paradigm" (93). Toni understands Chippering's intentions all too well and blackmails him. His confrontation with Toni escalates when her roommate discovers Toni's diary, which further incriminates Chippering. He agrees to write her thesis as well. The word *manipulator* joins many others from a list of words reminding Chippering of his past. His mock-pathetic outbursts reach a crescendo in his relationship with Toni when he insists that she treat him as a war hero. Having learned little from the encounter—and destined to repeat his mistakes—Chippering recounts, "it took a good portion of the afternoon, a greater portion of my spiritual resources, but in the end I succeeded in mollifying my hypersensitive young chippie. Flattery, I have learned, is the key" (93). Chippering loses his job over the perceived affair.

Once Chippering has been brought to his lowest point by those he had sought to humiliate, he discovers the truth of Lorna Sue, who, Herbie divulges, set the church fire all those years before. He concludes that "she doesn't want a real life. She wants worship" (312). One of Chippering's most profound statements is that, in giving his life to the vision of Lorna Sue as he remembers her as a young girl, "I had married a child" (331). The revelation offers perspective to Chippering, who continues his relationship with Mrs. Kooshof and for the first time calls her Donna, her given name. Still, the Tomcat, "untamed, thank the Lord, but learning how to love" (340), is bound not to change overnight. The past is a dangerous place for Chippering to live with two people like Herbie and Lorna Sue. In a moment of epiphany, he sees an "image of Lorna Sue herself: both middle-aged and impossibly young. How she managed to do this I do not pretend to know" (329).

CHARACTER DEVELOPMENT

Thomas Chippering is a comic character who muses incessantly on language, history, love, and lost opportunities. At the outset of *Tomcat*, Chippering reflects on his life and concedes, "It's a mystery. Four decades have passed, so much pain, so much horror, yet I cannot begin to understand the causes. All I know is this: I am alone now" (10). Novelist Jane Smiley surmises that O'Brien's primary challenge in creating a character so obsessed with language and the nature of being is "to write a whole novel in the voice of a man who is entirely deluded to begin with and gets worse. . . . It is an iffy proposition to let Chippering tell his own story. He does not care to let the other characters, no matter how major they are in the structure of the novel, say much or have much screen time" (11). The protagonist's solipsism—Chippering defines the world exclusively through the filter of his own experiences, with little regard for the thoughts and feelings of others—is the novel's primary focus.

On the surface, Chippering caricatures the soldiers who people O'Brien's early novels, a stark departure from the deadly-serious situations in *The Things They Carried* and *In the Lake of the Woods*. Still, Chippering describes himself in terms closely paralleling John Wade's own Vietnam experience in *Lake*. While Wade's alter ego as Sorcerer suggests his inability to distinguish fantasy from reality when called upon to do so after his wife's disappearance, Chippering muses, "to look at me, perhaps, one might conclude that I am incapable of violence, yet little could be more distant from the truth. I am a war hero. . . . No doubt my students would raise their Neanderthal eyebrows at this, even cackle in disbelief, for I cultivate the façade of a distant, rather ineffectual man of letters" (27). Chippering, like Wade, is not what he seems.

A character defined by his own contradictions, he admits in a rare candid moment that, far from being the quintessential man's man, "I was not cut out for the grim business of soldiering. I am a tall, somewhat gawky man. Athletically disinclined. A distinctive stride—pelvis forward, elbows sideward—an intellectual's abstract tilt to the jaw" (58). His primary defense is language, not nearly as effective a palliative, as it turns out, as Wade's magic in the earlier novel. Chippering describes a tree in his backyard to which Lorna Sue had attributed magic powers when they first fell in love. Now, Chippering understands, "over the years that twisted old apple tree had kept growing in my memory, magnifying itself as the objects of youth often do. And yet, now, in the graying bleakness of my middle age, the tree struck me as scrawny and forlorn and laughable. It held no magic. It meant nothing. It was a tree" (249). His one endearing characteristic is a profoundly inflated self-image. The reader, privy to Chippering's dissimulation through subtle (and not so subtle) cues that Chippering himself drops like crumbs in his story, feels sympathy toward the vanquished linguistics professor. In a sense, his treatment at the hands of Lorna Sue and Herbie, his oldest and dearest friends, amounts to a betrayal of his childlike trust and innocence. And even though the rela-

tionships have been damaged beyond repair, Chippering's desire to hold
on to those childhood truths mitigates judgment against him in his obsession for vengeance; or, as Heberle puts it, "Chippering's sob stories
parody trauma therapy itself; they satisfy his need to justify or feel sorry
for himself, but his mainly female listeners have problems of their own"
(283).

When Chippering and Mrs. Kooshof travel to Tampa so that Chippering
may exact his revenge on Lorna Sue, their relationship sours as well. Chippering understands, perhaps for the first time, the extent of his obsession
with Lorna Sue and the intertwined vagaries of language. When Chippering first sees Lorna Sue and Herbie in a Tampa hotel, he is surprised
by how much he misses Mrs. Kooshof and how his love for Lorna Sue
has become little more than "a hollowed-out version of the old love" (140).
But when Herbie shows the love ledger to Mrs. Kooshof, the relationship
takes a predictable turn. Also, Lorna Sue and her husband plan to humiliate Chippering in front of his students; Mr. Robert Kooshof, Mrs.
Kooshof's absent husband, calls and threatens Chippering from prison;
and his Vietnam nemesis Spider calls. Chippering recalls the events in his
typical bombastic language, which hides the confusion and disgrace of a
character who becomes increasingly pathetic as the novel moves toward
its conclusion. "I have reached the moral divide of my narrative: the
jumped-off cliff, the burning bridge, the stark and sinister sine qua non,"
Chippering intones. "Here, if you will, we approach that fatal intersection
at which my life took its turn toward chaos and desperation and what
others (dimwits) might call madness" (208).

The women whom Chippering pursues act as foils through which the
reader better understands the protagonist. The novel's female characters
are not as fully developed as Chippering himself, since Chippering tells
the story through the lens of his distorted observations. The strategy more
or less precludes much character development outside Chippering's own
solipsistic and self-serving frame of reference. The female characters are
conspicuous by their absence, begging to be heard through the constant
covering chatter of their suitor. Mrs. Robert Kooshof is Lorna Sue's coun-
terpart in the present, and Chippering treats her much as he must have
treated Lorna Sue. By refusing to use her first name in addressing her,
Chippering relegates her to the same list as the women, many of them
anonymous, detailed in his love ledger. Like Lorna Sue, Mrs. Kooshof has
secrets of her own—a husband in prison, a six-figure bank account, and
some past-life baggage among them—though Chippering is capable of

handling the details of Mrs. Kooshof's life in a way that eluded him in his relationship with Lorna Sue.

Chippering admits that he has fallen in love with the idea of Lorna Sue, not the woman herself, and he draws her character in the sorts of absolutes that force the reader to question his motives. Still, Lorna Sue, whom Chippering discovers late in life has underlying psychological issues, feels put upon by both Chippering and her brother, Herbie, to act as they remember her: the object of their collective worship. After Lorna Sue jams the tip of a fountain pen deep into her arm without flinching, she explains, "My whole life, Tommy—ever since we were kids—it's like I've been squeezed from two sides, these two walls pushing in. You and Herbie. And sometimes I just want to run away from both of you. Or else hurt you. That's the other alternative" (131). No wonder Lorna Sue leaves Chippering—who, she says repeatedly, too often acts like an 18-year-old—for a more predictable and banal existence with a Tampa tycoon.

Finally, Herbie Zylstra acts as a sort of Greek chorus for Chippering, reminding him that his actions have consequences and warning him on many occasions that he should stop pursuing Lorna Sue. Although Chippering cannot forgive Herbie for having betrayed him with Lorna Sue and similarly attempting to destroy his relationship with Mrs. Kooshof, Herbie is ultimately responsible for Chippering's epiphany at the novel's conclusion. Chippering describes Herbie in unflattering terms, positing that "in a later decade, Herbie would have been a candidate for Ritalin or some similar drug, gallons of the stuff, a long rubber hose running from pharmacy to vein" (7). Still, and despite his apparent treasonous actions toward Chippering, Herbie seems to have the best interests of his sister at heart and harbors no particular animosity for Chippering. The most difficult realization for Chippering does not concern his relationships with the women, who provide a convenient excuse for his anger toward Herbie, but rather the erosion of his relationship with his oldest friend, a symbol of the failure of his closest relationships throughout his life. "In a way, it seemed my old pal had willfully erased me from memory, along with our joint history," Chippering bemoans, "and I have since come to suspect that this was a means of wiping away his own shame, obliterating guilt by obliterating me. I was invisible to him: not even a ghost" (9). What Chippering does not understand is that the woman who has been the attention of both men throughout their lives is also the one who set the church fire all those years before. It is that flaw in Lorna Sue that finally allows Chippering to accept his own flaws and move on with his life. Chippering becomes cognizant enough of other people's thoughts and feelings to interact with them on their terms, as when he rids himself of Lorna Sue's memory: "For a man who lives by words, a man whose very being amounts to little more than language, it came as the ultimate satisfaction—indeed, the only vengeance that could ever make a difference—to stop and square my shoulders and return to Lorna Sue the parting gift of a long, cold, reptilian stare" (334).

The reader and an unnamed "other" who, Chippering posits, has suffered a similar heartbreaking loss, are also implicated in the story. As Chippering puts it, "All of us, no doubt, have our demons. One way or another we are pursued by the ghosts of our own history, our lost loves, our blunders, our broken promises and grieving wives and missing children" (22). The character whom Chippering addresses throughout, specifically in chapter 27, "You," is Chippering's alter ego, a person who similarly has been hurt. When Chippering addresses that person directly, he crosses the line into melodrama, the emotion of his response exceeding its motivation: "And you? Do you have a name? Better without. Unique as you are—and do not for a moment think otherwise—you also represent every brokenhearted lover on this planet, every stood-up date, every single mother, every bride left weeping at the altar, every widow, every orphan, every divorcee, every abandoned child, every slave sold down the river" (236). The novel's final paragraph addresses the narratee directly, imploring her to "embolden yourself. Brave the belief" (342). The protagonist's transformation is not complete, though the strides he has made toward finally establishing a healthy romantic relationship are significant. As O'Brien explains to Rosica, "[Chippering] gets some wisdom. He makes progress. . . . It would be silly to end the book with him utterly reformed, sort of toeing the politically correct line. . . . He begins to learn about himself, and he says near the end of the book, 'I'm taking two steps forward, and one back,' and that's a kind of progress."

THEMES

In *Tomcat*, O'Brien examines themes familiar from his first handful of works, albeit this time in a humorous context with very serious consequences: language, love, and religion define the characters and lead Chippering to a conclusion with which Paul Berlin *(Going after Cacciato)*, Jimmy Cross *(The Things They Carried)*, or John Wade *(In the Lake of the Woods)* might have been in agreement: "We had plowed this fallow ground before, and it struck me that nothing in our lives ever comes to absolute closure— not love, not betrayal, not the most inane episode of youth. We are surrounded by loose ends; we are awash in why and maybe. An absence of faith, one might call it" (333). From the outset, Chippering's stylized delivery and his erstwhile profession as a linguistics professor suggest the importance of language for much of what follows, in the plot and the philosophical grounding that round out Chippering's character. "To name it is to tame it" (144), he proclaims, and, despite repeated failures on his part to tame much of significance, including his own emotions, Chippering adheres to the notion. Recalling his childhood, he muses on his fascination for certain words—oddly, *corn* and *Pontiac* among them, and later *manipulation*—as he catalogs events not as sensory perception, but strictly in terms of language. From his earliest memories, Chippering was aware of language, recalling that "even back then, in a preknowledge way, I understood that language was involved, its frailties and mutabilities, its potential for betrayal" (4). He comes to understand the power of words and their effect on the individual, and he concludes, "Language is an organism that evolves separately inside each of us. It kicks like a baby in the womb. It whispers secrets to our blood" (262).

Only when Chippering begins his obsessive journey into the maze of language, however, does he become ineffective in maintaining his relationships. Words, he discovers, "are like embers. They smolder. They drop to the bottom of our souls, where for years they give off only a modest heat, and then out of nowhere a life-wind suddenly whips up and the words burst into red-hot, spirit-scorching flame" (37); still, the very language that Chippering prides himself on using so well also often fails him. Language supersedes memory and action, and because language only *represents* an event, it is even further removed from experience than memory. Chippering's version of reality, then, differs markedly from objective truth. Chippering, so involved with semantics (not unlike Cowling's fascination with language and the way it shapes the past and the present in *The Nuclear Age*), is unable to analyze the events of his life as separate from the words describing them. During his wandering in the Vietnam wilderness, he recalls, "I was no longer aiming at anything. Not even survival. Except for an occasional whimper, I had lost my capacity for language, the underlying grammar of human reason; I had lost the me of me—my name, its meaning—those particularities of spirit and personality that separate one from all, each from other" (147). By losing his language, he comes closest to his essential nature, to the elemental dichotomy of life and death.

Another of Chippering's pet words is *love*, and though he is incapable of remaining content in any relationship, he has clear notions of what love should be, and he draws a close connection between love and language: "The betrayal of love, in other words, seems also to entail a fundamental betrayal of language and logic and human reason, a subversion of meaning, a practical joke directed against the very meaning of meaning" (165). The reality, of course, is much different from Chippering's fantasy. Even after loosing himself from his relationship with Lorna Sue, he naively muses that with Mrs. Kooshof, "I was at peace. I was quietly and vastly content" (68); still, he can hardly hide his disdain for her unwillingness to follow every twist and turn of her suitor's convoluted tales, a condition he describes as "Mrs. Kooshof's intolerance for complexity, for the looping circuitry of a well-told tale, [which] symptomizes an epidemic disease of our modern world. (I see it daily among my students. The short attention span, the appetite limited to linearity. Too much *Melrose Place*.)" (70). Similarly, relationships with Toni and her roommate, the bartender and her friend, and a host of other women confirm Chippering's profound inability to connect with women in a meaningful, nonsexual way.

Chippering, despite his insatiable anger at his ex-wife and her new husband, is bound only to dream of revenge. His self-centeredness and general ineptitude prevent him from becoming dangerous, though he invokes his military training to illustrate his seriousness. Much as Wade in *Lake* goes to Vietnam only for Kathy's love, Chippering is motivated by his love for Lorna Sue specifically and women in general, even if he realizes that "Lorna Sue had never been mine. Not wholly. And it was never love" (140). Although Chippering prides himself on having "enjoyed carnal relations with a paltry four women" (158), he attributes great power to a more abstract notion of love, connecting it with his ability to make sense of his own life.

Chippering's notions of love are intimately connected with his childhood memory of Lorna Sue's crucifixion. The novel's religious overtones become clear when Chippering recalls how he and Herbie had used their airplane-cum-makeshift-wooden-cross many years before. Although Chippering is in no sense a religious person, he organizes his memories of Lorna Sue around the metaphor of religion. She is the object of worship for Chippering, her family worships her as they would a religious icon, and Chippering feels unworthy of Lorna Sue's attention to the point that he drives her away with what he considers to be a "modest little lie" (77). Chippering blames Herbie for a fire in the sanctuary of St. Paul's Catholic Church not because of some inherent flaw in Herbie's personality, but because of the profound influence on Chippering of the Zylstra family's attitude toward Lorna Sue. Pushed to the edge, Chippering posits that "the 1957 fire could be seen as a cruel but not unpredictable outcome of the pressures on Herbie's spirit. A mix of rage and guilt, no doubt, had made him try to burn religion out of his life and perhaps out of the world as a whole" (39). Instead, the fire is Lorna Sue's attempt at asserting herself as a religious object, though the stunt casts doubt on her stability and, should Chippering have found out, would have moved both their lives in much different directions.

In cataloging Lorna Sue's good points, Chippering connects what he perceives as his wife's piety with the Catholic Church, hence the act that he and Herbie perpetrated when they were children. Chippering recounts how "Lorna Sue missed only a single Sunday Mass in our many years together. She believed in the blood of Christ, its real presence, and accepted without question the doctrines of corporeal resurrection and immaculate conception" (109). He also couples the purplish stigmata on her hand with her sexuality, deeming it Lorna Sue's "most attractive feature" (111). For Chippering, unaware of Lorna Sue's deep-seated family issues, the girl and the truth are inseparable. When he learns otherwise, however, he bemoans, "How easy it is, I thought, to meddle in another human life. I had learned the hard way that truth is immaterial, that accusation alone is more than sufficient. (Gossip becomes fact; speculation become certainty; arraignment become its own life sentence.)" (136). Chippering's views on religion suggest what O'Brien has explored throughout his fiction, namely questioning why a benevolent and omniscient deity would allow such tragedy—Lorna Sue's infidelity and Chippering's subsequent inability to find happiness—to befall Chippering in his personal life. Chippering is able, finally, to uncover the causes for his anxiety and to examine his relationship with Lorna Sue in a more objective light: "Did I love her? I did. Was she still sacred? She was not" (334).

ALTERNATIVE READING: FEMINIST CRITICISM

Much of the impetus for feminist criticism in literature can be traced to the turn of the last century, though the women's liberation effort, particularly focused in the late 1960s and early 1970s and at times closely aligned with the counterculture and civil rights movements, profoundly affected the ways in which literary texts are interpreted. Betty Friedan, Katharine M. Rogers, Simone de Beauvoir, Mary Ellmann, Myra Jehlen, Kate Millett, Carolyn Heilbrun, Nina Baym, and Elaine Showalter are some of the many names associated with feminist and women's studies in literature, a movement that has assimilated theories from other disciplines—

cultural theory and sociopolitical theory among them—in order to examine the ways in which a text approaches matters of language, a society's treatment of women, and relationships, particularly those favoring the masculine impulse.

In his study of the convergence of literary theory and composition, Lester Faigley writes, "During the 1970s and 1980s different lines of feminist theory challenged the assumption that acts of writing are similar for men and women. Radical feminists such as Mary Daly and Adrienne Rich argued that women's experience is distorted by language that purports to be objective and disinterested. Language in their view does not merely name inequality, it reproduces it" (35). While the pervasive and diverse nature of feminist criticism makes a blanket definition difficult to pin down, one of the most common notions posits that the canon of literature is patriarchal, or male-centered, and that gender and identity are constructed by culture. At its base, feminist criticism studies the ways in which women are portrayed in literature and how language is used to define them.

In his first comic novel, O'Brien risks offending many readers with the introduction of a blatantly chauvinistic protagonist, though he defends Chippering's attitudes by invoking an aspect of literature that takes into account a character's most intense emotions. He tells Karen Rosica, "if people take offense at the book, they have to take offense at *Hamlet*, too. . . . Books that are any good, I think, are supposed to go to the raw parts of the human spirit and psyche, our fears and our terrors and our wishes and all the things that make us human. And often times the books will hit a ragged nerve in a person, but that's what literature is supposed to do." The novel was well received despite its subject matter, not the least due to the laughable extent to which Chippering goes to assert his manly right. O'Brien points out, "In the case of Tomcat, he's outraged at a woman leaving him. What he doesn't understand, of course, is that she should have left him. He was a total jerk. And it's that sense of blindness behind his outrage that was fun to explore in this book" (Rosica). Because of the obvious juxtaposition of male and female characters in the novel and Chippering's misogyny, a fitting alternative perspective would be to read the novel through a feminist lens.

One emphasis in feminist criticism is the relationship between language and the subject being depicted. Even though Chippering, as the story's narrator, divulges little about Lorna Sue's interior life, the fact that O'Brien creates such a pretentious and unappealing character (in fact, the reviews that lauded O'Brien for Chippering's character described him as so onerous as to be repulsively humorous) shifts the focus from Chippering's rants to his relationship with Lorna Sue, their childhood upbringing, and the matter of her crucifixion. That Lorna Sue has been violated—even if in the process she sustains only a minor wound that undoubtedly carries more significance for Chippering than any other of the novel's characters—is an indication of her acquiescence to Herbie and Chippering at the same time that it confirms much of what Chippering claims later is the family's unhealthy worship of Lorna Sue. She is, in one way, a religious icon. Though crucified in the manner of Christ, Lorna Sue symbolizes the Virgin Mary—pure, maternal, above reproach—to both her brother and his friend, and the nail penetrating her hand suggests the sexual relationship she will have with Chippering, as well as a pseudosexual relationship with her own brother.

Readers will recognize the irony in O'Brien's reversal of traditional gender roles: Chippering bemoans and records for posterity his partner's leaving, a cautionary tale for both Chippering and his ostensible addressee, a woman who has lost her own lover to an affair: "Over the past empty months, as your ex-husband combs the far-off beaches of Fiji, have you not felt exactly what I feel? A contradictory mix of despair and hope, longing and regret, ferocious hatred and barbaric love? Be truthful. Did you not conceive, if only briefly, your own plan of revenge? Did you not imagine hurting him as he hurt you?" (109). The novel contains many such digressions and callings-out, each one a cry for recognition from Chippering, whose own defense is a pathetic attempt at rationalizing his attitude toward feminists in derogatory terms. When Herbie and Lorna Sue's husband humiliate Chippering in front of his students by spanking him, Chippering blames the event on everyone but himself, haughtily declaring, "Right now, for that matter, I can hear the feminist flies buzzing at my buttocks, those jackbooted squads of Amazon storm troopers denouncing my indefatigable masculinity. Oh, yes, I can see the sorry spectacle—thousands of ill-mannered, cement-headed, shrill-voiced, holier-than-thou guardians of ovarian rectitude, each squealing with delight at my public humiliation" (213). Later, in a footnote, Chippering writes, "With women, I have learned, the fundamental function of language is rarely to impart intellectual content, or to share objective meaning, it is rather to give vent to some murky-headed sense of 'emotion'" (254).

Language, which plays an important role in developing the protagonist, also empowers Chippering by allowing him to define and describe his world through *his own* language, a male language. Clearly, Chippering uses language with the sole intention of convincing his audience—be they the characters he meets in the course of the novel or, in a metafictional sense, the readers of his story—that his story is the *real* story. Much of the comedy comes from the reader's immediate recognition of Chippering's duplicity.

That Chippering's story is the creation of a man is made clear, and the silences—the addressee of Chippering's many asides remains voiceless, as if Chippering offers a one-sided response to that woman (or to women in general)—become as important as the words on the page. Post-structural feminism is based upon the premise that language itself is gendered and that "gender difference dwells in language rather than in the referent, that there is nothing 'natural' about gender itself" (Elam, "Post-structuralist Feminisms" 242). Elaine Showalter observes that feminist theory has had implications "in literary theory where female space is the alternative linguistic and imaginative place from which women can speak" (36). None of the female characters in *Tomcat* are given that opportunity. Rather, Chippering's self-conscious and self-referential recording of his experiences ironically conveys his chauvinistic sentiments in a comic light.

July, July
(2002)

> That the United States was defeated in Vietnam is certain. But did
> that defeat truly mean what the antiwar movement seems to have
> persuaded everyone it meant? Do the policies that led the United
> States into Vietnam deserve the discredit that has been attached to
> them?
> —Norman Podhoretz, *Why We Were in Vietnam*

After more than 30 years of intense introspection spanning eight books,
O'Brien comes to a philosophical conclusion in *July, July* that, if not inevitable, is a likely evolution of the author's worldview: "Our politics
have become personal. The world has whittled itself down to basics" ("An
Interview with Tim O'Brien: *July, July*"). That succinct notion is the backdrop for *July, July*, a retrospective glance, by turns loving and critical, at
the people and events defining the Vietnam generation. In the novel, the
thematic continuity so important in O'Brien's fiction is complemented by
a strong temporal component that allows the author to assess the three
decades since his generation's participation in the Vietnam War. The result
is bittersweet nostalgia for a more unambiguous way of life.

The idea for the novel came from a magazine-writing assignment offered to O'Brien by Rust Hills, fiction editor at *Esquire*. Hills requested a
piece of short fiction, and O'Brien gave him a 600-word story that was

successful enough to encourage the author to cobble other pieces into his
seventh novel. O'Brien saw the collection—vignettes similar to the *Esquire*
piece, linked by a patchwork quilt of characters' shared experience—as
an organizational challenge on the order of that which he had faced with
The Things They Carried and *The Nuclear Age,* both of which offer varied,
oftentimes wildly disparate versions of the same reality. Perhaps not coincidentally, then, *July, July* met with a similar critical ambivalence to that
of *The Nuclear Age.* Critic Alan Davis credits O'Brien with powerful writing in the vignettes, asserting that "such stories, some haunting and others
absurd, collectively tell a story about a generation that could be extrava-
gantly idealistic and ridiculously foolish by turns. O'Brien, whose experience perhaps equips him better than most writers to glean what imperial
ambitions cost average Joes and Janes, writes at his best about an America
full of funhouse mirrors" (388). Still, Davis considers the synthesis of the
many short pieces into an ostensible novel to be artificial.

Even more difficult for O'Brien than seamlessly organizing the novel,
however, was the author's desire to write, really for the first time, strong
female protagonists. Despite the dearth of female leads in his fiction,
O'Brien, fascinated by the characters who return to Darton Hall College—
"especially the women" ("An Interview with Tim O'Brien: *July, July*")—
took on the task with passion. In creating those characters, O'Brien, always
a scrupulous craftsman, makes an uncharacteristic intuitive leap from not-
knowing to truth. He likens the act of writing the "other," in this case
female characters, to his trepidation at writing the thoughts and the feelings of the Vietnamese in his books. "This problem of not knowing the
other is compounded even more by problems of culture, problems of language, compounded by problems of not knowing the history behind this
culture," O'Brien says. "The same principles I'm talking about apply to
writing about women" (Shostak and Bourne 88).

O'Brien's decision was not without risk, and Jonathan Yardley points
out that "the pathos that is at the heart of the human condition often tips
over into bathos, and thus to tell the truth about how we live and what
we do is often to risk sentimentality, coincidence, melodrama and all the
other ingredients of the soap opera" (2). In order to balance descriptions
of disturbing events and his characters' reactions to those events, O'Brien
must speak with an authority that, by his own admission, he has not
earned. The tipping point between truth (or, in literary terms, realism)
and melodrama lies within a dangerously small margin of error. What
presumes to examine the human condition risks becoming meaningless
white noise, an unintelligible shout into a walkie-talkie. Yardley concludes

of the effort that "in moving from Vietnam to stateside, O'Brien hasn't gotten out of his depth—he's already provided ample evidence that he has a deep understanding of human nature and the human heart—but he appears to be out of his element" (2).

Although Yardley reads *July, July* in the context of O'Brien's earlier work and gives the author high marks for his ambition, not all reviewers were kind to the attempt. The novel garnered little of the effusive praise reserved for, of the later fiction, *The Things They Carried* and *In the Lake of the Woods*. David Gates, in easily the most disapproving of the reviews, posits that after having read what he considers to be a clichéd, facile premise acted out by one-dimensional characters, "these days, even the television shows his characters surely watch collude in a culture of knowingness and irony far beyond the ken of *July, July*" (6). In just the past handful of years, Gates's statement itself has become ironic, the self-reflexive and very public shaming of individuals on ubiquitous "reality shows" an indication of the voyeuristic quest for meaning in otherwise stagnant lives. In that sense, O'Brien is prescient of the need for such an examination as he presents in *July, July*. Introspection without any meaningful filters, as his characters illustrate upon their return to Darton Hall, can be as dangerous as it is liberating.

PLOT DEVELOPMENT

Because of the size of the novel's cast, *July, July* is O'Brien's most character-driven work, detailing events from middle-aged lives by describing "how these . . . characters dealt with those things over the past thirty years, long after the war ended. The erosion of ideals. Of the transformation of ideals" ("An Interview with Tim O'Brien: *July, July*"). Although the characters inhabiting the novel are not unlike many other of O'Brien's creations—the injured veteran David Todd recalls John Wade, Paul Berlin, or even the soldier Tim O'Brien in *If I Die*, and Grace Perry, the matronly college sweetheart and wife of protagonist Paul Perry in *Northern Lights*, could have roomed with Amy Robinson, Paulette Haslo, Jan Huebner, or any other of the women who return—the combinations and permutations for interaction so many years after the fact make the novel one of O'Brien's most visually stimulating, even if it lacks the stunning structural complexity and intensity of *Going after Cacciato* or *The Things They Carried*.

On Friday, July 7, 2000, a group of friends returns to the Darton Hall College gymnasium, outside Chicago, for their 30th reunion (in fact, the group graduated 31 years before, but due to a scheduling error, the reunion comes a year late; that error mirrors the scattered lives the friends have lived in their absence from one another). The names, some suggestive of salt-of-the-earth midwestern stock, could be any group of friends from a college yearbook in the late 1960s, their stories the stories of any young people raised in the shadow of war: David Todd, Marla Dempsey, Jan Huebner, Amy Robinson, Ellie Abbott, Billy McCann, Dorothy Stier, Spook Spinelli, Marv Bertel, and Paulette Haslo. Two of their classmates, they discover in the course of conversation, are dead: one, Karen Burns, a woman who has never found love, has been murdered in the desert in a side story that parallels the understated tragedy and near absurdity of Flannery O'Connor's "A Good Man Is Hard to Find"; the other, Harmon Osterberg, a dentist, drowns while committing adultery with Ellie Abbott, one of the reunion revelers.

July, July employs a structure similar to that of *The Nuclear Age*, the past and the present fused in alternating chapters whose digressions define characters' motivations and dreams. In *July, July*, however, the 10 characters who tell 10 different stories present a more complete picture of the intervening years. O'Brien draws on a common experience, the college reunion and the clichés attendant upon such events, to reveal the fates of the friends. Although the novel contains little of the magical realism characterizing *Cacciato* and the surreal mingling of truth and fiction in *The Things They Carried*, *July, July* does have a similar fragmented structure, the "Class of '69" vignettes interspersed with brief chapters detailing the lives of each of the novel's major players, from their college days to the present.

In a haze of recollection, the students rehearse for and perform the first acts of their adult lives. When back together, their thoughts turn immediately to the single event that they have in common: Vietnam. In Jan Huebner's flashback to the summer of 1969, O'Brien serves up a litany of the time's most memorable events interspersed with the mundane events of life:

> The nation's youth began converging on forty acres of farmland outside Woodstock, New York. Sharon Tate had been dead less than a week. Sanitation workers in Manhattan were sweeping up Neil Armstrong's ticker tape. But for Jan Huebner, as for most others, the summer of 1969 would later call to mind not headlines, nor global politics, nor even a war, but small, modest memories of small, modest things: rumpled beds and

ringing telephones and birthday cakes and dirty pictures and catchy tunes about everyday people. . . . Small, simple things, yes, but as in some great nationwide darkroom, the most ordinary human snapshots would be fixed in memory by the acidic wash of war—the music, the lingo, the evening news. (74–75)

The passage illustrates O'Brien's continuing attention to the individual, the power of the seemingly banal act to transform and define a life, of a world "whittling itself down to basics." By associating the details with the larger reality, "the acidic wash of war," O'Brien asserts both the individual's ability to transcend the brutality of war and the value of everyday experience to add perspective to such horror. Jan, for the first time in her life, "felt wanted and appreciated, even loved, for something beyond a laugh. . . . A morbid irony, Jan realized, but slaughter had given her a life. Napalm had made her happy. She hoped the war would never end" (63). Ironically, even as she skims the surface of life, paying fleeting attention to Neil Armstrong's moon walk, for instance, or commenting only briefly on movie actress Sharon Tate's death at the hands of Charles Manson's "family," David Todd, shot through both feet, simultaneously suffers on a river bank somewhere west of Chu Lai, deciding whether to live or die.

Memories of war form the novel's opening and closing, the circularity of the present-time story, the reunion, pointing out the war's residual impact on the partiers. When the revelers arrive at Darton Hall for the weekend, the Vietnam era's dynamism has metamorphosed into something different, something less, youthful energy and optimism dissipated by time: "The war was over, passions were moot, and the band played a slow, hollowed-out version of an old Buffalo Springfield tune. For everyone, there was a sense of nostalgia made fluid by present possibility" (6). In the aftermath of the reunion, as the friends prepare to leave with the knowledge that they may never see one another again, the mood turns somber, the war of their youth contrasted to the psychic wars that continue to haunt them: "Nixon was dead. Westmoreland was in retirement. That war was over. Now there were new wars" (319). The friends' stories, many told primarily through dialogue commenting ironically on the passage of time, detail the lives of the characters both during their time at Darton Hall and in the intervening years. The conversations take a different tack from those 30 years before. In the din of the gymnasium, old friends talk about "death, marriage, children, divorce, betrayal, loss, grief, disease:

these were among the topics that generated a low, liquid hum beneath the surface of the music" (8). The novel concludes at 3:11 A.M. on Sunday, July 9, as the friends—paired off, in some instances, and others having gone their separate ways—return to their lives. The principal tone is one of disappointment and a sense of wasted opportunity coupled with the improbable hope that so often accompanies misery in O'Brien's novels.

Though O'Brien's fragmented texts have always mirrored the complexities and the fragile psyches of his characters, experience has led O'Brien in a roundabout way, and through some difficult narrative terrain, to the more traditional, realist style that balances both *July, July* and *Tomcat in Love*, the author's preceding effort. Such a portrayal of lives irrevocably changed by war, however, inevitably leads O'Brien to examine the consequences of "certain blood for uncertain reasons." Never one to eschew the well-placed epigraph, O'Brien quotes Irish poet William Butler Yeats to lend atmosphere to his novel of parts: "We had fed the heart on fantasies, / The heart's grown brutal from the fare." Those lines and the novel's title evoke images of patriotism, revolution, freedom, and sacrifice in two eras linked by an inescapable history. The Julys of the title, separated by three decades, contrast battles against tyranny with an increasingly frantic and even more nebulous search for meaning and purpose. The friends seek a mantra for a generation whose extravagant dreams, O'Brien reminds us repeatedly, far exceed their ability to fulfill them.

CHARACTER DEVELOPMENT

Although the novel's characters represent different political views, socioeconomic circumstances, and life experiences, the most fully developed characters are the ones cogently linking the friends' past with the present. The most powerful story is that of David Todd, a star shortstop on the Darton Hall baseball team who was scouted by the Major Leagues before being drafted into the army. He is the sweetheart of Marla Dempsey—a woman, Todd discovers, incapable of fully loving anyone—and plans on marrying her when they graduate from college and he turns pro. Superficially, the relationship is ideal, a sure sign in O'Brien's fiction that something is amiss.

Todd's recurring flashback to the war and an injury that took his leg and destroyed his baseball career still threatens to overwhelm him, even as he returns for the reunion. The trauma is described in great detail, the scene of devastation—Todd is the only living soldier amid the carnage of a massacre, and he has plenty of time to relive the nightmare—contrasting neatly with the heroism of Neil Armstrong's voyage to the moon and his subsequent moon walk in July 1969. Instead of returning to the United States to adoring masses, as Armstrong undoubtedly will, Todd medicates himself with morphine, watches as ants slowly begin to eat his feet, and remarks disinterestedly about the death around him. Not coincidentally, his surname means "death" in German (the protagonist in *The Floating Opera*, the first novel of postmodern writer John Barth, is named Todd Andrews, and that character is not dissimilar to David Todd in *July, July*; Todd Andrews's mantra, like David Todd's, is that he has "no reason for dying (or for living)"). David Todd's condition reminds the friends returning for the reunion exactly what they needed so desperately to escape in the spring of 1969.

While Todd waits in the paddy to die, he hallucinates the character Johnny Ever, who takes on various guises, including that of an omnipotent deejay who gives Todd the option of living or dying. "I could run the future tape for you, but I think it might end up real, real depressing. Twenty-two years old, career finished, nobody gives a hoot about war wounds," Ever warns him. "Your bubble-gum cards, Davy, they won't fetch top dollar. Anyhow, if that's not enough, pretty soon you start dreamin' the bad dreams. Ten, twenty years down the pike, here comes the survivor guilt" (32). Ever purports to know everything about Todd's life, and the prognosis is bleak. He predicts a divorce from Marla Dempsey (correctly, it turns out, when Marla runs away with a stockbroker on a Harley). Even armed with such foreknowledge, however, Todd chooses life. For a time, Johnny Ever's admonitions seem to be little more than a figment of the soldier's wartime imagination. Todd and Marla enjoy a stable relationship, and the two take for granted the simple events of their lives together, as "they ate meals in front of the RV, chatted amiably, laughed sometimes, took vacations, planned an addition to their house, visited with friends, gave up cigarettes, started again, celebrated birthdays and anniversaries, listened to music, bought a Chevrolet, took up yoga" (294). They both soon realize, though, that "none of it was sufficient" (294). Jane Ciabattari comments on the importance of Todd's failure with Marla in terms of his exposure early on to life's more unsavory events. She also recognizes that O'Brien is too keen an observer of human nature to allow any of his characters a life free from adversity. "In this early loss of innocence," Ciabattari writes, "[David Todd] gets a jump on his classmates. But by reunion time, all of them have realized that nobody gets out alive—or unscarred" (4).

That innocence is stripped away in a surreal play-by-play narrated by

Ever, who acts as a counterculture Greek chorus—a similar capacity to the one the interchapters in the earlier *In the Lake of the Woods* or Addie and the townspeople in *Northern Lights* fill—standing outside events at the same time that he comments on them and, in this case, accurately predicts their ultimate outcome. Of Ever, O'Brien says, "I'm not sure if Johnny is an angel or a devil or a voice of conscience or just a weird metaphysical middleman. . . . Johnny is meant to lift the story out of time, to remind both the characters and the reader that human beings have gone through certain universal troubles and joys throughout history, and to remind us that those abiding mysteries and unknowns envelop all of human experience" ("An Interview with Tim O'Brien: *July, July*"). Ever—the name, like that of the protagonist David Todd, connotes a meaning far beyond the character's literal identity—epitomizes the era. He is a combination of oracle and rock-and-roll deejay who wholeheartedly advocates the attitude of living fast and dying with a pretty corpse. Still, he has the best interests of Todd at heart and views the situation with a sardonic wit that eludes Todd as he lies dying.

To now, with the notable exception of Mary Anne Bell in "Sweetheart of the Song Tra Bong" in *The Things They Carried*, and perhaps Grace Perry and Addie in *Northern Lights*, O'Brien's distaff characters have not been as fully developed as their male counterparts, hard-bitten men whose lives are often defined by the war and the women who remain in their stead. The most difficult aspect of writing the novel, O'Brien admits, was portraying strong female protagonists, "convincing, detailed, intelligent, compelling women. . . . For every man who went to Vietnam, or for every man who went to Canada, there were countless sisters and girlfriends and wives and mothers, each of whom had her own fascinating story, her own tragedies and suffering, her own healing afterward" ("An Interview with Tim O'Brien: *July, July*"). Despite that apparent incongruity in O'Brien's work generally, the female characters in *July, July* have been the more analyzed, often in less than flattering terms. Ciabattari contends that O'Brien's "sense of humanity does not seem to extend to his female characters, who are rarely as fully realized as his men" (4). Michiko Kakutani saves her most strident remarks for the author's depiction of women, writing that "with the exception of Marla, who is drawn with considerable sympathy and elan, the women in this book are all cartoonish parodies, depicted with the same sort of misogynistic energy that animated Mr. O'Brien's last novel, *Tomcat in Love*" ("When the Magic" E45).

Marla Dempsey is indeed intriguing for her enigmatic relationship with David Todd. While dating Todd in college, Marla has an affair with a married high-school teacher. When she confronts the man's wife, for reasons that even Marla herself has difficulty fathoming, she "realized that this woman's sad, unsurprised, washed-out face offered exactly what she'd needed, everything she'd run three miles for, which was to know that she would never be forgiven" (287). The event foreshadows the trials that she and Todd would undergo later when they marry. Marla is frightened by Todd's nighttime recollections of Vietnam, and she records the conversations he has with dead comrades and plays them back to him to prove the depth of his neurosis. The voice is his, barely recognizable as the same man who returned from the war physically and psychologically changed for the worse. The torment is confirmation of Johnny Ever's warning that Todd would eventually be visited by the men who died in Vietnam, and he would live with a survivor's guilt for the rest of his life. Marla, rationalizing her position, leaves Todd, telling him that her lover has "no rivers bubbling through his head" (295). Importantly, that relationship sours after a few years, and O'Brien glosses over the events leading to its disintegration. That O'Brien chooses not to detail the events of Marla's life in the interim, particularly given her eventual reconciliation of a sort with Todd, illustrates the transitory nature of romantic relationships and suggests the specific case that may be applied to Todd's (and O'Brien's) generation in general. The love O'Brien discusses both in interviews and in his fiction is not timeless, but rather mutable and inevitably the cause of much pain. Seen in that light, then, the David Todd/ Marla Dempsey plotline links the novel's other stories and acts as a touchstone for the others' lives.

The novel's remaining female characters are a class clown who marries the brother of a blackmailing dwarf; a 51-year-old virgin murdered by a psychopath; a cancer survivor who goes topless in her neighborhood; a woman married to two men simultaneously (with their permission); a 50-year-old honeymooner who, against her will, wins a quarter of a million dollars; and an adulterer whose lover drowns while they are together. Taken at face value, those characters may suggest that O'Brien, far from developing strong female characters, instead plays upon the sensational. Seen as variations on a theme, however, those additional stories combine to form a complete and engaging whole. Perhaps O'Brien is limited by the size of his cast (he has mentioned that to fully develop these characters would have taken 50,000 pages) or the novel's structure, the vignettes allowing for stylistic and narrative texture at the cost of depth. Still, the characters act out lives as real in their own way as the lives that many of O'Brien's generation have led, replete with death, disease, infidelity, success, disappointment, and pleasure. One of the most astute comments leveled at the novel questions the inability of his characters to find fulfillment, despite their best efforts, when Ciabattari writes, "It is strange that in this portrait of a generation in its prime, O'Brien does not include a single character who has moved beyond the loss of innocence to a deeper, more subtle understanding of the complexities of choice or a character who shows leadership, wisdom or the generosity to feed back into the younger generations through family life or work" (4).

THEMES

The themes in *July, July*—aging and mortality, difficulty adjusting to a changing society, the lingering effects of war, the consequences of youthful idealism, and the importance of memory in making meaning—are similar to those O'Brien has examined previously. The novel's retrospection, lives seen from not only a great distance, but through a span of years, expands upon those themes, giving his characters the authority of life experience and increasing the urgency with which they explore those issues. The themes are intimately related: the trauma of war cannot exist apart from lives made on the run in Canada, love is not possible without the inevitability of shattered relationships, middle-aged dreams die without memories to fuel them, affairs are meaningless when the adulterer fails even to respond with passion to her own betrayal.

As the friends gather to compare notes from their lives, Jan Huebner and Amy Robinson have a conversation that cuts to the heart of their attitude toward a 30th reunion. Amy, bemoaning their middle age, reminds Jan, "Used to be we'd talk about the Geneva Accords, the Tonkin Gulf Resolution. Now it's down to liposuction and ex-husbands. Can't trust anybody over sixty" (18). Amy's reference recalls the saying "Don't trust anyone over 30," a 1960s motto attributed to Jerry Rubin, counterculture icon and, along with Abbie Hoffman, a member of the infamous protest group the Chicago Seven. Even in moments little related to aging—after all, the characters are contemporaries—the issue arises. On meeting his old flame Dorothy Stier for the first time since he dodged the draft after college, Billy McMann comments on Dorothy's beauty. Her response, "I have breast cancer. I'm fifty-two. Fifty-three in a week" (105), epitomizes her attitude not only toward aging, but its consequences. Later, Billy watches Dorothy dance, and "it ought to have been embarrassing, which it partly was, because she was drunk and loud and fifty-two, almost fifty-three, with a husband and two grown boys" (108). Actions that would not have drawn a second glance in their youth are now cause for comment. The point is moot, perhaps—friends reveling for the first time in years and nothing more. Still, in a later vignette, Dorothy discusses her cancer and her past relationship with Billy, to which her neighbor comments shrewdly on missed opportunities: "Missed that flight for Canada. Went for handsome. Went for conservative. No-risk marriage, so to speak. And then all these years down the road, yikes, along comes cancer, eight nodes, enough to give a gal the middle-age willies. Certain what-ifs pop up" (200). That analysis is equally applicable to everyone who shares a story.

The war has affected the friends as well, and time, far from healing those wounds, acts as a repository for their memories. The scenarios arising from the war are as insidious for the noncombatant survivors as they are for the David Todds of the world. The characters who did not experience the war firsthand—the deserter Billy McMann or Marv Bertel, who stays behind to become a successful businessman, for instance—reconcile their beliefs and dreams with the expectations of society, despite their best efforts at remaining outside its influence. While McMann's discordant political views do not allow him to return to the United States after he emigrates to Canada, a choice that costs him his relationship with Dorothy Stier, Marv Bertel must face his own obesity and a lack of self-esteem by reinventing himself and, ultimately, paying the price for his hubris and deceit.

O'Brien implies that such behavior may be a form of survivor guilt not reserved exclusively for the combatant survivors of war, but also for anyone touched indirectly by the war, the specter of which, with the creeping unease and sense of time's slipping that it engenders, compels them later to make ill-considered decisions. One example is Amy Robinson's relationship with her husband, Bobby. Although the two have been together for four years, having met later in life, and Bobby has "been decent to her, assiduously decent, decent without flaw" (53), once they are married, the collective weight of their unspoken past makes the relationship, at least for Amy, implausible.

For O'Brien, relationships often hinge upon the sharing of ideals between lovers, a common vision directing lives. Ellie Abbott begins an affair with Harmon Osterberg, an old classmate, out of a sense of camaraderie and comfort missing from her marriage to Mark Abbott. The ideals that Ellie and Harmon held dear in college do little to preserve their relationship in the present. They discuss a future together, but "there was no real romance between them, no heat, but there was affection and good humor and the trust of co-conspirators. And there was also a shared history—the sticky ideals and illusions of 1969" (168). Although Ellie hesitates to admit the affair to Mark even after her lover has drowned, he discovers the infidelity and leaves her. Her response is typical of O'Brien's characters, a nearly pathological unwillingness to accept happiness. Her affair with Harmon, she realizes, "had been an experiment of sorts, a means of testing the proposition that she was more or less happily married, more or less content, more or less a lucky woman" (307). O'Brien's characters spend a great deal of time attempting to prove to themselves that they are still alive. A society that allows such uneventful lives to be perpetuated as the status quo, however, is difficult to transcend.

By telling the stories of 10 protagonists, none more or less important than any other, any of them wholly true or perhaps entirely fiction, O'Brien illustrates the importance of memory. The ten stories alternating with the "Class of '69" chapters are based on memory and constitute the most powerful of the novel's images. For David Todd, the stench of war is always fresh in his nostrils, and he relives that event from the moment he steps on campus and recalls with preternatural clarity how, even as he lay along the river, the place "already . . . had the feel of memory" (24). Memory affects each character differently, of course, and Billy McMann is ashamed to have waited so long to avenge the loss of Dorothy Stier: "He'd come here to get revenge, to inject grief into Dorothy Stier's iron heart, but as it turned out, he'd only hurt himself and Spook Spinelli" (208). Every character feels a similar passion, be it for revenge or fulfillment. That sentiment is echoed by Stewart O'Nan, who writes of Vietnam literature in general, "Memory serves some other purpose than conjuring mere terror or heartrending sorrow. It seems that as the years pass and the war recedes, more Vietnam authors are questioning memory, examining how it can be at once devastating and salvific, perhaps because with the dwindling of any worthwhile popular discussion concerning the war, veterans and their families are left with little but their own intimate recollections" (617).

Although the story of Marv Bertel is neither as heroic as Todd's nor as tragic as McMann's, it is, in its way, no less poignant. After years of being ignored by women because of his weight, Bertel goes on a diet and reinvents himself. Enamored with his secretary, Sandra, Bertel makes a regrettable decision, an utterance that "came to him exactly as all the other barroom lies had come, out of the old fatness, the new thinness, those deferred dreams and a job he hated and a stale marriage and a lifetime of mockery and humiliation and a craving for something better" (253). He claims to be a reclusive, world-famous writer (based on the American writer Thomas Pynchon). With Bertel's story, O'Brien explores the idea of the writer as a purveyor of truth and the organizer of reality. Bertel's reality—and O'Brien's, as the author of the novel—is similarly nebulous to that developed in *The Things They Carried:* all stories are true; all stories are fiction. Memory and reality serve us simply to fit our current situation. In Bertel's case, he flies away from the reunion with Spook Spinelli, with whom he has been in love since their college days. That love has been unrequited to now, though Bertel has a chance, slim as it is, at finding happiness with her. The relationship, of course, cannot last. The two die in a plane crash in a Nebraska cornfield, and the story moves to its inevitable conclusion, invoking the spirits of Spook and Marv, and "several million other survivors of their times, [for whom] there would also be the essential renewing fantasy of splendid things to come" (319). At the moment the novel ends, "Harmon Osterberg kicked a cantaloupe at Ellie Abbott, and Billy burned his draft card, and Karen Burns eyed a newly hired professor of sociology. It was 3:11 a.m., Sunday morning, July 9, 2000, but over the bleak flaming grasslands it was July now, July always" (322). Memory, reality, the past, and the present become inseparable.

Other writers who tackle the issue of return, survival, and perseverance are Bobbie Ann Mason (*In Country*), Louise Erdrich (*Love Medicine*), Larry Heinemann (*Paco's Story*), Yusef Komunyakaa (*Dien Cai Dau*), and Robert Olen Butler (*The Alleys of Eden* and *On Distant Ground*), to name a few. One remarkable aspect of the literature about Vietnam to come out of the post-Vietnam period is its diversity. The novels, poetry, drama, and essays are written from a number of points of view illustrating the strength of Vietnam's grasp on our collective psyche. Perhaps one of O'Brien's strongest arguments for writing the book was to give voice to the relative normalcy of people who are often seen, as Kakutani and Gates so readily see them, as characters removed from their historical context. The films of the Vietnam era, which invariably render the same themes on much less demanding terms, do a disservice to writers such as O'Brien by perpetuating the Vietnam stereotypes without fully exploring the mind of the Vietnam veteran or the noncombatants who nonetheless suffer. *First Blood, Full Metal Jacket,* and *Apocalypse Now,* among many successful Vietnam films, have brought war into the mainstream, in the process desensitizing viewers—and readers—to the more subtle and insidious social and psychological conditions that persist long after the shooting stops.

ALTERNATIVE READING: NEW HISTORICISM

By the time O'Brien's characters, and O'Brien himself, had graduated from the thinly veiled Macalester College (in *July, July,* Darton Hall College) in the spring of 1969, Vietnam had a reputation as a miasma into which America was leading its young men: in March of that year, President Nixon had begun secret bombing raids on communist camps in Cambodia; in May, 11 days of fighting for Hamburger Hill took a heavy toll on American soldiers; in August, American troops refused to fight the North Vietnamese at Queson; and in November, the largest antiwar protests of the Vietnam era took place in Washington, D.C., with 250,000 marchers, including veterans who had begun to see the war in a negative light. The view of the war as unnecessary and destructive would continue to gain strength until America's divestment in 1975. In many ways, those attitudes toward the war exist even today (see chapter 3 for a discussion of new-historical criticism).

The height of political activism against the war and the Establishment—and also the bloodiest year of fighting, with more than 14,000 Americans soldiers killed and 150,000 wounded, while 500,000 troops remained in-country—came in 1968. The 10 friends who were juniors at Darton Hall that year would have been steeped, both in and out of the classroom, in a burgeoning counterculture that questioned the war, as well as in the voice of the opposition. No wonder O'Brien's characters, even half a lifetime after their graduation from Darton Hall, recall that time with confusion, regret, and a continued sense of hopelessness.

In November 1969, journalist Peter R. Kann published an essay in the *Wall Street Journal* detailing Vietnam's contradictory impulses:

> "Progress" is measured here in many ways. The Air Force computes the tonnage of bombloads dropped. The Army tots up enemy bodies. Pacification planners neatly categorize hamlets on computerized evaluation charts. Psychological warriors conduct mini-Gallup Polls among taxi drivers. Economists plot curves on the shipments of rice. Embassy officers sip tea with Saigon legislators and seek to divine their Delphic utterances.

Kann's conclusion: "And still, Vietnam seems to defy analysis" (*Reporting Vietnam* 401). On the home front, much of what Kann and others observed in Vietnam would likely be better known in general, but hardly more comforting, whispers through the grapevine. Earlier that spring, Jeffrey Blankfort wrote of the impact of the war on Beallsville, a small

Ohio town accustomed to bringing its young men home in flag-draped caskets, recalling, "I went to Beallsville a little more than month after the town had buried its fifth son, Naval Corpsman Robert Lucas, in a plot of ground overlooking the high school where he and the four other boys had been schoolmates. Three of them now lie with him in the same graveyard and another is buried a few miles away" (*Reporting Vietnam* 396).

In the same way that *The Nuclear Age* follows William Cowling through the angst of the cold war, Vietnam, and the threat of nuclear annihilation, *July, July* reprises the lives of characters who, having had much different experiences over the intervening decades since their last meeting, return to compare notes, some poignant and some humorous. When taken as a whole, such memories define the postwar experience for O'Brien's generation. The important difference between *The Nuclear Age* and *In the Lake of the Woods*, which describes a similar situation with the psychologically scarred John Wade, is that *July, July* attempts, through the study of the individual case, to present an overview of a society yet to rebound fully from the events of the war. When Ellie Abbott leaves her husband for a weekend to have an affair with Harmon Osterberg in Minneapolis, she seeks the fulfillment that has eluded her, and "she did not contemplate turning back" (167). A metaphor for "the sticky ideals and illusions of 1969," Ellie's past is writ large in her relationship with Harmon. When he drowns off Loon Point during their clandestine meeting, Ellie dispassionately watches the paramedics work over his lifeless body and wonders "how she'd ever come to care for such a man, someone so wet and dead, whose swimming trunks had slipped below the knees and whose buttocks looked wrinkled and fishy white in the bright morning sunlight" (168).

The high ideals O'Brien's generation saw as their own—the same ideals that they assumed were mutually exclusive from those of the war makers—become ironic and inconsequential when juxtaposed with death. Humiliation, O'Brien implies, supersedes (or at least precedes) humility. Most of the friends have survived, though their lives will never be the utopias they had envisioned for themselves as younger people. In some ways, those events are etched in our collective memory, as in the powerful images of war articulated not only in Vietnam fiction, but in the poems of John Balaban, Kevin Bowen, W. D. Ehrhart, Bruce Weigl, and others who were inexorably changed by their war experiences. In some ways, the act of forgetting can be the single most difficult, and paradoxically the most gratifying, response to the war. It is the forced act of remembering and sharing that makes O'Brien's novel a testament to the Vietnam generation.

Although some reviewers have criticized *July, July* for its clichéd portrayals of those events, the critical response seems to be as much a veiled critique of a generation as a studied response to the novel. Perhaps a more productive avenue for exploring the novel would be to identify the novel's audiences: middle-aged readers would certainly remember and likely relate to the stories that O'Brien's characters tell; anyone too young to recall the Vietnam era would do well to read the novel with a historical context in mind. O'Brien's characters, pat as their reactions may be to the war and its aftermath, persevere despite what Dorothy Stier sees when she walks into the banquet room at the reunion, and "it crossed her mind that these people were strangers, complete aliens, like a new life form dredged up from the bottom of the sea. And they'd always been strangers. Except by an accident of birth, this was not Dorothy's generation. She didn't fit. The generation didn't fit her" (273). Such malaise is pervasive in O'Brien's work. Even Janice Ketch, a minor character in the novel, accuses Darton Hall alumna Paulette Haslo, the pastor of Janice's church, of having an affair with her husband, Rudy. Janice has fallen into the same rut that defines the lives of so many of O'Brien's characters. "It was as if she'd been on a four-decade train journey with the man, sharing a compartment, watching the miles go by, never speaking," O'Brien writes. "Total strangers, Janice realized. The man's very identity would forever remain the purest guesswork: a bumbler, a child, a cheat, a hopscotch player, a lifelong whittler of ducks" (156).

Regardless of the stories they have to tell, the characters' sole stay against chaos is memory. O'Nan draws a connection between the time elapsed since Vietnam and the increasing reticence on the veterans' parts to discuss their memories on the subject. Clearly, not all of O'Brien's stories are related directly to the war; however, the silences defining the lives of the characters in *July, July* are similar enough to those of the Vietnam veterans described by O'Nan to be remarkable. He writes, "There's a loneliness, an unwillingness to speak or unearth the past. It's not merely that America won't listen, it's that for his own sake the vet hesitates to make the private public, and instead keeps it inside" (615). Because of that need for privacy—or conversely, a fear of being judged by society—many of the war's adverse consequences have become cultural clichés: increased drug use by veterans; the government's perceived lackadaisical response to caring for vets with injuries and chronic diseases; a counterculture that eroded American mores and values; a facile response to combat-induced psychological distress, including post-traumatic stress disorder. Those clichés have hindered serious exploration of the psychological consequences of the war from the perspective of both participants and non-participants.

O'Brien's book balances the two, relying primarily on the dreamlike sequences involving David Todd for its Vietnam context and the various voices of the other characters to ground the novel in the more recognizable milieu of Middle America. Todd's return to America is accompanied by visits to a therapist, and O'Brien's description clearly points up the irony of the treatment, as "twice a month, David went to see a VA psychiatrist, a woman his own age, also a veteran of the sixties, with whom he'd share a couple of joints and vigorous assurances that Master Sergeant Johnny Ever was no angel, no devil, no ghost, no middleman; that, in fact, the man at the microphone was none other than David himself" (293–94). Vietnam reached the height of its ferocity in the late 1960s, and the war is remembered not for the nearly 60,000 young Americans and countless Vietnamese who lost their lives, but rather as political anathema. Such a view does little to reconcile firsthand literary accounts of the war with the views substituting a popular notion of the war with little regard for the reality that O'Brien relates. The importance of memory in the literature of the Vietnam War—and particularly in O'Brien's fiction—in creating that reality cannot be overstated. As an adjunct to history, such fiction is crucial to any nuanced understanding of the war by future generations.

Bibliography

PRIMARY SOURCES (CHRONOLOGICALLY ARRANGED)

Books

If I Die in a Combat Zone, Box Me Up and Ship Me Home. New York: Delacorte, 1973.
Northern Lights. New York: Delacorte, 1975.
Going after Cacciato. New York: Delacorte, 1978.
The Nuclear Age. New York: Knopf, 1985.
The Things They Carried. Boston: Houghton, 1990.
In the Lake of the Woods. Boston: Houghton, 1994.
Tomcat in Love. New York: Broadway, 1998.
July, July. Boston: Houghton, 2002.

Selected Essays, Articles, and Book Chapters

"Medals! Medals! Everyone's Got Medals." *Los Angeles Times* 18 Mar. 1973: C17.
"The Crumbling of Sand Castles." *Washington Post* 18 Nov. 1973: C1 + .
"Darkness on the Edge of Town." *Feature* Jan. 1979: 42–49.
"The Violent Vet." *Esquire* Dec. 1979: 96–104.
"We've Adjusted Too Well." *The Wounded Generation: America after Vietnam.* Ed.
    A. D. Horne. Englewood Cliffs, NJ: Prentice, 1981. 205–07.
"The Magic Show." *Writers on Writing.* Ed. Robert Pack and Jay Parini. Hanover,
    NH: Middlebury College P, 1991. 175–83.

"Ambush." *Boston* Apr. 1993: 62–67 + .

"The Vietnam in Me." *New York Times Magazine* 2 Oct. 1994: 48–57.

"The Mystery of My Lai." *Facing My Lai: Moving beyond the Massacre.* Ed. David
    L. Anderson. UP of Kansas, 1998.

"Tim O'Brien, President's Lecture, 21 April 1999." Brown University. 27 Aug. 2003
    <http://www.stg.brown.edu/projects/WritingVietnam/obrien.html>.

"A Letter to My Son." *Life* 15 Oct. 2004: 14–15.

SELECTED SECONDARY SOURCES

Books and Film

Anisfield, Nancy, ed. *The Nightmare Considered: Critical Essays on Nuclear War Lit-
    erature.* Bowling Green, OH: Bowling Green State U Popular P, 1991.

Appy, Christian G. *Patriots: The Vietnam War Remembered from All Sides.* New York:
    Viking, 2003.

Baskir, Lawrence M., and William A. Strauss. *Chance and Circumstance: The Draft,
    the War, and the Vietnam Generation.* New York: Knopf, 1978.

Beidler, Philip D. *American Literature and the Experience of Vietnam.* Athens, GA: U
    of Georgia P, 1982.

———. *Re-Writing America: Vietnam Authors in Their Generation.* Athens, GA: U of
    Georgia P, 1991.

Berman, Art. *From the New Criticism to Deconstruction.* Urbana, IL: U of Illinois P,
    1988.

Bertens, Johannes Willem. *Literary Theory: The Basics.* London: Routledge, 2001.

Calley, Willam. *Lieutenant Calley: His Own Story.* New York: Viking, 1971.

Christopher, Renny. *The Viet Nam War, The American War: Images and Representations
    in Euro-American and Vietnamese Exile Narratives.* Amherst, MA: U of Mas-
    sachusetts P, 1995.

Cox, Karen Castellucci. *Isabel Allende: A Critical Companion.* Westport, CT: Green-
    wood Press, 2003.

Ebert, James R. *A Life in a Year: The American Infantryman in Vietnam, 1965–1972.*
    Novato, CA: Presidio, 1993.

Engel, Susan. *Context Is Everything: The Nature of Memory.* New York: Freeman,
    1999.

Faigley, Lester. *Fragments of Rationality: Postmodernity and the Subject of Composition.*
    Pittsburgh, PA: U of Pittsburgh P, 1992.

The Fog of War. Dir. Errol Morris. Perf. Robert S. McNamara. Sony, 2003.

Gilman, Owen W., Jr., and Lorrie Smith, eds. *American Rediscovered: Critical Essays
    on Literature and Film of the Vietnam War.* New York: Garland, 1990.

Groden, Michael, and Martin Kreiswirth, eds. *The Johns Hopkins Guide to Literary
    Theory and Criticism.* Baltimore, MD: Johns Hopkins UP, 1994.

Halberstam, David. *The Making of a Quagmire.* New York: Random, 1965.

Heberle, Mark A. *A Trauma Artist: Tim O'Brien and the Fiction of Vietnam.* Iowa City, IA: U of Iowa P, 2001.

Hellmann, John. *American Myth and the Legacy of Vietnam.* New York: Columbia UP, 1986.

Herzog, Tobey C. *Tim O'Brien.* New York: Twayne, 1997.

Jones, James. *Viet Journal.* New York: Delacorte, 1974.

Kaplan, Steven. *Understanding Tim O'Brien.* Columbia, SC: U of South Carolina P, 1995.

Karnow, Stanley. *Vietnam: A History.* New York: Viking, 1983.

Maraniss, David. *They Marched into Sunlight: War and Peace, Vietnam and America, October 1967.* New York: Simon, 2003.

Martin, Andrew. *Receptions of War: Vietnam in American Culture.* Norman, OK: U of Oklahoma P, 1994.

McNamara, Robert S. *In Retrospect: The Tragedy and the Lessons of Vietnam.* New York: Random, 1995.

Merrill, Robert. *Joseph Heller.* New York: Twayne, 1987.

Morrison, Wilbur H. *The Elephant and the Tiger.* New York: Hippocrene, 1990.

Neilson, Jim. *Warring Fictions: American Literary Culture and the Vietnam War Narrative.* Jackson, MS: UP of Mississippi, 1998.

Newman, John. *Vietnam War Literature.* Metuchen, NJ: Scarecrow, 1982.

Olson, James S., and Randy Roberts. *Where the Dominos Fell.* New York: St. Martin's, 1991.

Paris, B. J. *Third Force Psychology and the Study of Literature.* Rutherford, NJ: Fairleigh Dickinson UP, 1988.

Pizer, Donald. *The Theory and Practice of American Literary Naturalism: Selected Essays and Reviews.* Carbondale, IL: Southern Illinois UP, 1993.

Podhoretz, Norman. *Why We Were in Vietnam.* New York: Simon and Schuster, 1982.

Reporting Vietnam: American Journalism, 1959–1975. Intro. Ward Just. New York: Library of America, 1998.

Ringnalda, Don. *Fighting and Writing the Vietnam War.* Jackson, MS: UP of Mississippi, 1994.

Searle, W. J., ed. *Search and Clear: Critical Responses to Selected Literature and Film of the Vietnam War.* Bowling Green, OH: Bowling Green State U Popular P, 1988.

Staton, Shiley. *Literary Theories in Praxis.* Philadelphia: U of Pennsylvania P, 1987.

Takiff, Michael. *Brave Men, Gentle Heroes: American Fathers and Sons in World War II and Vietnam.* New York: Morrow, 2003.

Taylor, Mark. *The Vietnam War in History, Literature and Film.* Tuscaloosa, AL: U of Alabama P, 2003.

Tegmark, Mats. *In the Shoes of a Soldier: Communication in Tim O'Brien's Vietnam Narratives.* Uppsala, Swed.: Uppsala, 1998.

Thompson, Hunter S. *Fear and Loathing in Las Vegas.* New York: Random, 1972.

Vernon, Alex. *Soldiers Once and Still: Ernest Hemingway, James Salter, and Tim O'Brien*. Iowa City, IA: U of Iowa P, 2004.

Welling, Philip H. *Vietnam in American Culture*. Boston: Twayne, 1990.

Wilson, James C. *Vietnam in Prose and Film*. Jefferson, NC: McFarland, 1982.

Wolfe, Tom. *The New Journalism*. New York: Harper, 1973.

Articles, Essays, and Book Chapters

Amato, Joseph, and Anthony Amato. "Minnesota, Real and Imagined: A View from the Countryside." *Daedalus* 129.3 (Summer 2000): 55–80.

Bates, Milton. "Tim O'Brien's Myth of Courage." *Modern Fiction Studies* 33.2 (1987): 263–79.

Beidler, Phil. "Bad Business: Vietnam and Recent Mass-Market Fiction." *College English* 54.1 (1992): 64–75.

Bonn, Maria. "Can Stories Save Us? Tim O'Brien and the Efficacy of the Text." *Critique* 36.1 (1994): 2–15.

Cadzow, Hunter. "New Historicism." Groden and Kreiswirth 534–39.

Caldwell, Gail. "The Summer of Our Discontent." *Boston Globe* 13 Oct. 2002: D6.

Dahlin, Robert. "Philip Caputo: Facing Evil Vietnam to Suburbia." *Publishers Weekly* 29 Jan. 1996: 80–81.

DeCoste, Damon Marcel. "Modernism's Shell-Shocked History: Amnesia, Repetition, and the War in Graham Greene's *The Ministry of Fear*." *Twentieth Century Literature* 45.4 (1999): 428–51.

Elam, Diane. "Poststructuralist Feminism." Groden and Kreiswirth 242–47.

Epstein, Renee. "Talking Dirty: Memories of War and the Vietnam War Novel." *Massachusetts Review* 34.3 (1993): 457–70.

Franklin, H. Bruce. "Plausibility of Denial: Tim O'Brien, My Lai, and America." *Progressive* 58.12 (1994): 40–44.

Freedman, Samuel G. "The War and the Arts." *New York Times* 31 Mar. 1985: 50 + .

Goluboff, Benjamin. "Tim O'Brien's Quang Ngai." *ANQ: A Quarterly Journal of Short Articles, Notes, and Reviews* 17.2 (2004): 53–58.

Grossman, Mary Ann. "Fighting Words." *St. Paul Pioneer Press* 30 Apr. 1995: 1E.

Heller, Joseph. "Joseph Heller Replies." *Realist* 50 (1964): 30.

Herzog, Tobey C. "Tim O'Brien's True Lies (?)." *Modern Fiction Studies* 46.4 (2000): 893–916.

———. "Writing about Vietnam: A Heavy Heart-of-Darkness Trip." *College English* 41.6 (1980): 680–95.

Jarraway, David R. "Excremental Assault in Tim O'Brien: Trauma and Recovery in Vietnam War Literature." *Modern Fiction Studies* 44.3 (1998): 695–711.

Jones, Dale W. "The Vietnams of Michael Herr and Tim O'Brien: Tales of Disintegration and Integration." *Canadian Review of American Studies* 13.3 (1982): 309–20.

Kearns, George. "Revolutionary Women and Others." *Hudson Review* 39.1 (1986): 121–34.

Kneale, J. Douglas. "Deconstruction." Groden and Kreiswirth 185–92.

Liparulo, Steven P. "'Incense and Ashes': The Postmodern Work of Refutation in Three Vietnam War Novels." *War, Literature and the Arts: An International Journal of the Humanities* 15.1–2 (2003): 71–94.

Mahaffey, Vicki. "Modernist Theory and Criticism." Groden and Kreiswirth 512–14.

McCay, Mary. "The Autobiography of Guilt: Tim O'Brien and Vietnam." *Writing Lives: American Biography and Autobiography* 39 (1998): 115–21.

Nelson, Marie. "Two Consciences: A Reading of Tim O'Brien's Vietnam Trilogy: *If I Die in a Combat Zone, Going after Cacciato,* and *Northern Lights.*" *Third Force Psychology and the Study of Literature.* Ed. Bernard J. Paris. Rutherford, NJ: Fairleigh Dickinson UP, 1986. 262–79.

Newmiller, William. "A Real Good War Recollection and Conversation with Sam Halpert." *War, Literature and the Arts: An International Journal of the Humanities* 15.1–2 (2003): 152–59.

Oldham, Perry. "On Teaching Vietnam Literature." *English Journal* 75.2 (1986): 55–56.

Palo, Michael F. "'Dad, What Did You Do during the War?': A Postmodernist (?) Classroom Exercise." *History Teacher* 33.2 (2000): 193–212.

"Politics of the Sputnik." *New York Times* 10 Oct. 1957: 32.

Probst, Robert E. "Reader-Response Theory and the English Curriculum." *English Journal* 83.3 (1994): 37–44.

Reeves, Charles Eric. "Myth Theory and Criticism." Groden and Kreiswirth 520–23.

Ringnalda, Don. "Fighting and Writing: America's Vietnam War Literature." *Journal of American Studies* 22 (1988): 25–42.

———. "Tim O'Brien's Understood Confusion." *Fighting and Writing the Vietnam War.* Jackson, MS: UP of Mississippi, 1994. 90–114.

Robinson, Daniel. "Getting It Right: The Short Fiction of Tim O'Brien." *Critique* 40.3 (1999): 257–64.

"Round the World in 96 Minutes." *New York Times* 6 Oct. 1957: 193.

Schroeder, Eric James. "The Past and the Possible: Tim O'Brien's Dialectic of Meaning and Imagination." *Search and Clear: Critical Response to Selected Literature and Films of the Vietnam War.* Ed. W. J. Searle. Bowling Green, OH: Bowling Green State U Popular P, 1988. 116–34.

Showalter, Elaine. "Women's Time, Women's Space: Writing the History of Feminist Criticism." *Tulsa Studies in Women's Literature* 3.1/2 (1984): 29–43.

Shuman, R. Baird. "The Past as Present: Reader Response and Literary Study." *English Journal* 82.5 (1993): 30–32.

Smith, Lorrie N. "The Things Men Do: The Gendered Subtext in Tim O'Brien's *Esquire* Stories." *Critique* 36.1 (1994): 16–40.

Spender, Stephen. "The Modern as Vision of the Whole." *The Idea of the Modern in Literature and the Arts*. Ed. Irving Howe. New York: Horizon, 1967. 50–58.

Taylor, Gordon O. "American Personal Narrative of the War in Vietnam." *American Literature* 52.2 (1980): 294–308.

Taylor, Mark. "Tim O'Brien's War." *Centennial Review* 34.2 (1995): 213–30.

Vizinczey, Stephen. "Condemned World, Literary Kingdom." Rev. *Armies of the Night*, by Norman Mailer. *Times Saturday Review* 21 Sep. 1968.

Wilhelm, Albert E. "Ballad Allusions in Tim O'Brien's 'Where Have You Gone, Charming Billy?'" *Studies in Short Fiction* 28.2 (1991): 218–22.

Zins, Daniel L. "Imagining the Real: The Fiction of Tim O'Brien." *Hollins Critic* 23.3 (1986): 1–12.

Articles on Individual Works and Reviews

If I Die in a Combat Zone

Gottlieb, Annie. *New York Times Book Review* 1 July 1973: 10+.

Glover, Elaine. *Stand* 15.3 (1974): 49–50.

Horner, Carl S. "Challenging the Law of Courage and Heroic Identification in Tim O'Brien's *If I Die in a Combat Zone* and *The Things They Carried*." *War, Literature and the Arts* 11.1 (1999): 256–67.

"Tale of Battle." *Times Literary Supplement* 19 Oct. 1973: 1269.

Waters, Chris. "Everyman-at-Arms." *New Statesman* 4 Jan. 1974: 23–24.

Wesley, Marilyn. "Truth and Fiction in Tim O'Brien's *If I Die in a Combat Zone* and *The Things They Carried*." *College Literature* 29.2 (2002): 1–18.

Northern Lights

Brown, Rosellen. *New Republic* 7 Feb. 1976: 27–28.

Deck, John. *New York Times Book Review* 12 Oct. 1975: 42.

Donahaugh, Robert H. *Library Journal* 15 June 1975: 1241.

Roripaugh, Robert A. *Western American Literature* 11 (Summer 1976): 177–79.

Sale, Roger. *New York Review of Books* 13 Nov. 1975: 31–32.

Going after Cacciato

Calloway, Catherine. "Pluralities of Vision: *Going after Cacciato* and Tim O'Brien's Short Fiction." Gilman and Smith 213–24.

Couser, G. Thomas. "*Going after Cacciato*: The Romance and the Real War." *Journal of Narrative Technique* 13.1 (1983): 1–10.

Freedman, Richard. "A Separate Peace." *New York Times Book Review* 12 Feb. 1978: 1+.

Froelich, Vera P. "O'Brien's *Going after Cacciato*." *Explicator* 53.3 (1995): 181–83.

Herzog, Tobey C. "*Going after Cacciato:* The Soldier-Author-Character Seeking Control." *Critique* 24.2 (1983): 88–96.

Kinney, Katherine. "American Exceptionalism and Empire in Tim O'Brien's *Going after Cacciato.*" *American Literary History* 7.4 (1995): 633–53.

McWilliams, Dean. "Time in O'Brien's *Going after Cacciato.*" *Critique* 29.4 (1988): 245–55.

Raymond, Michael W. "Imagined Responses to Vietnam: Tim O'Brien's *Going after Cacciato.*" *Critique* 24.2 (1983): 97–104.

Saltzman, Arthur M. "The Betrayal of the Imagination: Paul Brodeur's *The Stunt Man* and Tim O'Brien's *Going after Cacciato.*" *Critique* 22.1 (1980): 32–38.

Slabey, Richard. "*Going after Cacciato:* Tim O'Brien's 'Separate Peace.'" Gilman and Smith 205–12.

Slay, Jack, Jr. "A Rumor of War: Another Look at the Observation Post in Tim O'Brien's *Going after Cacciato.*" *Critique* 41.1 (1999): 79–85.

Vannetta, Dennis. "Theme and Structure in Tim O'Brien's *Going after Cacciato.*" *Modern Fiction Studies* 28.2 (1982): 242–46.

Wilson, Robert. "Dreaming of War and Peace." *Washington Post Book World* 19 Feb. 1978: E4.

The Nuclear Age

Clute, John. *New Statesman* 11 Apr. 1986: 24.

Foertsch, Jacqueline. "Not Bombshells but Bookcases: Gendered Illness in Nuclear Texts." *Studies in the Novel* 31.4 (1999): 471–88.

Kakutani, Michiko. "Prophet of Doom." *New York Times* 28 Sep. 1985: 12.

Lipez, Richard. "In the Shadow of the Bomb." *Washington Post Book World* 13 Oct. 1985: 9.

Lochte, Dick. *Los Angeles Times Book Review* 3 Nov. 1985: 16.

Marcus, James. "A Hole Is to Dig." *Nation* 2 Nov. 1985: 450+.

Montrose, David. *Times Literary Supplement* 28 Mar. 1986: 342.

Paley, Grace. "Digging a Shelter and a Grave." *New York Times Book Review* 17 Nov. 1985: 7.

Romano, John. "Blue over the Bomb." *Atlantic Monthly* Oct. 1985: 105–6.

Schwininger, Lee. "Ecofeminism, Nuclearism, and O'Brien's *The Nuclear Age.*" Anisfield 177–85.

The Things They Carried

Bunting, Josiah. "Vietnam, Carried On." *Washington Post* 23 Apr. 1990: B3.

Caldwell, Gail. "Following the Point Man in a New Kind of War." *Boston Globe* 4 Mar. 1990: B49.

Calloway, Catherine. "How to Tell a True War Story: Metafiction in *The Things They Carried.*" *Critique* 36.4 (1995): 249–57.

Cario, Laura. "Regarding the O'Brien Paintings . . . " *War, Literature and the Arts: An International Journal of the Humanities* 15.1–2 (2003): 40–43.

Chen, Tina. "Unraveling the Deeper Meaning: Exile and the Embodied Poetics of Displacement in Tim O'Brien's *The Things They Carried*." *Contemporary Literature* 39.1 (1998): 77–99.

Eder, Richard. "Has He Forgotten Anything?" *Los Angeles Times Book Review* 1 Apr. 1990: 3.

Harris, Robert R. "Too Embarrassed Not to Kill." *New York Times Book Review* 11 Mar. 1990: 8.

Kakutani, Michiko. "Slogging Surreally in the Vietnamese Jungle." *New York Times* 6 Mar. 1990: C21.

Kaplan, Steven. "The Undying Uncertainty of the Narrator in Tim O'Brien's *The Things They Carried*." *Critique* 35.1 (1993): 43–52.

King, Rosemary. "O'Brien's How to Tell a True War Story." *Explicator* 57.3 (1999): 182–84.

Loose, Julian. "The Story That Never Ends." *Times Literary Supplement* 29 June 1990: 705.

Mehren, Elizabeth. "Short War Stories." *Los Angeles Times* 11 Mar. 1990: E1.

O'Gorman, Farrell. "*The Things They Carried* as Composite Novel." *War, Literature and the Arts* 10.2 (1998): 289–309.

Smiley, Pamela. "The Role of the Ideal (Female) Reader in Tim O'Brien's *The Things They Carried:* Why Should Real Women Play?" *The Massachusetts Review* 43.4 (2002–03): 602–14.

Timmerman, John H. "Tim O'Brien and the Art of the True War Story: 'Night March' and 'Speaking of Courage.'" *Twentieth-Century Literature* 46.1 (2000): 100–14.

Volkmer, John. "Telling the Truth about Vietnam: Episteme and Narrative Structure in *The Green Berets* and *The Things They Carried*." *War, Literature and the Arts* 11.1 (1999): 240–55.

Wetherell, W. D. "Dubious Martyrdom." *Chicago Tribune* 11 Mar. 1990: 5.

In the Lake of the Woods

Danziger, Jeff. *Christian Science Monitor* 4 Nov. 1994: 13.

Eder, Richard. "Vanishing Act." *Los Angeles Times Book Review* 2 Oct. 1994: 3.

Elsen, Jon. "Doing the Popular Thing." *New York Times Book Review* 9 Oct. 1994: 33.

Iyer, Pico. "Missing in Contemplation." *Time* 24 Oct. 1994: 74.

Kakutani, Michiko. "A Novel with a Complex Strategy." *New York Times* 7 Oct. 1994: C31.

Kerrigan, Michael. "Memories of War." *Times Literary Supplement* 21 Apr. 1995: 20.

Klinkenborg, Verlyn. "A Self-Made Man." *New York Times Book Review* 9 Oct. 1994: 1+.

Melley, Timothy. "Postmodern Amnesia: Trauma and Forgetting in Tim O'Brien's *In the Lake of the Woods.*" *Contemporary Literature* 44.1 (2003): 106–31.

O'Rourke, William. "Into Troubled Waters." *Chicago Tribune Books* 16 Oct. 1994: 1+.

Piwinski, David J. "My Lai, Flies, and Beelzebub in Tim O'Brien's *In the Lake of the Woods.*" *War, Literature and the Arts: An International Journal of the Humanities* 12.2 (2000): 196–202.

Tomcat in Love

Kakutani, Michiko. "Shell Shock on the Battlefields of a Messy Love Life." *New York Times* 15 Sep. 1998: E7.

Nicholson, David. "Laughs of the Red-Hot Lover." *Washington Post* 1 Sep. 1998: B1.

Smiley, Jane. "Catting Around." *New York Times Book Review* 20 Sep. 1998: 11–12.

Walker, Tom. "*Tomcat* a Purging for Tim O'Brien." *Denver Post* 25 Oct. 1998: G3.

Ybarra, Michael J. "Caught Up in Conflict." *Los Angeles Times* 30 Sep. 1998: E1.

July, July

"An Interview with Tim O'Brien: *July, July.*" vjbooks.com. 13 Jan. 2004. <http://www.vjbooks.com/interviews/obrien_tim_interview2.htm>.

Ciabattari, Jane. "Casualties of the Class of '69." *Los Angeles Times Book Review* 3 Nov. 2002: R4.

Davis, Alan. "A Day Late and a Dollar Short." *Hudson Review* 56.2 (2003): 385–90.

Dayley, Glenn. "Familiar Ghosts, New Voices: Tim O'Brien's *July, July.*" *War, Literature and the Arts: An International Journal of the Humanities* 15.1–2 (2003): 316–22.

Gates, David. "Everybody Must Get Sloshed." *New York Times Book Review* 13 Oct. 2002: 6.

Grossinger, Harvey. "A Chill in July." *Houston Chronicle* 24 Nov. 2002: 25.

Kakutani, Michiko. "When the Magic of Youth Turns into Midlife Misery." *New York Times* 11 Oct. 2002: E45.

Shea, Mike. "Days of Their Lives." *Texas Monthly* 30.10 (2002): 108+.

Yardley, Jonathan. "Tim O'Brien Forsakes the Jungles of Vietnam for Dispatches from the Home Front." *Washington Post* 13 Oct. 2002: T2.

Interviews and Profiles

Birnbaum, Robert. "Author of *July, July* Talks with Robert Birnbaum." 5 Nov. 2002. 17 Mar. 2004 <http://www.identitytheory.com/printme/obrienprint.html>.

Blades, John. "Prisoners of War." *Chicago Tribune* 9 Dec. 1994, Tempo sec.: 1–2.

"Bold Type: Interview with Tim O'Brien." *Bold Type* 2.7 (1998). 13 Jan. 2004 <http://www.randomhouse.com/boldtype/0998/obrien/interview.html>.

Bruckner, D.J.R. "A Storyteller for the War That Won't End." *New York Times* 3 Apr. 1990: C15+.

Caldwell, Gail. "Staying True to Vietnam: Writer Tim O'Brien Aims for the War's Nerve Center." *Boston Globe* 29 Mar. 1990: 69+.

Capuzzo, Mike. "A Novelist's Inner War." *Philadelphia Inquirer* 27 Oct. 1994. G1+.

Coffey, Michael. "Tim O'Brien: Inventing a New Form Helps the Author Talk about War, Memory, and Storytelling." *Publishers Weekly* 16 Feb. 1990: 60–61.

Cryer, Dan. "Talking with Tim O'Brien: Goodbye to All That." *Newsday* 16 Oct. 1994: 32.

Edelman, Dave. "My Full Interview with Tim O'Brien." 21 May 2004 <http://www.dave-edelman.com/interviews/obrien-full.cfm>.

Grossman, Mary Ann. "Reality Doesn't Matter." *St. Paul Pioneer Press* 11 Mar. 1990: 1D.

———. "Secret Life of Tim O'Brien." *St. Paul Pioneer Press* 17 Oct. 1994: 1C.

"An Interview with Tim O'Brien." *Reading Guides:* In the Lake of the Woods. 15 Mar. 2004. <http://www.penguinputnam.com/static/rguides/us/lake_of_the_woods.html>.

Kahn, Joseph P. "The Things He Carries: Vietnam's Sins Still Haunt Tim O'Brien." *Boston Globe* 19 Oct. 1994: 69+.

Kaplan, Steven. "An Interview with Tim O'Brien." *Missouri Review* 14.3 (1991): 95–108.

Lannon, Linnea. "In War, Reality Becomes Surreal." *Detroit Free Press* 17 Apr. 1991: 3E+.

Lee, Don. "About Tim O'Brien." *Ploughshares* 21.4 (1995–96): 196–201.

McCaffery, Larry. "An Interview with Tim O'Brien." *Anything Can Happen: Interviews with Contemporary American Novelists.* Ed. T. LeClair. Urbana, IL: U of Illinois P, 1983. 262–78.

McNerney, Brian C. "Responsibly Inventing History: An Interview with Tim O'Brien." *War, Literature, and the Arts* 6.2 (1994): 1–26.

Marquiss, Twister. "Westward Ho! (Chi Minh): Tim O'Brien and the Wounding of the American Cowboy Mythos." *Southwestern American Literature* 29.2 (2004): 9–15.

Mehegan, David. "New Terrain." *Boston Globe* 8 Oct. 2002: E1.

Muro, Mark. "Believer in the Grand Theme." *Boston Globe* 10 Oct. 1985: 85–86.

Naparsteck, Martin. "An Interview with Tim O'Brien." *Contemporary Literature* 32.1 (1991): 1–11.

Rosica, Karen. "Interview with Tim O'Brien—From Life to Fiction." 15 May 2004 <http://www.lighthousewriters.com/newslett/timobrie.htm>.

Sawyer, Scott. "In the Name of Love: An Interview with Tim O'Brien." *Mars Hill Review* 4 (Winter–Spring 1996): 117–26.

Schroeder, Eric James. "Two Interviews: Talks with Tim O'Brien and Robert Stone." *Modern Fiction Studies* 30.1 (1994): 135–64.

Schumacher, Michael. "Writing Stories from Life." *Writer's Digest* 71 (April 1991): 34–39.

Shostak, Debra, and Daniel Bourne. "*Artful Dodge* Interviews Tim O'Brien." *Artful Dodge* 17 (1991): 74–90.

Slater, Judith. "An Interview with Tim O'Brien." *Short Story Review* 4.2 Spring 1987: 1–5.

Streitfeld, David. "The Writer Wounded by Friendly Fire: Vietnam Vet Tim O'Brien, Still at War with Himself." *Washington Post* 25 Nov. 1994: B1.

Tambakis, Anthony. "An Interview with Tim O'Brien." *Five Points: A Journal of Literature and Art* 4.1 Fall 1999: 95–114.

"Tim O'Brien: Past Interview." *bookreporter.com*. 24 Apr. 2004. <http://www.bookreporter.com/authors/au-obrien-tim.asp>.

Weber, Bruce. "War and Peace." *Esquire* Sep. 1985: 269.

———. "Wrestling with War and Love: Raw Pain, Relived Tim O'Brien's Way." *New York Times* 2 Sep. 1998: E1 +.

Other Works in the Vietnam Tradition

Apocalypse Now. Dir. Francis Ford Coppola. Zoetrope, 1979.

Baker, Mark, ed. *Nam: The Vietnam War in the Words of the Men and Women Who Fought There.* New York: Berkley, 1981.

Caputo, Philip. *A Rumor of War.* New York: Ballantine, 1977.

Coming Home. Dir. Hal Ashby. United Artists, 1978.

The Deer Hunter. Dir. Michael Cimino. Columbia, 1978.

Downs, Frederick. *The Killing Zone: My Life in the Vietnam War.* New York: Berkley, 1978.

Ehrhart, W. D. *Passing Time: Memoir of a Vietnam Veteran against the War.* Amherst, MA: U of Massachusetts P, 1995.

Glasser, Ronald J. *365 Days.* New York: Bantam, 1971.

Greene, Bob, ed. *Homecoming: When the Soldiers Returned from Vietnam.* New York: Ballantine, 1990.

Herr, Michael. *Dispatches.* New York: Knopf, 1977.

Kopit, Arthur. *Indians.* New York: Hill, 1969.

Kovic, Ron. *Born on the Fourth of July.* New York: Pocket, 1976.

Marshall, Kathryn, ed. *In the Combat Zone: An Oral History of American Women in Vietnam, 1966–1975.* New York: Viking, 1988.

Mason, Robert. *Chickenhawk.* New York: Penguin, 1983.

Myers, Thomas. *Walking Point: American Narratives of Vietnam.* New York: Oxford UP, 1988.

O'Nan, Stewart. *The Vietnam Reader: The Definitive Collection of American Fiction and Nonfiction on the War.* New York: Anchor, 1998.

Platoon. Dir. Oliver Stone. Orion, 1986.

Rabe, David. *The Basic Training of Pavlo Hummell/Sticks and Bones.* New York: Viking, 1973.

———. *Streamers.* New York: Knopf, 1977.

Santoli, Al. *Everything We Had: An Oral History of the Vietnam War by Thirty-Three American Soldiers Who Fought It.* New York: Ballantine, 1981.

Ung, Loung. *First They Killed My Father: A Daughter of Cambodia Remembers.* New York: HarperCollins, 2000.

Walker, Keith, ed. *A Piece of My Heart: The Stories of Twenty-Six American Women Who Served in Vietnam.* New York: Ballantine, 1985.

Webb, James. *Fields of Fire.* New York: Bantam, 1978.

Weigl, Bruce. *Song of Napalm.* New York: Atlantic Monthly, 1988.

Index